'SOUND THE TRUMPET AMONG THE NATIONS!'
(Jeremiah 51:27)

D1331796

Other books by the same author:

The Trumpet Sounds For Britain (Vol 1)
The Trumpet Sounds For Britain (Vol 2)
The Trumpet Sounds For Britain (Vol 3)

'Sound the Trumpet Among the Nations!'

(Jeremiah 51:27)

David E. Gardner

ISBN 0 9518308 0 5

Production and Printing in England for
CHRISTIAN FOUNDATION PUBLICATIONS
East Barnet Village, Herts EN4 8UY.
by Nuprint Ltd, Harpenden, Herts AL5 4SE.

Contents

The National, World and Middle East Situation Today
Viewed Biblically and Prophetically

The Story of How This Book Came to be Written

It was while I was preaching in the Manchester and Stockport area on the state of the nation and of the world today against the background of all the Bible prophecies of the end days in which we are living and of the nearness of the Lord's return, that it became apparent that a number of Christian medical students were attending all my meetings. One of these, Nicholas Heredotou, told me in a conversation after one of the meetings, that he would be going to St Andrews University, Scotland, for two years and when he had arrived there he would arrange for me to preach along the same lines in the university itself. This he eventually did, early in 1990, by which time he had got the full backing of the university authorities and the keen support of several members of the St Andrews University Christian Union. He set about this task single-handed, and with tremendous enthusiasm, which to my mind was even more remarkable since he was not even English, neither was he a Scot, but was a Greek by nationality!

Nicholas had arranged for an all-day Saturday major preaching occasion to take place in one of the university's largest lecture halls, and he had made it plain within the university itself and throughout St Andrews that it was to be a preaching *only* occasion, with just a brief word of welcome, an opening prayer after which I would go straight into the preaching. He also made it plain by leaflets, advertisements and by word of mouth that the preaching of a whole series of connected and inter-related messages would be undertaken between 10 am and approximately 8:30 pm, with suitable breaks in between, and that all the messages would be professionally recorded on cassette tapes. The day then arrived.

The Lord undertook wonderfully for the whole of the day. There were those present who had come all the way from Surrey and from Manchester, together with St Andrews University students and some of its professors, as well as those from different parts of Scotland and from the town of St Andrews itself. The listening was intense throughout the whole of the day. People of all age groups were obviously being gripped by the message. And when at about 8:30 pm the preacher indicated that perhaps he ought to draw to a close, a great cry went up, 'Why must you stop? We want to hear more. We've got this hall until 10 o'clock, why do you have to stop now? We want you to go on.' So I did, for about another hour, and they still would have taken more!

It seems that the impact on St Andrews of the day's preaching was considerable. I was told the next day that people all over St Andrews were talking about the messages. Arrangements were made with the university and by Nicholas for fifty sets of the six cassettes containing all the messages to be run off. All fifty sets had gone before ever it became possible to let it be known that they were available!

Then a most surprising thing happened. Someone who seeks to witness for the Lord behind the scenes in Parliamentary circles phoned and asked for a full set of the St Andrews tapes in order to listen to them. This person stayed in for a whole day to listen to all of the tapes. Having done that this person phoned again and said, 'David, these tapes are absolutely fantastic. You make it so plain from the Bible what is the meaning and significance of all that we see happening in the world today. Please would you let me have another full set that I can send to the Prime Minister, because I regard it as an absolute *must* that she listens to them, and I will tell her so in a covering letter (the Prime Minister at that time being Mrs Margaret Thatcher) and please would you let me have another full set that I can send to the Speaker of the House of Commons because I believe it is an absolute *must* that he listens to them also.' Then this same person promptly ordered another eighteen full sets to send to people in leadership and to others in positions of authority.

But that was not all. This same person phoned again a few

days later and said, 'David, I want you to come to my house. I have invited a certain publisher to come at the same time and I want him to listen to some of these tapes in your presence.' So I went. This publisher sat listening to the tapes for over an hour. Then he suddenly said, with great enthusiasm, 'The entire message on these tapes needs to be published in book form, and very quickly. Will you write it all up with that in mind?' He even said, 'A set of these tapes needs to be taken over to America, and people in leadership over there should listen to them also.'

I immediately set about writing up the message exactly as it had been preached, because that is how it was strongly requested that it should be done. This task took me a whole month. But then there was a serious hold-up. The Gulf Crisis intervened. I was then requested to preach further messages on 'The Prophetic Significance of the Middle East Situation', bringing the St Andrews messages up to date. Operation Desert Storm followed, together with a renewed emphasis on the so-called 'Peace Initiatives' between Israel and the Palestinians, which immediately brings Israel and Jerusalem into prophetic significance once again. So further messages have been preached along these lines and have been incorporated into the message of this book to bring it as up to date as possible as it now goes into print.

My prayer is that now the publication of all these messages in book form has become possible, the Lord will cause it to reach the greatest number of people possible in as many countries of the world as possible, to prepare the hearts of as many people as possible for the greatest event ever yet to take place in the whole of human history, namely, the glorious return to this world of every true believer's Lord and Saviour Jesus Christ, the Saviour of the world.

I wish to express my deep and heartfelt gratitude to Dr Brian J. Taylor, Proprietor of Christian Foundation Publications, for his kind co-operation in getting this book published, and to Rodney Shepherd of Nuprint, Harpenden, for doing everything possible to ensure that the book gets out quickly.

David E. Gardner

Chapter One

Setting the Scene

As I begin this series of addresses on 'The State of the Nation and of the World Today Viewed Biblically and Prophetically', may I draw your attention to two verses of Scripture which are most applicable. One is Hosea 8:1, which says, 'Set the trumpet to thy mouth.' This was a command from Almighty God, given to the Prophet Hosea, to warn the nation of Israel of a coming judgment of God upon it. And we need such a trumpet call today, because a judgment of God is soon coming on the nations.

The second Scripture is from Micah 3:8, which says, 'But truly I am full of power by the spirit of the Lord, and of judgment, and of might, to declare unto Jacob his transgression, and to Israel his sin'—or, as would be very appropriate to say today, 'To declare unto the nation of Britain her transgression, and to the British people their sin.' For this is what urgently needs to be done today, in the full power of the Spirit of God, and to bring Britain's people to deep and heartfelt *repentance*.

I have been greatly looking forward to this visit to St Andrews and to its university, and I would like to take this opportunity to say how grateful I am to Nicholas Herodotou for so kindly arranging it, and to the university authorities for so kindly allowing us the use of this hall and all its facilities.

Scotland has always had a very real place in my heart. In my Royal Navy days, when I was on board the Cruiser HMS *Southampton*, the Flag Ship of the Second Cruiser Squadron, Home Fleet, our Squadron was often operating from Rosyth, and also from Scapa Flow. We frequently re-oiled in Sollum

Voe up in the Shetlands, on our way to The Northern Patrol in the Denmark Straits. Then later, after I was transferred to submarines, we enjoyed rest-cures over in Campbeltown, Tobermory, and on the Island of Bute, after hazardous North Sea patrols.

In my nationwide 'Trumpet Sounding' ministry during the past few years, I have already preached right up in the Orkneys for a period of about ten days; in Glasgow City Hall for a whole Saturday (10 am to 10 pm, with suitable breaks); then I have preached in the Methill and Kirkcaldy area in the Kingdom of Fife; then over on the Outer Hebrides (on the Islands of Lewis, Harris and Scalpay), where, by invitation of the local believers, I delivered no less than fifteen major addresses in the course of a fortnight! Then, when I arrived back in Inverness from Stornoway, I also spoke at short notice to a crowded house-meeting one evening, and on my way back to London from there I was invited to preach in a church and then at a crowded house-meeting on the Mull of Kintyre.

A few years ago, also, I was invited to be the main speaker when the Perth Convention was re-inaugurated. So this is by no means my *first* preaching occasion in Scotland!

I am also deeply aware that a study of history reveals that when God has been pleased to visit the British Isles with revival, it has almost invariably started in Scotland.

Columba, for instance, brought pure, New Testament Christianity to Iona, and then to the mainland of Scotland, before ever Christianity came to England. It was as early as in AD 563 that Columba brought that pure, New Testament form of Christianity to Scotland—the Apostolic form.

The Reformation came to Scotland under John Knox, and such people, before it came to England. Then there were the Scottish Revivals under powerful preachers like Robert Murray McCheyne, whose system of daily Bible readings I use regularly. Scotland also experienced revival on the Isle of Lewis and in the Outer Hebrides in 1947.

And you might be interested to know that when the Secretary of the Perth Convention—the Revd Hill—came to London to discuss with me the part I was being invited to play in the re-inauguration of the Perth Convention, he said to me, 'We are expecting nothing short of *God coming down* during the re-inauguration of this convention, so will you have that in mind as you prepare your messages?' But Scotland was not ready for revival then. The question is: Is it *now*?

The British Isles desperately need a revival of pure, true, New Testament Christianity again today. It needs *God coming down* in mighty Holy Ghost power. Britain needs a visitation of God, for this is the only thing which will touch our national situation today. And when I talk about revival I mean God coming down in such an awesome way that there is a sense of His presence everywhere, and for miles around, with the result that people everywhere come under deep conviction of sin and begin to cry out to God for *mercy*, and God does, in five minutes, what it would take fifty years of evangelism to do. That is what I mean when I talk about revival. And if God is going to send such a revival today, and only *He* can do it, why should it not begin again in Scotland? Why not indeed!

But we need the *fire of God* if this is to happen again today. We need a *baptism of fire*. John the Baptist said of Jesus, 'He shall baptize you with the Holy Ghost, *and with fire*' (Matthew 3:11). We need such a baptism today.

So at the outset of this day's preaching, may we pray that the fire of God may come down upon us all, and upon the preacher also, that we all may be endued with power from on high, and be so full of power by the Spirit of the Lord, and of judgment and of might, that these messages may be used to declare unto Britain her transgression, and to the people of Britain their sin, as we set the trumpet to our mouth to warn the nation, and the world, of a coming judgment—and of what else is to come.

Now I would remind you that the subject today is 'The State of the Nation and of the World Today Viewed Biblically and Prophetically'. This needs, therefore, to be quite a comprehensive address, or series of addresses. And it is not just a fad that this overall title has been chosen.

We live in most momentous times. People all over the British Isles today are deeply troubled about everything that is going on around them. They are deeply troubled about all that is going on in our own nation. Yes. They are deeply troubled by all that is going on in the Church and in the churches. They are deeply troubled about what is happening to our nation and to its Church. There is no doubt about that.

But what many people are even more troubled about today is what is going on in the world, and what is happening to the world. They see and hear about what is happening in the Middle East, in the Soviet Union, in Armenia, in Azerbaijhan, in Latvia, in Estonia, in Romania, in Central Asia, in Poland, in East Germany, in Hungary, in West Germany, in China, in Hong Kong, in Japan, in Pakistan, in India, in Kashmir, in Yugoslavia, in the Lebanon, in Syria, in Iraq, in Israel, and so on. Ferment, unrest and upheaval are evident everywhere! And they are saying, 'Whatever is happening to the world? Where is it all heading?' They are asking those questions in the supermarkets now.

Gorbachev, soon after he came to power, said, in an interview with *Time* magazine, published on 9th September 1985, 'The situation in the world today is highly complex, *very tense*, I would even go so far as to say it is *explosive*.' He could not have been more right. There is tension everywhere, and ferment.

And we've got an explosive situation in the Middle East right now. That powder keg could go up at any moment.

In view of all this, the problem of *all* problems as we enter into the last decade of this present century is: What is going on in the context of *world* history? What lies behind it all?

And, of course, to find the answer to that question we must turn to the Bible, and to the revelation which God gives us in the Bible. For the only answer to that question is to be found in the Bible. You won't find it anywhere else.

You won't find it in the philosophers, for instance. You won't find it in the history books. You won't find it in science, or in medicine. You won't find it in humanism, or in materialism.

You won't find it either by 'hearing a voice' (in inverted commas—this is the language now being used in some Christian circles) or by 'seeing pictures' (again in inverted commas—this is the language being used in other Christian circles today; language which is far removed from New Testament language). You won't find it by 'seeing a vision', or by 'seeing auras', or anything of an etherial or psychic nature such as that, or by anything which has to do with seances, or is of the same nature as happens in seances.

You won't find it in 'extra revelation', or so-called 'new

revelation', nor in any far-fetched, way-out pseudo-prophecies which have their origin in the imagination as the result of '*visualising*' and which have little or no relation to the Scriptures, or to what the Bible says. (The practice of 'visualising' is a practice which has infiltrated many of our churches and fellowships from the Eastern Religions.) You won't find it in the realm of hypnotism, hallucinations, by telepathy, or by taking 'a trip'.

You won't find it in any of these things. But you *will* find it in the Bible: this '*more sure word of prophecy*', as the Apostle Peter calls it in 2 Peter 1:19; this God-breathed, Divinely inspired, totally inerrant, infallible Word of God.

That, therefore, is why we stress that our comprehensive subject, 'The State of the Nation and of the World Today', is being viewed biblically and prophetically. It will also include 'The Situation in Europe Today and in the Middle East'. In this Book, the Bible, these things are *revealed*. The answer to our question is revealed. Christianity is a revealed religion—a God-revealed religion. And we must never forget that. We would not know a thing about it, otherwise.

> As it is written, Eye hath not seen, nor ear heard, neither have entered into the heart of man, the things which God hath prepared for them that love him. But God hath revealed them unto us by his Spirit (1 Corinthians 2:9–10).

Nobody can deny that things on the Continent of Europe, in Israel and the Middle East, in the Far East even, and indeed throughout the whole world, are happening at such a rapid and breath-taking rate today that it is almost impossible to keep up with them. In fact, I have to update parts of this message almost every day! Things are happening so fast!

'The signs of the times' which are mentioned many times in the Bible, especially in the sayings of Jesus, are multiplying so rapidly, and world affairs are developing so quickly, that it seems they are heading up to some climax of gigantic proportions. So much so, that I am obliged to ask myself: Are we fast heading towards the climax of the ages, and towards 'the coming great day of God', of which God's holy prophets have spoken almost ever since the world began? This is what the

Prophet Joel referred to as 'the great and the terrible day of the Lord' (Joel 2:31), which the Apostle Peter quoted in his sermon on the Day of Pentecost (see Acts 2:20). He referred to it there as 'That great and notable day of the Lord', which was coming. If so, there is certainly an urgent need to 'Set the trumpet to [one's] mouth' (Hosea 8:1), which is why I struck that note right at the beginning.

However that might be, I have had it very strongly laid upon my heart that the most relevant prophetic Scripture for this present momentous day in which we live is to be found in Haggai 2:6–7. I will read it from the Authorised Version of the Bible (the King James Version), which I believe is still the most accurate translation of the Bible that there is for preaching, teaching and devotional purposes, which is why I always preach and teach and quote from it. It reads:

> For thus saith the Lord of hosts; Yet once, it is a little while, and I will shake the heavens, and the earth, and the sea, and the dry land; and I will shake all nations, and the desire of all nations shall come.

Friends, that is what God is going to do! And I believe it will be very soon. I believe we are hard up against that. That passage of prophetic Scripture is basic to the whole of this message that I am proclaiming everywhere, today. I will keep coming back to that.

And as I proceed, I want you to bear in mind this principle: God never judges unless He first *warns*. And God is warning, right now. He is warning this nation. He is warning all the nations. He is warning the whole world of what is coming— and maybe very soon.

I would like to follow that reading from Haggai 2:6–7, with its New Testament equivalent in the Epistle to the Hebrews 12:25–29, which shows us very clearly that what God says in Haggai 2:6–7 is *still future*. It has still to be fulfilled. So God is talking about something which is still ahead of us. But maybe not very far ahead of us. It could happen at any moment.

Hebrews 12:25–29 says:

> See that ye refuse not him that speaketh.

That means Jesus, when it is read in the context of the rest of the chapter: 'See that ye refuse not him—Jesus!'

> For if they [which, in the context of the whole chapter, is referring to the children of Israel, who were gathered around Mount Sinai when God came down on the mountain to give Moses the Ten Commandments—as recorded for us in Exodus 19], if they escaped not who refused him that spake on earth, much more shall not we escape, if we turn away from him that speaketh from heaven: whose voice then [at Sinai] shook the earth: but now he hath promised, saying, Yet once more I shake not the earth only, but also heaven. And this word, Yet once more, signifieth the removing of those things that are shaken, as of things that are made, that those things which cannot be shaken may remain. Wherefore we [Christians that means, and only Christians, only truly born-again Christians, for it was Christians here that were being written to—Hebrew Christians in this case], Wherefore we [believers] receiving a kingdom which cannot be moved, let us have grace, whereby we may serve God acceptably with reverence and godly fear: for our God is a consuming fire.

And then I would like to follow that reading with another related Scripture from 2 Peter 3:10–11. We have been talking about 'The coming great day of God', 'The great day of the Lord that is coming', 'The great and terrible day of the Lord,' 'The great and notable day of the Lord'. And these verses from 2 Peter 3:10–11 say:

> The day of the Lord will come as a thief in the night; in the which the heavens shall pass away with a great noise, and the elements shall melt with fervent heat, the earth also and the works that are therein shall be burned up. Seeing then that all these things shall be dissolved, what manner of persons [what kind of persons] ought ye to be in all holy conversation and godliness?

Friends, all these Scriptures are talking about the day of the Lord which events in the world today are fast heading up to! I stress—maybe soon. Maybe sooner than we expect. World events today are fast 'bringing us into focus', so to speak, with it, and are bringing certain major prophetic Scriptures, like those to which I have already referred, into focus with it. They are talking about 'The coming day of God', and what some Scriptures refer to as 'The great and terrible day of the Lord'.

It is coming. It is going to be a mighty visitation of God; a mighty visitation of God *in judgment*—and upon the nations, the Gentile nations.

And I would suggest that where such a subject as 'The State of the Nation and of the World Today Viewed Biblically and Prophetically' is concerned, especially in the light of the fast-approaching 'climax of the ages', there is no more relevant Scripture than Haggai 2:6–7, which, no doubt, is why the Lord has laid it so heavily on my heart as the background Scripture against which the whole of today's preaching should be set.

I repeat:

> For thus saith the Lord of hosts: Yet once, it is a little while, and I will shake the heavens, and the earth, and the sea, and the dry land; And I will shake *all nations*, and the desire of all nations shall come.

This says it *all*! It speaks to both our national situation, and to the international situation in a nutshell, so to speak. And it speaks to both of them today, in the context of these most momentous days in which we live. Anybody with an all-seeing eye, certainly any truly born-again believer, with the eye of perception—of spiritual perception—can see very clearly that this is what is soon to happen, especially if they know their Scriptures, which, unfortunately today, many of them don't!

God will shake all nations. And all nations includes Britain! And that includes Scotland! It also includes Wales. And furthermore it includes Ireland! And God is going to shake all nations in judgment. That is the message of the hour! Then the desire of all nations shall come. The desire of all nations is the Lord Jesus Christ.

God will shake all nations in judgment in a way in which I propose to show from the Scriptures. And then the Lord Jesus Christ, my Saviour, will return, literally, and in Person, identified by the nail-marks in His hands, and in His feet. Bishop of Durham and all other disbelieving bishops and archbishops and church leaders, I will have you know. This is the message of the Bible.

And His return could be far nearer than we think. Everything that is happening on the world scene today is fast-paving the way for His glorious return. It is all heading up to that. That is the great culminating point to which Almighty God is working; it is what the prophets of the Bible describe as 'The consummation of all things'. And some of us here today may even see it take place. That, my dear friends, is what lies ahead of us, and maybe immediately ahead of us.

So the question is: Are we ready for it? Are we ready for Him—Jesus? And what are we doing to prepare others for it? And for Him? These are questions which need to be asked at this present time.

Now, if you turn to Haggai 2:6–7 you will notice that Haggai 2:6 begins with the words 'For thus saith the Lord.' 'Thus saith the Lord,' I repeat that. This, therefore, is no 'way-out' prophecy which has nothing to do with what the Bible says, like a number of so-called prophecies' (in inverted commas) which are being trotted out in some Christian circles today. Listen! All prophecies should be well and truly in line with what the Bible says, and should be seen and heard to be.

And why? Why! Because Isaiah 8:20 says:

> To the law and to the testimony: if they speak not according to this word [this word means the Bible], it is because there is no light in them.

And Amos 3:7 says:

> Surely the Lord God will do nothing, but he revealeth his secret unto his servants the prophets.

And his servants, the prophets, are those who proclaim from this Word of God—the Bible—what God is saying. It is what the Apostle Peter described as 'a *more sure* word of prophecy' (2 Peter 1:19).

In these days in which we live it needs to be stated very clearly that 'this more sure word of prophecy'—the Bible—

never has to be tested. It is certain. It is sure. It is irrefutable. It is bound to be fulfilled. The thing which God has said shall come to pass. There is no 'if', or 'perhaps', or 'maybe' about it. That which God has spoken shall be done.

I repeat, 'if they speak not according to this word, it is because there is no light in them.' These are *false* prophets, who do not speak according to this Word. We read in the Bible that the false prophets of Isaiah's, Jeremiah's, and Ezekiel's day prophesied by the methods and techniques used in divination and sorcery. They used occultic powers—psychic powers in other words—demonic powers. They indulged in listning to 'voices' outside of themselves, the voices of evil spirits, of demons. They even resorted to telepathy. So it was not under the power and inspiration of the Holy Spirit that they spake. And much false prophecy today comes from similar sources.

But it is according to this Word, according to 'this more sure prophecy', taken from the Word of God, the Bible, that I aim to speak to you all today. And so we come to the subject, 'The State of the World and of the Nation Today, Viewed Biblically and Prophetically.'

Chapter Two

The State of Our Own Nation Today Viewed Biblically

I deliberately take first, the state of our own nation of Britain today. What is God saying to Britain and about Britain today? Inevitably, I will be dealing also, in a measure, with the appalling state of the Church, because the state of the Church is intricately linked with the state of our nation.

In answering the question: What is God saying to Britain, and about Britain, and to the British people today?, an appropriate text would be Isaiah 58:1:

> Cry aloud, spare not, lift up thy voice like a trumpet, and shew my people their transgression, and the house of Jacob their sins.

That is what urgently needs to be done. Britain, as a nation, needs to be confronted with her transgression, and the British people with their sins—all of them. This is the first step that needs to be taken before ever beginning to pronounce the cure.

We are a nation which is ripe for judgment. There is no question at all about that. And we are a nation which is ripe for judgment because of our sins, and because of our blatant transgressions which are being committed, quite unashamedly, right out in the open, now, for everyone, even the children, to see.

In presenting Britain's case, by way of making a diagnosis, I will make the following points first.

We are unquestionably a nation upon which the hand of

Almighty God has rested in blessing, for some reason best known to Himself, all down the centuries of our national history. This fact is irrefutable. It is unarguable. I have dealt with this in great detail in Volumes 1 and 2 of *The Trumpet Sounds for Britain*. The hand of Almighty God, in blessing, can be traced throughout our long history in at least four ways.

First, God has given these islands Christian foundations from the very earliest times—either directly from Pentecost or shortly after Pentecost. For instance, before Sir Winston Churchill wrote his *History of the English-Speaking Peoples*, he had an army of researchers at work trying to discover when Christianity was first brought to this country. They found their task impossible. Christianity was already here when the first missionaries arrived.

Indeed, there is quite a remarkable chain of evidence to support the fact that Christianity was brought to these islands at a very early stage. A whole chain of evidence shows that well over 550 years before ever Augustine landed with his Roman form of Christianity, God had caused the pure, New Testament, Apostolic form of Christianity to come to these islands.

History books erroneously claim that Christianity in these islands began with Augustine. That is what has been taught for far too long. However, that idea is false, utterly false. I want to blow the idea sky-high! Most of the history books are blatantly wrong at this point. So has been, and still is, most of the teaching in schools, colleges and in universities, even in some Bible Colleges and Theological Colleges.

Augustine did not arrive on these shores until AD 596, and by the time he arrived, a very ardent and virile form of Christianity was flourishing and growing in Wales, in Scotland, and in the North of England, as I will go on to show. And furthermore, he knew it! He also knew that there were Christian bishops here when he landed, even before he set out. And so did those who sent him. So it is quite wrong to say Christianity in Britain began with Augustine. Nothing could be further from the truth. It was here at least 550 years before Augustine arrived; that is, over half a millennium before he arrived!

The question, therefore, is: When did it arrive, and in what form? The answer is: It could have come direct from Pentecost or very soon after, and I will give very good reasons why it could have, a little later.

But this much can be firmly and irrefutably established, that early Christianity in Britain dates at least as far back as the period of the Roman occupation of these islands. In the year AD 43 the Roman Emperor Claudius—the Claudius Caesar who is several times mentioned in the Acts of the Apostles—landed with his Roman legions in Kent, only ten years after the crucifixion, resurrection, ascension of our Lord Jesus Christ, if we can quote AD 33 as the date of our Lord's crucifixion, and only ten years after the Day of Pentecost.

That is how early the period of the Roman occupation of Britain began. So British history was running parallel with all the events of the New Testament even then! Then from AD 43 onwards, Britain remained one of the 45 provinces of the great Roman Empire for 400 years, until the year AD 407. That was 189 years before Augustine arrived!

I notice that one historian after another that I have read, says that the Roman occupation of Britain gave time for the Christian faith to be planted. They also add that it was within that period that there arose a British Church which sent its bishops to the early Church Councils. This settles the matter pretty conclusively. Early Christianity would have had to be quite strongly developed and established to be in a position to do that! So there had arisen a British Church in these islands long before Augustine was even born, or thought of!

G. M. Trevelyan, the English historian, wrote:

> When the last of the Roman legions left these shores, and the Romans passed out of the story of Britain, they left behind them just three things of value, and the first of these was Welsh Christianity.

This establishes beyond any shadow of doubt that Christianity was already here well within this period of Roman occupation. His use of the term 'Welsh' Christianity also furnishes us with a clue as to what type of Christianity it was.

But there are strong indications that Christianity was here even earlier than this. I will explain this statement as follows.

The rise of the great Roman Empire paved the way for the spread of the Gospel. Once Julius Caesar had planted its power firmly and widely on the north side of the Alps and into Gaul, he caused the Empire to be stretched right across the world from East to West. Roads were then built by the Romans across this great Empire.

All historians, each in his turn, give testimony to the fact that the great Roman Empire, which arose after Julius Caesar, became the arena for the propagation of Christianity, which travelled to the four corners of civilisation very quickly by the roads built and guarded by the Roman soldiers. Churchill, in his *History of the English-Speaking Peoples*, writes, 'There were no obstructions of frontiers, laws, currency, or nationalism to hinder it.'

Then, fifty-five years before the birth of our Lord Jesus Christ in Bethlehem, Julius Caesar first landed in Britain, in 55 BC. This prepared the way for the conquest of Britain under Claudius Caesar in AD 43. But the landing of Julius Caesar, fifty-five years before the birth of Jesus Christ, also opened the way for the arrival of the Gospel. G. M. Trevelyan records that from the time of Julius Caesar's departure from these shores, a peaceful penetration of Britain by travellers from Rome and from other and more distant parts of the Roman Empire began (including from all the Mediterranean countries), and continued between Julius Caesar's departure from Britain and Britain's conquest by Claudius.

Added to this, all the events concerning Christianity's beginnings in the Roman province of Judaea can be placed within a significant and specific timetable.

Luke tells us in his Gospel, for instance, that the birth of our Lord Jesus Christ took place in Bethlehem in the days of the Roman Emperor Caesar Augustus, who was Emperor from 31 BC to AD 14. So he was Emperor at the actual time of Jesus' birth.

Caesar Augustus was succeeded by Tiberius Caesar, who was Emperor from AD 14 to AD 37. He would still have been Emperor at the time of Jesus' crucifixion, therefore.

In Tiberius Caesar's fifteenth year, John the Baptist arrived on the scene.

Our Lord began His earthly ministry when He was about thirty years of age according to Luke's account of all this. His crucifixion and resurrection took place three years later. Forty days after that, His ascension into heaven took place. The

Holy Spirit came upon the 120 disciples in the Upper Room in Jerusalem on the Day of Pentecost, 40 days after our Lord Jesus's ascension.

All the main events in our Saviour's life, therefore, took place within the two historic points of Roman and British history to which I have already referred, namely, the landing in Britain by Julius Caesar in 55 BC, and the invasion of Britain by Claudius Caesar. So if we place the crucifixion of our blessed Lord in the year AD 33, the gap, in years, is very narrow indeed between the crucifixion, resurrection and ascension of our Lord (and Pentecost), and Claudius Caesar's invasion of Britain. That gap was only a matter of ten years.

Why do I get so excited about this? Why! Because I find that G. M. Trevelyan, the historian, makes this very significant statement:

> The hundred most important years in the history of the world were not wholly blank *even in Britain*. While Julius Caesar was being murdered and avenged, while the loves of Antony and Cleopatra were raising the question of the relation of East and West inside the Roman World, while Caesar Augustus was busy constructing the Empire, while Jesus Christ was *preaching* and while Paul was being converted—throughout all this period, far in the north, Roman traders and colonists, working from the base of the Romanized province of Gaul, were establishing settlements in the interior of Britain and gaining influence at the courts of its tribal kings.

While Jesus Christ was preaching they were doing that! While He was working His miracles also, that means!

I get so excited about this because it was preparing the way for an early arrival of the Gospel; a very early arrival of the Gospel indeed!

Notice what it says. The Romans were establishing settlements in Britain even before Jesus Christ was born! Merchants and traders were travelling backwards and forwards between the Mediterranean countries, and were coming, with merchandise and produce, right into the interior of Britain, to the settlements which they had established there, throughout the time of Jesus' childhood and earthly ministry, while He was preaching and working miracles, at the time of His crucifixion, resurrection and ascension, and at the time of the outpouring of the Holy Spirit on the Day of Pentecost! So news of these happenings could have been brought here by these merchants and traders even as early as that! And they wouldn't have kept quiet about His miracles if any of them had heard about them, or even witnessed them!

I am persuaded, therefore, that there is no reason whatsoever why faith in Jesus Christ, in terms of a personal belief and trust in Him, could not have been brought to Britain direct from Pentecost, or at least, very soon after it, even if not before Pentecost.

But let's now look at what happened at Pentecost.

• 'There were dwelling at Jerusalem Jews, devout men, out of every nation under heaven,' says Acts 2:5. They could easily have included people from those settlements in Britain if 'every nation under heaven' included Britain.
• The Holy Spirit came down on the 120 disciples.
• This great multitude of Jews rushed together to see what had happened. (There had been a great sound from heaven like a rushing mighty wind to attract them!)
• Peter preached his first sermon out in the streets of Jerusalem under the power of the Holy Spirit.
• 3,000 of them were converted; then 5,000! Then many more.

But they didn't stay there. They returned to the various nations from where they had come. The thousands who had been converted took their new faith with them—the Christian faith. Furthermore, they went back indwelt by the Spirit of Jesus. And if any of them had, indeed, come from Britain, they returned to Britain carrying the Spirit of the Lord within them. Some of them were merchants and traders. They were Jews! This was their livelihood! But they were now new creatures in Christ Jesus, filled with the joy of the new life, which they would have wanted to share with others along the trade routes. They would have been so filled with the Holy Spirit that they would surely have taken the Gospel wherever they went, to be discussed and talked about, and the news about Jesus would be carried very far afield.

What is more, they had come as families and groups. The Jew is noted for his strong family ties and family allegiances. We are given an insight into the way they travelled, as families, in the account of how Jesus was taken up to Jerusalem at the age of twelve. On the return journey to Nazareth 'the child Jesus tarried behind in Jerusalem; and Joseph and his mother knew not of it,' says Luke 2:43. But then it says, 'But they, supposing him to have been in the company, went a day's journey; and they sought him among their kinsfolk and acquaintance' (v 44). So it must have been a considerably large company! They travelled that way in those days. The multitude of Jews who went up to Jerusalem for the Feast of Pentecost had travelled in families and in groups. So they would have returned in families and groups, but now as Christian groups and families, those of them who had been converted.

On their return they would have used these Christian groups as nucleii for establishing Christian churches in the various countries, towns and cities from whence they had come. These cities and towns were situated all along the main highways and trade routes throughout the provinces of the Roman Empire, and that is one of the explanations of why Christianity spread so quickly.

When Paul the apostle arrived at Ephesus on his missionary journeys, for instance, he found there was a group of Christian believers already there. And long before he arrived in Rome he knew there was a Christian church already there because he wrote to them! Hence his Epistle to the Romans. Moreover, he said to them in the opening section of that Epistle, 'I thank my God through Jesus Christ for you all, that your faith is spoken of throughout the whole world.' Such was the impact that the Christian faith was making in those early days of Christianity. In such a way was it spreading. It could have been spoken of in Britain.

That letter from Paul the apostle to the Christians at Rome was written in approximately AD 56, and Britain had already been a province of the Roman Empire for twelve years by them. So there is no reason why the faith in Christ could not have been taken by newly converted Jewish merchants and traders from Pentecost along the trade routes and right through to those settlements in the interior of Britain, and even into the courts of its tribal kings.

The Apostle Paul arrived in Rome in AD 60. He had said in his Epistle to the Romans that he intended to go to Spain from there (see Romans 15:24). In Rome he was held in open imprisonment, but had freedom to preach there for two years (see Acts 28:30–31). It is believed he was released from this open imprisonment after two years and that he fulfilled his intention of taking the Gospel as far west as Spain. If that is so, the Gospel could very quickly have reached Britain from Spain, either by the sea route across the Bay of Biscay and round the coast of France, or overland through the Roman province of Gaul, and thence across the Channel to Britain, especially as this had been a route taken by merchants, traders and colonists ever since Julius Caesar's landing in 55 BC.

But there are documents which go even further than this. The historian, Eusebius, who is sometimes referred to as the 'Greek father of ecclesiastical history', and who lived from AD 264 to AD 349, makes this very significant statement:

> The apostles passed beyond the ocean to the isles called the Brittanic Isles.

He says the Apostles did! To which I must immediately add that if they did, then it follows that the Gospel which they brought here with them was the Apostolic Gospel, and that that was what they preached here! It was pure Christianity, in other words—New Testament Christianity! It would have been no false form of it. Eusebius made that statement at least 300 years before Augustine was to arrive.

Then a man named Gildas, who was a Celtic priest, and one of the earliest historians of the conquest of Britain by the Roman Emperor Claudius, and others, testified that:

> Britain received the Gospel in the latter part of the reign of Emperor Tiberius.

Gildas was saying there were Christians here in Britain as early as that!

I have already pointed out that Tiberius reigned as Emperor from AD 14 to AD 37. That is a known fact of history.

Therefore if Britain received the Gospel in the last part of his reign, it must have been shortly after the crucifixion, resurrection and ascension of our Lord, and the coming of the Holy Ghost on the 120 disciples on the Day of Pentecost. If the crucifixion took place in AD 33, which is the usual date quoted, it would leave only five years before 'the latter part of the reign of Tiberius' had come to an end. So it would have to be somewhere between AD 33 and AD 37 that 'Britain received the Gospel', to quote the words of Gildas.

In addition I discover that the Venerable Bede also speaks of an early Christian mission to Britain, dating from that very early date of AD 37.

Also Tertullian, writing in AD 190, 407 years—or thereabouts—before Augustine, said:

> The extremities of Spain, the various parts of Gaul, the regions of Britain have received the Christian faith.

Notice he includes 'the regions of Britain'!

I have also discovered that several early church historians have identified these Apostles who 'passed beyond the ocean to the isles called the Brittanic Isles'. Theodoretus, for instance, wrote in a book dated AD 435 (162 years before Augustine arrived here or was even born!):

> Paul, liberated from his first captivity at Rome, preached the Gospel to the Britons, and to others in the West.

'To the Britons,' he wrote!

Sophronius, who was Bishop of Jerusalem in AD 600 (three years after Augustine landed), says:

> Paul, doctor of the Gentiles, passed over the ocean to the island that makes a haven on the other side, even to the lands of the Britons, even to Ultima Thule.

So *he* didn't believe that Christianity in Britain began with Augustine!

Then once again, Arnoldus Mirmannus, yet another early church historian, stated:

> Paul passed to Britain in the fourth year of Nero [AD 59], and there preached, and afterward returned to Italy.

In addition to this, early church historians and writers such as Eusebius, state:

> Peter went to Britain during the expulsion of the Jews from Rome under Claudius.

Peter did!

This expulsion of the Jews from Rome, under the Emperor Claudius, according to the most reliable dating, was in AD 54. It is referred to in Acts 18:1–2. And this Emperor Claudius, by the way, is the same Claudius who landed in Britain with his Roman legions in AD 43 and so began the period of Roman occupation of these islands. Eusebius's statement, if it is true, would mean that Peter would have come to Britain in AD 54, or soon after, if he came here during the expulsion of the Jews under Claudius.

So 'the apostles who passed beyond the oceans to the isles called the Brittanic Isles' included the Apostle Paul, and the Apostle Peter according to these authorities.

It was firmly held by all these early church historians, therefore, that the Christian faith was being preached and planted in Britain not many years after Jesus ascended into heaven, and certainly during the early stages of the Roman occupation of Britain. They even say that the Apostle Paul and the Apostle Peter were among those who brought it here, and they must have had good and reliable authority for saying that.

But if they did, do you realise what that means? It means that if this was indeed the case, then we know what Gospel they would have preached here!

The Apostle Paul would have preached the same Gospel which he had been preaching everywhere else, and as is recorded in many places in the Acts of the Apostles, and in all his Epistles. Furthermore, he would have preached the kind of sermon that he preached on Mars Hill, which is recorded for us in Acts 17, especially as there was Druid worship, the worship of Mithras, and of Thor and Woden here. Namely:

The times of this ignorance God winked at; but now commandeth all men every where to repent; because he hath appointed a day in the which he will judge the world in righteousness by that man whom he hath ordained; whereof he hath given assurance unto all men, in that he hath raised him from the dead (Acts 17:30–31).

The burden of his preaching would have been the same as it was when he came to Corinth:

I determined not to know anything among you, save Jesus Christ, and him crucified (1 Corinthians 2:2).

He would not have preached about faith in a city! He would have preached Jesus, and the resurrection! He would have preached, also, what he had already expounded fully in writing in his Epistle to the Romans, in his Epistle to the Ephesians, in his Epistles to the Philippians, Colossians, Galatians, Corinthians, and in 1 and 2 Thessalonians, and in all his other Epistles: namely, pure, unadulterated, Holy Ghost-revealed Christianity, and no false form of it. He might even have left copies of his Epistles behind!

The Apostle Peter would also have preached sermons similar to those we find recorded in the Acts of the Apostles. And he would have preached what he had already committed to writing in the two Epistles of Peter. And if, as many authorities claim, Peter dictated to Mark all the contents of Mark's Gospel for him to write down, he would have shared with his hearers in Britain all those events and details of the Lord's life and earthly ministry which are recorded in Mark's Gospel, and certainly the events concerning Jesus' crucifixion, resurrection, ascension into heaven, and the coming of the Holy Ghost on the Day of Pentecost, and upon himself! After all, Peter was very much involved in that mighty outpouring of the Holy Spirit. The Holy Spirit had come upon him!

In other words, what the Apostle Paul and the Apostle Peter, and any others who were with them, would have brought here and would have preached and taught here, would have been what the Apostle Jude described as 'the common salvation'—salvation through faith in Jesus Christ and through His atoning and reconciling death on the cross.

That faith was the faith which was common to them all: common to Matthew, Mark, Luke, and John and to all the other Apostles. It was what was common to each one, and every true believer in these early New Testament days, and was what was common to all of the New Testament churches everywhere. There was only one faith, only one Gospel. It was common to everyone, everywhere. It was, in fact, 'The faith which was once delivered unto the saints' (Jude 3). And it was the faith *as* it was once delivered to the saints. There were no corruptions of it. It was the New Testament faith—the original Apostolic faith; the pure New Testament form of Christianity.

There is, therefore, a very strong case for saying that under the controlling influence and direction of an Almighty God, Christianity arrived in Britain very early, and in its purest form. All the evidence points that way.

I suggest it could have arrived here during the ten-year interval between Pentecost and Claudius Caesar's conquest, and even before Britain became a Roman province, perhaps not very long after the Day of Pentecost. It certainly seems to have begun to be established here at least as early as the Roman occupation of Britain in AD 43. And if that is true, it establishes beyond question the form of Christianity it was.

But I need to go further and say that the Christianity which God had graciously brought to these islands so early, was taking root and spreading to such an extent during the period of the Roman occupation of Britain, that Churchill, in his *History of the English-Speaking Peoples*, thrilled with excitement, and caught up with the spirit of its onward march, proclaimed with great exuberance, 'The new creed was winning victories everywhere'! And this was in the Britain which, long before the days of Julius Caesar, and before the birth of our Lord Jesus Christ at Bethlehem, had been the chief centre of ancient Druid worship, the worship of the gods of Thor and Woden, and where human sacrifices were being made.

I only wish we could say, with equally great exuberance, that that same Christian faith is winning victories everywhere in Britain today! It is the other faiths and religions that are. They are even penetrating our Cathedrals!

In the year AD 367, the Picts from Scotland, the Scots from Ireland, and the Saxons from Europe all seemed to work in conjunction with one another, for all fell together on Britannia. At the same time, the Roman legions had to withdraw, because the Roman Empire itself was being assailed by invading hordes. Then in the year AD 442, a mass migration of assaulting barbarians from North Germany also descended on Britain. A period of terrible carnage and destruction began, and from this time onwards the curtains closed down on our history. The period of the Dark Ages had been ushered in, and a long dark night fell upon Britannia. The next 200 years of our history are left almost entirely blank.

Churchill laments: 'England was once again a barbarian island. It had been Christian, it was now heathen.' He was acknowledging it had been Christian! Therefore *he* didn't believe that Christianity in Britain began with Augustine! We are still talking about a period of our history which was at least 155 years before Augustine arrived!

Although the curtains closed down on our history, although a long dark night fell upon Britannia, although the period of the Dark Ages had been ushered in, God had preserved and nurtured more than a remnant of that already existing Christian Church—the Christian Church that had been established in Britain these hundreds of years before Augustine. For in the face of the terrible barbarian onslaught, the British Church had fallen back with other survivors upon the western parts of the island, and had taken refuge behind the Welsh mountains. There, under the hand of God, it continued to be spiritually led, nurtured, and encouraged, throughout this dark period, by Christian missionaries who kept coming over from the Continent to ensure that faith was sustained. In this way Christianity in the British Isles was preserved during the long period of these barbarian invasions. The point is, it was still there! As one historian has put it:

> There, far to the West, whilst the rest of Britain was being savaged and shaken by these ferocious hordes, cut off from the rest of the world by the barbarian flood, but defended by its mountains, there remained this tiny Christian realm.

It was an example of the glorious fulfilment of the Lord Jesus' utterance: 'I will build my church; and the gates of hell shall not prevail against it' (Matthew 16:18). All else had been devastated and destroyed, but there was one thing that remained—the Church of Jesus Christ!

Moreover, this Christian faith, driven back behind the Welsh mountains, got such a hold over the Welsh, that by the fifth and sixth centuries they had come to regard Christianity as their distinguishing mark.

But then came the resurgence of this Christianity, and the story of how it began to flourish and to spread once more. To understand about this, we must come now to the story of Patrick.

Patrick was a native of the western part of this country. He lived in the Severn Valley. A band of raiders came from Ireland across to the Severn Valley when he was still a lad, carried him away captive to Ireland, and sold him into slavery. There, in his loneliness, he was converted to Jesus Christ. He managed to make his escape, and persuaded the captain of a ship to take him on board. Thus he found his way to some islands off Marseilles. There he came under the care of Bishop Germanus of Auxerre and, after fourteen years of preparation and training, sailed back to Ireland in AD 432.

All this happened to Patrick long before the mass migration from North Germany to Britannia had begun. His return to Ireland in AD 432 was still 165 years before Augustine arrived. But God was preparing His instrument.

Ten years after Patrick's return to Ireland, in AD 442, Britain was plunged into night. That long period of darkness began. In his *History of the English-Speaking Peoples*, Winston Churchill wrote these sombre words:

> Far away in the centre of the world where Christianity had had its origin [ie, Judaea, Jerusalem and Palestine], men remembered that Britain had been Christian once, and might be Christian again.

Ireland, however, had been spared the waves of barbarian Saxons from the Continent and the mass migration from North Germany. And Patrick was now back in Ireland, and had been for over ten years. At a certain point, this is what we read of him:

Then came Patrick, and gathered together those Christians that remained, and through them, he proceeded to convert whole regions of Ireland to Christ.

God used Patrick to establish Christian churches over there.

When this had eventually been accomplished in Ireland, God brought Columba, imbued with the same fire and evangelistic zeal, from Ireland, to set up his group of beehive huts on the island of Iona.

In AD 563, still thirty-four years before Augustine arrived, Columba used his Iona base to send out swarms of missionaries over Western Scotland and Northern Britain. An ardent and vital movement of Christianity was therefore set afoot in the north, which spread quickly to the kingdom of Northumbria in the East, and the British Kingdom of Strathclyde in the West.

Columba became the founder of the Scottish Church. So the Scottish Church, too, was in existence before Augustine arrived!

Furthermore, it is important to stress at this point that the history books do not refer to the time of Patrick and Columba as the coming of Christianity to Britain—rather, they refer to it as the return of Christianity to Britain. That is why I myself referred to it as the resurgence; it was the resurgence of the already, long-existing Christian faith and British Church.

Equally important is it to stress that it is the historians (who have no particular axe to grind), not the theologians, who tell us that the form of Christianity which Columba brought to Iona, to Scotland, and to Northern England, had travelled from its original source in the Middle East (namely from Jerusalem and the Holy Land), through Northern Ireland, to its new home in Scotland and the North of England, without touching at any moment the centre at Rome.

Again, that means that it was pure New Testament Christianity, the original Apostolic Christianity. It was, therefore, this form of Christianity upon which that early Scottish Church, and the Church in Northern England was founded. It was this form of Christianity that became known as 'Irish' or 'Celtic' Christianity; 'Irish' because Columba brought it from Ireland.

I believe it is also important to explain that under Patrick's leadership, this Celtic Christianity had taken the form of loosely knit communities of devout Christians, who separated themselves from the rest of mankind, and lived in beehive huts made of wattle, clay, and turf. The huts were often grouped together in a fortified village or kraal on some rocky mountain or remote island, under the supervision of an outstanding Christian leader. That is what is meant when we talk about God using Patrick to establish 'churches' over in Ireland. It is not what we mean by the word 'church', in terms of one building where people worship, as we see it today. The purpose of this separation into groups of fortified wattle huts was to so build themselves up in the faith that they could go out and convert whole areas and regions to Jesus Christ.

These Christian communities were by nature, missionary bases, and in essence, this form of Christianity was independent. It was free from outside control, just as each and every Christian church in the New Testament was free from outside control. Never at any time in the New Testament was there even the beginnings of an idea that all churches should be brought under one supreme head. So the wattle-hut, kraal-type centres of Christianity which Patrick and Columba had established as missionary bases, were, like the New Testament churches, equally free of any outside control. And at this early period there was no association in any way with the universal organisation of the papacy, although many of the continental churches had by this time become linked with it.

To continue the story:

It is a fact of history that Rome, from a very early stage, had followed with deep interest the results of Columba's labour in Scotland and the North of England. It had seen that the Christian movement which was breaking out in the northern parts of the far-off islands of Britain was ardent and zealous, and full of fervour. Rome was excited about the spread of the Gospel there. But it became deeply disturbed because the faith seemed to have been separately planted, and viewed with deep concern the fact that, from the very outset, the Church in Britain was independent of any control from Rome.

Gregory was Bishop of Rome at the time when it was decided that it was the Bishop of Rome's duty to see that all

Christians in every country should be brought under one earthly head. Therefore Gregory, and the ecclesiastical statesmen who were gathered together in Rome, sent Augustine to England in AD 596, not only to spread the Gospel in England further, but also to bring about an effective union between British Christians and what, in the Roman view, was the main body of the Church.

I stress that this was when there was already a very live form of Christianity in Scotland, and when Columba had founded the Scottish Church. There was also a very live form of Christianity in the North of England by this time, brought there by Columba and his missionaries. Behind the Welsh mountains, too, there was a flourishing Church, which for a very long time by now, even as far back as the period of the Roman occupation of Britain, had been sending its bishops to the various Councils of the Church. And there was a very virile form of Christianity in Ireland! Added to all of which, a resurgence of the original Christianity which had been brought here early, and which had become very strongly and firmly established during the long period of the Roman occupation of Britain, was, by the time Augustine arrived, more than beginning to take place. So how anybody could possibly say Christianity in Britain began with Augustine I just don't know! It is flying in the face of historical facts. There had been a very long history of Christianity in Britain by the time that Augustine arrived.

The truth of the matter is that after he had landed, and following the conversion of King Ethelbert of Kent, and after he had founded the see of Canterbury and had made it a solid base for the subsequent spread of Roman Christianity over this island, Augustine set about this other task of bringing about Gregory's desired union of British Christians with the Church at Rome.

From the outset, his attention became focussed in a westerly direction, for his first attempt was directed towards the British Church, which, during the barbarian invasions, had been so miraculously preserved behind the Welsh mountains. He summoned a conference of its British Christian bishops and Welsh representatives at the mouth of the River Severn. But the bishops were in no mood for throwing themselves into the strong embraces of Rome.

When Augustine claimed to have supremacy over all Christians in Britain by virtue of his Roman commission, they adamantly rejected his claim. They had defended the faith for so long against all the terrible cruelties and oppressions which the barbarians had levelled at them, and had remained independent, so why should they now subject themselves to being controlled from overseas? Why lose their freedom?

When Augustine threatened that if they did not submit, the Saxon armies in England would be used to bring the whole influence and prestige of Rome against them, they saw Rome in its true light. (It was one of the earliest indications that Rome intended to get what it wanted by force of arms if necessary.) That finished the matter as far as the British bishops and Welsh representatives were concerned, and the conference broke up in enmity.

Augustine's attempt to bring about a union had totally failed, and, with it, Rome's very first step in the direction of making Britain a Roman Catholic country. All further efforts by Augustine in this direction were virulently repulsed. This is historical fact, proven historical fact. Such infinite pains, therefore, did Almighty God take to ensure that these islands were established on Christian foundations, and on New Testament Apostolic Christian Foundations at that.

The second way in which the hand of Almighty God can be seen in blessing on this nation's history is in restoring those pure, New Testament, Apostolic, Christian foundations whenever they have been in danger of being destroyed or of becoming lost.

We have only to think of the glorious Reformation, then of the time of the Puritans, then of the Great Awakening which was brought about under the preaching of Whitefield and Wesley, then of the Moody Revival, and of the great Welsh Revivals, and of the Scottish Revivals, to establish that fact. I can only deal with all this in outline.

Third, the hand of Almighty God can also be seen at work in blessing in our history by causing these islands to be founded on Christian, and Bible-based laws ever since the time of King Alfred the Great, and even before then—up until the early 1960s and 1970s that is. So much was this the case that when I was a boy, the law of the land was absolutely in line with all of the Ten Commandments, and the Ten

Commandments were absolutely in line with the law of the land. The one could not be distinguished from the other. But look at the situation now!

Then the fourth way the hand of Almighty God can unquestionably be seen in blessing on this nation's history is in bringing about mighty and miraculous deliverances, especially when these islands were in danger of being invaded.

- At the time of the Armada, for instance, in 1588.
- At the time of the Gunpowder Plot which aimed at blowing up the King and Parliament in 1605.
- At the time of the Glorious Revolution in 1688.
- At the time when Napoleon had his armies mustered in France opposite Dover, ready to invade this country, only to be defeated by Nelson at the Battle of Trafalgar.
- During the 1914–18 war.
- During the 1939–45 war, when we saw the miracles of Dunkirk; the miracles which God wrought during the Battle of Britain which saved this country from Hitler's invasion, and many other miracles also, all of which I have recorded in detail in Volume 2 of *The Trumpet Sounds for Britain*.

We are indeed a nation which has long enjoyed a rich Christian heritage, and which has seen miraculous act of deliverance after miraculous act of deliverance all down the centuries of our history.

After all the mighty miracles which God wrought on this nation's behalf during the 1939–45 war, our King and national leaders and Service Chiefs proclaimed, 'We have been saved for a purpose, and now we need humbly to seek what that purpose is, and when we have done so, we need faithfully to fulfil it.' All this needs to be forthrightly stated when making an accurate diagnosis of the state of our nation today, and of the appalling state of its Church and its churches.

The tragedy is that we didn't seek to find out what that purpose was for which we had been saved. Somehow we 'missed the boat'. We turned away from God. We proceeded to put Him right out of the picture, and to keep Him out. We jettisoned our national Christian faith which had stood us in such good stead for so long.

And Parliament proceeded to put on our Statute Book anti-

God and anti-Christian laws, and laws which make legal things which the Bible specifically declares are an abomination in the sight of the Lord:

• such as legalised homosexuality from a certain age—sodomy, in other words. That is what the Bible calls it. And it refers to those who practise such foul and filthy behaviour as sodomites.

• such as easy divorce, which God says, 'I hate' (see Malachi 2:16).

• such as legalised abortion, which has resulted in no less than three and a quarter million living human creatures being put into hospital incinerators, many of them while they were still alive, since the United Kingdom Abortion Act was put on to our Statute Book in 1967, *and* with the Royal Assent if you please! And all to cover up the consequences of human sin, spelt with capital letters, because a very high percentage of these infants were conceived outside of holy wedlock. And this wholesale, legalised destruction of them has made this nation an exceedingly blood-guilty nation, because we have the blood of all these three and a quarter million children on our hands, and God is going to require that blood at the hands of the nation in terms of judgment. Let us make no mistake whatsoever about that. That is what the Bible teaches.

Listen to what Isaiah 26:20–21 has to say:

> Come, my people, enter thou into thy chambers, and shut thy doors about thee: hide thyself as it were for a little moment, until the indignation be overpast.

The indignation! That is what is coming, my friends! It is 'The great and terrible day of the Lord', to which I have already referred several times. It is 'The coming day of wrath'—what John the Baptist described as 'The wrath to come', and what Isaiah described as 'The day of vengeance'. That is what Isaiah is talking about when he says, 'hide thyself . . . until the indignation be overpast.'

Then he goes on to describe it still further:

> For, behold, the Lord cometh out of his place to punish the inhabitants of the earth for their iniquity: the earth

also shall disclose her blood, and shall no more cover her
slain.

We need to look at those stern and challenging words
again. What do they say?

'The Lord cometh out of his place.' What for? 'To punish.'
We say we must not talk about punishing people today. But
God talks about punishing!

It says, 'The Lord cometh out of his place *to* punish.' To
punish whom? 'The inhabitants of the earth.' What for? 'For
their iniquity.'

'The earth also shall disclose her blood, and shall no more
cover her slain.' What does that mean? It means that in that
day, all the blood of those who have been slain in terms of
violence, in terms of genocide, in terms of mass abortion, in
terms of brutal murder and such like, will be laid bare before
Almighty God. All will be brought out into the open. There
will be no more 'cover-up'. And God will require all that
blood at the hands of those that shed it.

Judgment *on blood-guiltiness* is what Isaiah 26:21 is talking
about. And where that blood has not been requited 'at the
hand of him that shed it', in terms of his forfeiting his life for
the life that he has taken, then God will require that blood at
the hand of his nation, of his country. That is what the Bible
teaches. So there is no question but that God is going to
require the blood of those three and a quarter million lives
that have been taken by legalised abortion, at the hand of this
nation in terms of some terrible form of judgment.

And yet we *still* persist in deliberately going down this
wrong road. The House of Lords voted, by a huge majority, in
favour of experimenting on living human embryos on 8th
February 1990. And that, despite the fact that the Duke of
Norfolk, and others, stated very clearly that human life begins
at the moment of conception, and continues to the moment of
indisputable death. Even bishops, and one archbishop, voted
in favour of experimenting with, and then destroying, these
unborn babies! Fleet Street, on the other hand, in an indignant
leading article in *The Sunday Telegraph* on 11th February 1990,
said of the House of Lords vote:

They don't think of themselves as having voted to

destroy unborn babies. They think of themselves as having voted to promote research on the causes of genetically carried diseases. In truth they were doing both. They were voting to sacrifice unborn babies on the altar of humanitarian research.

The article continues:

How strange it is that as society gets more and more squeamish about hanging murderers it gets ever more ruthless about destroying unborn babies.

That comment came from Fleet Street and Wapping, *not* the Church!

At the same time that it was putting all these anti-God and anti-Christian laws on to our Statute Book, Parliament abolished capital punishment, making us even more a blood-guilty nation, and thus causing the nation to invite Divine retribution even more.

Then, Roy Jenkins, when he was Home Secretary, introduced the permissive society, as a result of which anything became permissible.

By instigating these changes, Parliament was guilty of causing an escalation of the catastrophic moral and spiritual landslide which has been going on, completely unarrested, ever since.

Moreover, to make matters worse, the Church in our land has got further and further away from God and from the true, New Testament, Apostolic Gospel of our Lord Jesus Christ. It has got further and further away from the Bible—from belief in the Bible, and from what the Bible teaches. And it has done all this, largely in favour of ecumenism. Essential, basic, biblical doctrines have been deliberately set on one side in order to bring about a *false* unity.

The Established Church has even removed the Ten Commandments from the inside walls of their church buildings, where they had had a prominent place for so long, and where everybody, including the children, could see them and read them, and be guided by them. It also removed them from its church services where they used regularly to be read, Sunday by Sunday, so that now they are rarely, if ever, mentioned any more, or being taught.

The Bible says:

> If the foundations be destroyed, what can the righteous do? (Psalm 11:3).

And the foundations have been destroyed. All of them. There are none of them left, any more.

As a result of all this, and a lot more that I could mention, God is *angry* with us as a nation.

Psalm 119:126 says:

> It is time for thee, Lord, to work: for they have made void thy law.

We have become a nation and a people, therefore, that has forsaken the Lord.

And Ezra 8:22 says:

> The hand of our God is upon all them for good that seek him; but his power and his wrath is against all them that forsake him.

Who can stand against God's power and God's wrath? No one. Certainly not Britain!

We are therefore, now, a people *living without God*. And listen! All our troubles stem from there. So we are, in fact, a God-*less* nation and a God-*less* people, with God-*less* political parties, all of them. None of them speak about God any more, or make any mention of Him. We have even reached the stage where the London *Evening Standard* carried a full-page article inside its Monday 4th December 1989 edition in which it said:

> The Archbishop of York manages to speak in the House of Lords on morality *without mentioning God*! We have Bishops who do not believe in what the Church has always taught, who cast doubt upon the Resurrection, deny the Virgin Birth, and laugh at those who uphold the orthodox faith. So the very people who ought to be

upholding the faith are seen by everybody to be under-
mining it.

The article goes on to say that in the November 1989 General Synod, they spent most of the time arguing about their
internal problems, and hardly any time in preparing to proclaim the good news of Jesus Christ crucified, risen, and
coming again. Fleet Street and Wapping emblazoned all this in
a major article entitled, 'Does *anyone* remember God?'! Not
Christian leaders!

I say we are a God*less* nation, and a God*less* people, with
God*less* leaders, both in State and Church. And the Epistle to
the Romans 1:18 says:

The wrath of God is revealed from heaven against all
ungodliness and unrighteousness of men.

Are you listening, people of Britain?
Are you listening, national leaders?
Are you listening, Church leaders?
Are you listening, British Parliament?
Are you listening, 10 Downing Street?
Are you listening, Buckingham Palace?
The wrath of God is revealed from heaven against all this.

At present we have the terrible scandal of the 'secret'
Church of England Report being leaked, which urges the
Church to look at the possibility of blessing homosexual 'mar-
riages' (which, the Report notes, some priests are already
prepared to do unofficially); a Report which speaks of placing
foster children with homosexual couples to be brought up and
looked after by them; which warns *against* a strict heterosexual
bias in schoolteaching; which slyly suggests that homosexuality
is normal; and which advocates the ordination of homosexual
clergy.

This 'secret' Report, when leaked, caused *The News of the
World*, of all papers, to speak out in consternation, and pub-
lish that a Member of Parliament, Mr Harry Greenway, had
called on the then Archbishop of Canterbury, Dr Runcie, to
quit because of it. Mr Harry Greenway had said that the
Archbishop's response, when he heard of the leak, was
'vacillating, out of touch, and *failing in his duty*'. The

Archbishop said limply that the Report was 'not an accepted policy document' but was 'still being considered by the bishops'. *The News of The World*, asked:

> What does the Archbishop of Canterbury think he is playing at? He is supposed to be leader of the established church, the most influential cleric in the land. How alarming that he does not rush to condemn a shocking report from the Church of England's gay maffia ['the homosexual rights campaigners', as other newspapers described them]. Shouldn't that Report be ripped up and robustly condemned by the Archbishop? Why does he not speak out? He should heed the clamour for him to quit.

I noticed that at that time, all the other newspapers took their readers back to the Church of England General Synod of 1987. At that Synod a resolution was passed, whose author was the Bishop of Chester, the Right Reverend Michael Baughen, which very feebly and weakly condemned homosexual genital acts as 'falling short of the Christian ideal and demanding repentance'.

How pathetic and weak that resolution was! Michael Baughen is an evangelical. Or was! Why did he not come right out into the open at that General Synod, *as a bishop*, and declare that homosexual genital acts constitute *blatant sin*, and that they are an abomination in the sight of the Lord? That is what God says about it. Michael Baughen knows his Bible. Why did he not come right out into the open and declare that that is what God says about it? God said of sodomy, in Sodom and Gomorrah, that it was *wicked*, and *sin against the Lord exceedingly* (Genesis 13:13) and that it was *very grievous* (Genesis 18:20). And God does not regard it any differently today. God doesn't alter. God does not suddenly 'go modern'. God does not change with the times. And why did not the Bishop of Chester say so, at that General Synod when he had the opportunity?

Following hard on the heels of that 'leaked' Church of England Report, the very same week-end, *The Sunday Times* of 11th February 1990 had a front page article announcing that the Labour Party is planning to reduce the age of consent for homosexuals to sixteen if it wins power at the next General

Election. And I am not being political here, I am merely quoting facts. The *Sunday Times* article says that Neil Kinnock has abandoned his intention to veto a call by his Party Conference for lesbians and gays to have sex, lawfully, at the same age as heterosexuals. The article says:

> Labour campaigners on gay rights, believe that a uniform age of consent would win the support of a majority of Labour MPs, and would be approved by a Labour-dominated House of Commons, despite Tory opposition.

In other words, it would be a good vote catcher, making capital of sheer wickedness, filth, and iniquity! How much lower can we sink as a nation, as a people?

Then that very same weekend, 11th February 1990, an Inquiry had to be set up about rent boys visiting a top security mental hospital, Broadmoor, so that gay inmates can have sex with them, for a payment. But it does not only go on at Broadmoor!

Friends! How rotten, really, are we, as a nation, as a people, as individuals? I ask you. All this is but the tip of the iceberg. This is what we, ourselves, can see. But what God, with His all-seeing eye can see, is *horrendous*.

The Bible says:

> *The wrath of God* is revealed from heaven against all [this] (Romans 1:18).

The wrath of God! How much do we hear about this these days? When did we last hear it preached? Do you know, for the last fifty years or more, we have been preaching the Love of God to the exclusion of all His other attributes, to our peril.

God *is* a God of love, yes.

> For God so loved the world that he gave his only begotten Son, that whosoever believeth in him should not perish, but have everlasting life (John 3:16).

But that is only a part of the truth. He is also a *holy* God, a righteous God, a God of judgment and of justice, a God who can by no means look upon sin; and He is a God who must judge sin. He is therefore a God who can be provoked to anger, and to indignation by sin. And when he is provoked to anger by sin, the Bible declares that He is a God of wrath, and a *consuming fire*!

'Oh!' you say, 'Christianity is all about the love of God.' Is it? I repeat, is it?

What was the message of John the Baptist, the forerunner of our Lord Jesus Christ? It was 'Flee from the wrath to come.' Or rather, it included that.

It included also:

> And now also the axe is laid unto the root of the trees; therefore every tree which bringeth not forth good fruit is hewn down, and cast into the fire. I indeed baptize you with water unto repentance: but he that cometh after me is mightier than I, whose shoes I am not worthy to bear: he shall baptize you with the Holy Ghost, and with fire: whose fan is in his hand, and he will throughly purge his floor, and gather his wheat into the garner; but he will burn up the chaff with unquenchable fire (Matthew 3:10–12).

Is that all about love?

Then what does John the Beloved Disciple, the Disciple of Love, say in chapter 3 verse 36 of his Gospel? He says:

> He that believeth on the Son hath everlasting life: and he that believeth not the Son shall not see life; but the *wrath of God abideth on him*.

The wrath of God! Is that all about love?

And what did the Apostle Paul write to his early Christian converts in Thessalonica in 1 Thessalonians 1:9–10? He wrote:

> Ye turned to God from idols to serve the living and true God; and to wait for his Son from heaven, whom he raised from the dead, even Jesus, which delivered us from *the wrath to come*.

The wrath to come, is mentioned here again.

Indeed, I have seen from a detailed study of the Acts of the Apostles that when Peter, and Paul, and others, preached the Gospel of salvation, they always preached it against that background—the background of the wrath to come. They told their hearers what it was that they needed to be saved from, namely, the wrath to come. They needed to be saved not only from their sin, not only from the penalty of their sin, not only from the power of sin in their lives, not only even from the very presence of sin, but *also* from the ultimate consequences of their sin, namely the judgment of their sin on the Day of Judgment, and from an eternity in hell when the penalty for their sin would be finally executed. And that is what Jesus did when He died for them on the cross, and when He paid the penalty in full for their sin so that they would never have to pay it. That is what it means to be delivered, from the wrath to come.

What did the Apostle Paul write to the Ephesian Christians in the Epistle to the Ephesians 5:3–7? He wrote:

> But fornication, and all uncleanness, or covetousness, let it not be once named among you, as becometh saints; neither filthiness, nor foolish talking, nor jesting, which are not convenient.... For this ye know, that no whoremonger, nor unclean person, nor covetous man, who is an idolater, hath any inheritance in the kingdom of Christ and of God. Let no man deceive you with vain words: for *because of these things* cometh *the wrath of God* upon the children of disobedience. Be not ye therefore partakers with them.

There it is again—the wrath of God! The Apostle Paul made great emphasis of that in his writings.

And what does Revelation 6:12–17 talk about? It talks about Jesus opening the sixth seal; it talks about the heavens departing as a scroll; it talks about every mountain and island being moved out of their place as a result of a great earthquake; and it talks about all classes of men everywhere, from the highest to the lowest, saying to the mountains and rocks;

> Fall on us, and hide us from the face of him that sitteth on the throne [that is God Almighty], and from *the wrath*

of the Lamb [that is Jesus]: for *the great day of His wrath* is come; and who shall be able to stand?

In other words, the passage talks about that great day of His wrath which is coming, the Great and Terrible Day of the Lord.

Then Revelation 15:1 speaks of seven angels having the seven last plagues: and it says:

For in them is filled up *the wrath of God*.

In no way, therefore, can you say, 'Christianity is all about the love of God.' It isn't. There is this other side of it. To say otherwise is to be unbalanced. It is also to create a Gospel after your own imagination and according to your own liking.

So what is the teaching of the Bible? It is balanced teaching. It says that on the one hand there is the *goodness* of God; on the other hand there is the *severity* of God. The Apostle Paul, in the Epistle to the Romans 11:22 said:

Behold therefore the *goodness* and the *severity* of God.

He held these aspects together, in perfect balance. He was balanced in his teaching and preaching.

We, too, in our preaching and teaching should be perfectly balanced. We should faithfully and uncompromisingly present the two sides of God's nature: that God is a God of love, but that He is also a God of wrath, of judgment and justice, and a Holy God. That is balanced teaching—well balanced teaching—and we should *never* present just the one side of the truth and keep quiet about the other. We must never be lopsided! And we most certainly must not sentimentalise the Gospel.

We have, therefore, become a nation and a people that has forsaken the Lord, and are now a people *living without God*. We are an *un*godly, God*less* people. And:

The wrath of God is revealed from heaven against all *un*godliness and unrighteousness of men (Romans 1:18).

And this wrath is being revealed against all *our un*godliness and *un*righteousness as a nation, and it has been doing so for some time.

For instance, it would seem that God has given us up, as a peoples *to uncleanness*, through the lusts of our own hearts, to dishonour our own bodies between ourselves. That is one way in which the wrath of God is revealed from heaven against all ungodliness, as Romans 1:24 teaches. It would seem that for the same cause, God has given us up, as a people, to vile affections, so that even women change the natural use into that which is against nature. And so lesbianism has prolife-rated to an alarming degree in the nation, just as Romans 1:26 teaches that it will when God gives people up.

It would seem also that the same is happening to men. God has given them up, so that:

> Likewise also the men, leaving the natural use of the woman, burned in their lust one toward another, men with men working that which is unseemly, and receiving in themselves that recompence of their error which was meet (Romans 1:27).

So homosexuality has also proliferated at an alarming rate in our nation, and with it aids, ie, people receiving in them-selves that 'recompence of their error which is meet'. It is all a manifestation of the wrath of God being revealed from heaven against all ungodliness and unrighteousness.

Because we, as a people, did not like to retain God in our knowledge, God has given us over, as a people, to a repro-bate, immoral, unprincipled mind, to do those things which are not convenient, being filled, as a people, with all unrighteousness, fornication, wickedness, adultery, covetous-ness, theft, maliciousness, envy, murder, violence, deceit, dishonesty and all manner of foul and filthy practices as Romans 1:28–32 teaches will happen. And again, it is the wrath of God from heaven being manifested. This is all part of the diagnosis of Britain's case. When will we learn, and *repent* and turn back to God?

But we are also a nation and a people which has *forgotten* God. Psalm 9:17 says:

> The wicked shall be turned into hell, and *all the nations that forgot God*.

And Britain has forgotten God.

In 1988, for instance, this nation celebrated the 400th anniversary of the defeat of the Spanish Armada. But during those celebrations, no mention whatsoever was made of the part which Almighty God played in that defeat, when 'He blew with His winds and they were scattered.' It was entirely omitted. And no doubt deliberately.

In fact, a huge exhibition was mounted in Greenwich called 'The Armada Exhibition'. When you eventually got to the end of the exhibition there was a printed statement which read rather sneeringly, 'the myth spread abroad that God gave the victory to the Protestants'! A myth! Even the Spaniards admitted at that time that it was a judgment of God upon themselves. It is of deep significance to learn that, in the view of the Spanish priests of that time, the first essential step towards the revival and recovery of the Spanish nation was not to refashion or rebuild its sorely stricken navy, or even to attempt to restore the nation's economy. It was rather to seek to propitiate an angry and jealous God. That was Spain's first priority. (See the full historical account of the defeat of the Spanish Armada in Volume 2 of *The Trumpet Sounds for Britain*.) Surely, that is a salutary lesson which Britain needs to learn today.

Then, in 1988 also, we celebrated the 300th anniversary of the Glorious Revolution of 1688, with the Queen herself delivering a major speech in the Palace of Westminster. But no mention whatsoever was made of the fact that it was a miracle of God which enabled William of Orange to come to this country in order to preserve the Protestant succession to the throne. William's country, the Dutch United Provinces, was, at that time, in danger of being attacked by France, and he could only sail to this country when he was sure that the French army would be occupied elsewhere. Right at the crucial moment the French armies suddenly turned in another direction, away from the Dutch United Provinces, just as Hitler suddenly turned to attack Russia on 22 June 1941, averting the danger of his invading this country. Thus William was free to sail to England, and God gave him a favourable wind, which the authorities in this country described as a 'Protestant wind'.

No mention whatsoever was made, either, during the 1988 300th anniversary ceremonies, of the *real* issue in the coming of William of Orange. The Queen, in her speech, made great mention of the Bill of Rights, but that was not the real issue which was involved. The real issue indisputably was whether or not this country should remain a Protestant Christian country, or whether it should become a Roman Catholic country. On 5th November 1688, the anniversary of 'Gunpowder Day', as William sailed into Brixham in Devon, he ordered a large white flag to be hoisted at his masthead to signify that he had come in peace, and his personal standard conveyed the message, 'For the Protestant religion and liberty.' But no mention whatsoever was made at the 1988 anniversary ceremonies of the fact that it was 'For the Protestant religion' that William of Orange came. That fact was entirely left out, and no doubt deliberately so. This is sheer deception, and should be repented of, and put right on any such future occasion.

Another example of how we, as a nation, have forgotten God is the way in which we celebrate Guy Fawkes' Night. Fireworks go off all over the country, and bonfires blaze away everywhere. 'Remember, remember, the fifth of November,' they say. But we have completely forgotten what it is that we should remember. What we *should* remember on every Guy Fawkes' Night, is a mighty deliverance of God of the first magnitude which God brought about on behalf of this country on the night of 5th November 1605.

The background to what happened is as follows. The purpose of the Spanish Armada was to invade this country, dethrone Queen Elizabeth I, who was a strong Protestant Queen, and place instead a Roman Catholic on the throne so as to bring this country once again under the supremacy of the Pope of Rome, as it had been before the glorious Reformation. But after the Armada's defeat in 1588, the Roman Catholic party in Britain, which was led by the Jesuits, worked continuously for a counter-revolution. Churchill, in his *History of the English-Speaking Peoples*, states that this was so.

King James I was a Protestant king with very decided views on religion. The Pope regarded him as a heretic. In those days all true believers were regarded by the Roman Catholic

Church as heretics, as they still are today, although they use the term 'the separated brethren'. Because the Pope regarded King James I as a heretic, he forbade allegiance to him.

The air, at that time, was charged with plots. A group of Roman Catholic gentlemen of the Jesuit party plotted to blow up King James, the whole of his Parliament, and the royal family, by gunpowder, when they were all assembled together at Westminster for the equivalent of our State Opening of Parliament.

Robert Catesby, a gentleman called Percy, and Guy Fawkes, were the chief conspirators. Garnet, the English Provicial of the Jesuits, to quieten their consciences, gave them the go-ahead to carry out this dastardly and bloody deed. They hoped that a Roman Catholic uprising would follow, and that a Roman Catholic regime might be established with Spanish help. By the night of 5th November 1605, Guy Fawkes had filled one of the vaults under Parliament with no less than thirty-six barrels of gunpowder, mingled with many iron bars, to create the maximum amount of havoc and destruction. But then something happened which can only be interpreted as a mighty intervention and overruling of God.

Ten days before the session of Parliament was due to open on 6th November, an anonymous letter was handed to the servant of a Roman Catholic Peer, Lord Monteagle, warning him to abstain from attending Parliament on 6th November, because some terrible blow was to be dealt by unseen hands. Lord Monteagle laughed at this letter and treated it as a hoax. However, he showed it to Robert Cecil (Lord Salisbury), who was the Secretary of State. He in turn, paid little attention to it, but he handed it to the King. King James was struck with the seriousness and earnest style of the paper. He mused over it for a while; then suddenly saw the implications of its message. He immediately ordered the vaults under Parliament to be examined. The inspection took place on the night of 5th November—the very night before Parliament was due to meet.

About midnight, Sir Thomas Knevett, the equivalent of our Sergeant at Arms, and some officers, entered the vault with stealthy steps, and caught Guy Fawkes red-handed, coming out of the door with a darkened lantern in his hand. He had just finished laying the train of gunpowder which was later to be ignited to cause the explosion. Matches for firing this train of gunpowder were taken from his pocket. He was led away, was interrogated, and was later executed for treason. He had revealed the names of the other conspirators while under interrogation. Some of these were hunted down, captured, tried and eventually executed for treason. Some were slain in an attempt to escape.

I want you to notice this. So grateful was the nation to Almighty God for this wonderful and mighty deliverance that public thanksgivings were offered in every church throughout the country. And later, a Service of Thanksgiving was annexed to *The Book of Common Prayer* and Liturgy of the Church of England by command of His Majesty King Charles, James I's successor, and was ordered to be used on every anniversary of 5th November until that Thanksgiving Service was withdrawn from *The Book of Common Prayer* in 1864. I myself have seen a copy of *The Book of Common Prayer* to which this Service of Thanksgiving was annexed, and in its opening prayer it describes what happened on the night of 5th November 1605 as, 'the wonderful and mighty deliverance brought about, not by our merit, not by our foresight, but by Thy mercy and by Thy Providence.'

But all we do now, on 5th November, is to let off fireworks and light bonfires! We, as a nation, have forgotten entirely the deliverance of Almighty God of the first magnitude which God granted to this nation on that night of 5th November 1605. It would have been a far greater explosion than the Brighton bomb explosion, with far greater casualties.

The Bible says: *Beware* lest thou forget the Lord (Deuteronomy 6:12). But That is exactly what we *have* done, as a nation. We leave God out, entirely, from the 5th November celebrations.

What is more, when we hold Battle of Britain services in Westminster Abbey every September, we never even make mention of the great miracles which God wrought during the actual Battle of Britain in 1940. Nor, at any of the Victory Day anniversary services which are held in our Cathedrals and churches, do we ever make mention of the other mighty miracles which God wrought on this nation's behalf during the 1939–45 war. The part that God played, which was considerable, is never so much as referred to any more. So there is no question but that we are a nation and a people that has forgotten God.

The Bible says:

> Remember his marvellous works that he hath done (1 Chronicles 16:12).

But that is exactly what we haven't done. We have forgotten them all. We don't consider they are worth so much as a mention.

Worse even than that, we are also a nation and a people which has been *defying* God, and which has been deliberately and wilfully going against Him. By placing anti-God, and anti-Christians laws on our Statute Book, for instance. So Britain is a God-defying nation today, and, as such, I believe she is on a collision course with God.

I am a former Royal Naval person, and I know what it means to be on a collision course. You have to do something about it pretty quickly or there will be an almighty crash, and there will be casualties.

2 Chronicles 15:2 says:

> The Lord is *with* you, while ye be with him; and if ye seek him, he will be found of you; *but*, if ye forsake him, he will forsake you.

There is a condition attached to that statement. So we need to ask, therefore: Is Britain now a God-*forsaken* nation as well as a God-*less* nation? If we are, then we are a God-*abandoned* nation, simply because we, as a nation, have abandoned Him.

Isaiah 1:4 says:

> They have forsaken the Lord, they have provoked the Holy One of Israel unto anger.

So to forsake the Lord in such a way provokes God to anger.

Added to which, Isaiah 5:24 says:

> Because they have cast away *the law of the Lord* of hosts, and despised the word of the Holy One of Israel. Therefore is *the anger of the Lord* kindled against his people,

and he hath stretched forth his hand against them, and hath smitten them.

When it says, 'He hath stretched forth his hand against them', it means in *judgment*. That is why He has smitten them.

And we need to realise that He smites with *catastrophies* sometimes, and with *tragedies*, and with *disasters*. The Bible teaches that! He smites with national tragedies, national calamities and national disasters! This also is part of the diagnosis of Britain's case. For we have had such national catastrophies, calamities, tragedies, and disasters. We have had a whole list of them.

We've had the King's Cross underground station inferno, for instance. And they still don't know what caused it. The staff of the London Underground tell me that it remains an unsolved mystery.

We've had the Bradford Football Stadium inferno for another.

Do you know I find that in the Book of the Prophet Amos, God says, seven times over in chapters 1 and 2, 'I will send a fire,' or 'I will kindle a fire...and it will devour the palaces thereof,' and this and that. '*I* will send a fire,' says the Lord.

Then we have had the Hillesborough Football Stadium disaster, the Lockerbie air crash, the Manchester air crash, after which the Queen asked in anguish, 'Why another air crash?'

We've had the Clapham train disaster, followed almost immediately by one at Glasgow.

We've had the Piper Alpha oil rig disaster, another inferno, which killed 167 men, and which the investigators said ranks third in world disasters, next to the Chernobyl nuclear accident and the poison gas tragedy in India.

Then came the Zeebruger *Herald of Free Enterprise* ferry disaster.

Then the 110-mile-per-hour hurricane which hit London, and the South and South-east of England in October 1987, ripping up 15 million trees and bringing power lines down everywhere. The Stock Exchange, the Bank of England, and the whole of the City of London had to close down because all the computers were put out of action, and because staff could not get in as all London main line railway stations were brought to a standstill and there were no trains. There was chaos everywhere!

My Bible Reading that very morning was from Amos 3:6, which says:

> Shall there be evil in a city, and *the Lord* hath not done it?

A leading article in *The Daily Telegraph* that same morning said:

> In John Bunyan's day, that hurricane would have been attributed to God expressing His immense displeasure at Britain.

Fleet Street and Wapping were saying that, you notice! Not the archbishops and bishops! Not the Free Church leaders! But Fleet Street! Wapping!

And at that time Muslim waiters in a London hotel said to me with looks of alarm on their faces, '*God* is speaking, Sir. *God* is speaking.'

A year later the Outer Hebrides and the west coast of Scotland were hit with the same kind of fierce hurricane. I saw some of the damage it caused on the islands of Lewis, Harris, and Scalpay when I was over there in July 1989.

After that, we had a major disaster in the Thames with the sudden sinking of the passenger boat *The Marchioness*, full of revellers early one Sunday morning, when a sand barge collided with it. And they still don't know how it happened. This is another unsolved mystery!

Then ever since mid-December of 1989, gale after gale, and winds of storm force and hurricane force, have battered and slashed these islands, wreaking havoc and destruction everywhere. In fact, if you study the reports, they seem to present a picture of a *rising crescendo* of hurricane-force gales. Here is a list of some that appeared in the national daily newspapers:

• *Monday 18th December 1989*. 'South and West Coasts of Britain from Hampshire to the Hebrides hit by winds gusting up to hurricane force that whipped up high tides and caused widespread flooding. Nine people feared drowned.'
• *Friday 26th January 1990*. '38 killed as Storm wreaks havoc.

Roads, rail, and power in chaos in the worst storms to have battered Southern Britain since the hurricane of October 1987.'

● *Tuesday 30th January 1990.* '100 mile per hour storms batter the West of England for second time in five days.'

● *Friday 2nd February 1990.* 'The most severe flooding in 20 years disrupts the West Country as gales *again* swept South-West England.'

● *Saturday 3rd February 1990.* 'Scotland bore the brunt of the latest storm-force winds.... January storms now reported to have brought down more than three million trees.'

● *Thursday 8th and Friday 9th February 1990.* 'Roads in Wales and Southern England blocked by floods and trees brought down by winds of up to 100 miles per hour. Thames bursts its banks. Storms battered Southern England and Wales a fortnight after hurricane-force winds killed 47 people.'

● *Monday 12th February 1990.* 'Winds of up to 98 miles per hour hammered the South West, causing the worst flooding in Gloucestershire for 43 years.'

Many are saying, 'There is something *unusual* about all this.' And they tell us there is *more to come*!

Scotland, also, has been severely battered by fierce hurricanes and gales, but I do not have the details to quote.

This is only *part* of the list of catastrophies, tragedies, and disasters which we, as a nation, have been experiencing during the last few years. The list is *endless*.

We find ourselves asking, 'Whatever is going to happen next?'

And the question which has been on the lips of many has been: *Why?* Why is all this battering and bruising happening to us?

I believe the Bible gives a very clear answer in 2 Chronicles 7:21–22, which says:

> [Someone will say,] Why hath the Lord done thus unto this land...? And it shall be answered, Because they forsook the Lord God of their fathers...therefore hath he brought all this evil [or calamity] upon them.

Oh that it were possible to get this message across to our

national leaders, to our Sovereign, to the Prime Minister, to Parliament, and to our Church leaders—Established Church leaders and Free Church leaders alike!

The situation is so serious that I sometimes have to ask myself: Has God had to withdraw His protecting hand from these islands? It is a question which needs to be asked. Is *that* why so many of these national calamities and tragedies have been allowed to happen to us?

I asked myself that question again as we began to get news that people, including children, were being savaged by Rottweiler dogs. And when an outstanding MP was assassinated. I ask, 'Was that a sign that God has withdrawn His protection?'

And what about this rising crescendo of hurricanes and storms which the man in the street is saying are unusual?

More recently there has been the spate of IRA bomb explosions on the mainland of Britain. The further question needs therefore to be asked: Has God begun to hand us over to 'the enemy within'? And since there is no sign of *repentance* anywhere, I have to ask myself yet another question: Is God saying to Britain, today, as He did in Jeremiah's day, 'In vain have I smitten [them]; they received *no* correction'? (Jeremiah 2:30). I rather think that He *is* saying that. Almighty God has a controversy with Britain, you see.

We need to remember that the Lord Jesus said,

> To whomsoever much is given, of him shall much be required (Luke 12:4).

I believe that applies to nations as well as to individuals. I believe it certainly applies to Britain. I fear the days of the United Kingdom may well be numbered. We have been weighed in the balances and have been found wanting. The writing has been on the wall for some time now. I fear that we have passed the point of no return. God's hand is stretched out in judgment against us. And it is not being withdrawn. The wrath of God has gone forth into the land, and it has been manifesting itself in all the ways I have already mentioned. And I fear a worse judgment of Almighty God is still to come on these islands.

The most urgent question, therefore, which needs to be asked in Britain today, by our Sovereign, by our Church and *celebrations?*

national leaders, and by Parliament, is: *What must be done to turn God's fierce anger away?* It is a question that must be asked and then be urgently answered. Therefore, please take notice of this:

Lamentations is what is most urgently needed in Britain today. Lamentations, not celebrations. X

No matter what Christian newspaper or magazine I pick up today, it is celebrations, celebrations, celebrations which are constantly being talked about. Huge, expensive advertisements appear, announcing this celebration, or that celebration. It seems the Christian world today has an obsession for them—a craze.

I believe Almighty God is sick to death of all these celebrations. He said to the people in the Prophet Isaiah's time:

> *To what purpose* is the multitude of your sacrifices unto me? saith the Lord: I am full of the burnt offerings of rams, and the fat of fed beasts [I am fed up to the teeth with them, in other words]; and I *delight not* in the blood of bullocks, or of lambs, or of he goats. When ye come to appear before me, *who hath required this at your hand*, to tread my courts? Bring *no more vain* oblations [note the word 'vain']; incense is *an abomination* unto me; the new moons and sabbaths, the calling of assemblies, I cannot away with [cannot put up with, in other words]; *it is iniquity*, even the solemn meeting. Your new moons and your appointed feasts *my soul hateth*: they are *a trouble unto me*; I am weary to bear them. And when ye spread forth your hands, *I will hide mine eyes from you*: yea, when ye make many prayers, *I will not hear*: your hands are full of blood (Isaiah 1:11–15).

In Britain's case the blood of three and a quarter million aborted children plus all the blood which has been brutally shed in Northern Ireland.

Is God saying the same thing today concerning all these celebrations, concerning all the *lightness* that goes on in many of our church services, concerning all the *entertainment* that goes on, and concerning all the ear-splitting, blasting *noise* that is being created during what is naively described as 'going into worship', when with tom-tom music, regular jungle-beat music forms 'the accompaniment'? Is He saying, 'To what *purpose* is it all? I delight not in it. Who hath required *this* at your hand? Bring no more of these *vain* things unto Me. They are *an abomination* unto Me. I cannot away with them. *It is iniquity*. Your appointed feasts or *festivals* My soul hateth. They are a trouble unto Me. I am weary to bear them. When you spread forth your hands, I will hide Mine eyes from you. When you make many prayers I will not hear.' Is He saying all that? I rather think He may be, at least at times.

The question certainly needs to be asked: Is all this serving and worshipping God *acceptably*, with *reverence*, and with *godly fear*, as Hebrews 12:28 says we should? I repeat what I said at the beginning. Our situation in Britain today is so desperate that only *God coming down* in mighty Holy Ghost revival power will touch the situation today, if, indeed, that is going to happen at all. But that will not happen until there are *lamentations, weepings, wringing of hands, howlings*, and crying out to God *in desperation* that He will have *mercy*.

That will not happen, either, unless and until there is *repentance*—deep and heartfelt repentance. But where is it? I don't see it taking place anywhere. We need to be literally crying out to God for this. We desperately need a mighty visitation of God on this country. That, too, is part of the diagnosis of Britain's tragic condition today.

But we need to realise that the Bible clearly shows there are *two kinds of visitations of God* which are possible. And both of these need to be clearly stated, not just one of them. One is a visitation of God *in judgment*. The other is a visitation of God in which He pours out His *blessing* in Holy Ghost power.

To state it another way. There are two ways in which God can shake the nation, or the district, and/or shake the world. He can shake the nation, and/or the World with some kind of awful catastrophe or calamity as He visits in judgment.

It could take the form of a total economic collapse. Right now the world economy and the national economy is teetering on the brink of collapse. Bankers expect it to happen at any moment. Meanwhile, share prices keep jumping up and down like a yo-yo. Something serious has only to happen on Wall Street or to the Japanese yen, and the world economy would collapse like a pack of cards.

Or it could take the form of an earthquake. The scientists

tell us that a major earthquake in the British Isles is long since overdue, and when it happens, they say, it is likely to take place in the Thames basin because of the number of subterranean disturbances that have been going on in that region for a number of years now. The whole of London would be seriously affected and devastated if such a major earthquake were to take place. The Thames barrier would be smashed like matchwood, and a wide area of London would be flooded as a result of tidal waves. Indeed, for some years now, God has been saying to me, in the Spirit, concerning the buildings and palaces in Whitehall, 'There shall not be left one stone upon another that shall not be cast down.'

When I was in Scotland in March and April of 1990, I heard from several sources that a major earthquake is expected in Dundee. So the British Isles could be visited with a major earthquake within a measurable length of time, and if it were, it would be a visitation of the judgment of God on the British Isles.

Or the shaking of the world and of the country could take the form of this planet being hit by a giant asteroid from outer space. *The Daily Telegraph* reported on its front page, on Friday 21st April 1989, that the earth narrowly escaped being struck by a giant asteroid weighing 400 million tons, which could have killed 100 million people. It was travelling at 50,000 miles an hour and only missed this planet by four hours! That really would have shaken the world had it hit it! The impact, the scientists say, would have had about the same effect as if all the nuclear weapons in the world had exploded at the same time and in the same place. But then on Wednesday 11th July 1990, *The Daily Telegraph* reported, again on its front page, that an asteroid sped past the earth the day before (10 July), and came even closer. The report said that 'the asteroid, estimated to measure 300 feet to 1,000 feet in diameter, made one of the closest crossings of earth's orbit observed in 50 years.' So it came even closer than did the one in April 1989. Such a major catastrophe, therefore, is not beyond the realm of possibility.

Such are some of the catastrophies or calamities with which God could shake the world in judgment.

Whatever form it may take, He *is* going to do it in some way, because He has *promised* that He will, as we have already seen from the Scriptures, both Old and New Testaments; that is, this *more sure* word of prophecy. He has clearly stated His intentions in Haggai 2:6–7 and in Hebrews 12:26–27, which I have already quoted more than once. So it is going to happen, because God has promised it. And the thing that God has spoken shall be done.

But the *other* way that God can shake a nation, or a district, town, city, community or church is by coming down in mighty Holy Ghost power, as He did on one occasion at the time of the Acts of the Apostles, when, after a company of the Lord's *true* disciples had prayed:

> The place was shaken where they were assembled together: and they were *all* filled with the Holy Ghost, and spake the word of God *with boldness* (Acts 4:31).

The whole place reverberated and shook as *God came down* upon them in mighty Holy Ghost power—and they were all filled with *the fire of God*. That is what the Church of God everywhere so desperately needs today—*a mighty baptism of Holy Ghost fire* to burn up all the dross, and to burn away everything which is impure in every believer's heart. Our God is a *Consuming Fire*. He is also *Light*—dazzling light. No impurity can survive in His presence. Do you hear me, all you who only talk about sentimental love?

The question really is: Which of these two kinds of visitations of God, or shakings of God, is it going to be?

We don't know. Who can tell? 'Who can tell if God will turn...and turn away from his fierce anger, that we perish not?' to quote Jonah 3:9.

But we need to fulfil the conditions if that is, indeed, going to be the form of visitation, and not the other. We need to do what the king and people of Nineveh did, over whom Jonah had courageously pronounced a coming judgment. We need to turn, every one of us, from our evil way, and *repent* of every sin and wickedness, even of the violence which is in our hands, or in our hearts—and even do it in sackcloth and ashes to show that we mean business. Then we need to cry mightily to God that He will have *mercy*, and come down in mighty Holy Ghost revival power before ever He comes down and shakes the world in judgment, as He has promised that He will do.

It is the people of Britain who need to repent in this way—all 56 million of them—not just the church in Britain. There is a lot of wrong teaching being put across today about this matter of repentance, even in 'National Days of Prayer and Repentance' circles. Often the emphasis is that *the Church* must repent. This is based on a wrong use of 'Judgment must begin at the house of God.' So the rest of the population is being let off repenting. But 1 Peter 4:17 does not say, '*Repentance* must begin at the house of God.' It says:

> For the time is come that *judgment* must begin at the house of God—and if it first begin at us, what shall the end be of them that obey not the gospel of God? And if the righteous scarcely be saved, where shall the ungodly and the sinner appear?

No! We need to get the teaching right. The teaching of the Bible is that now:

> God…commandeth *all men, everywhere* to repent: because he hath appointed a day, in the which he will judge *the world* in righteousness by that man whom he hath ordained; whereof he hath given assurance unto all men in that he hath raised him from the dead (Acts 17:30–31).

And when it says '*all men everywhere*', it means all men everywhere, not just the Church.

Nineveh was a heathen city. There was no Church there. Under the preaching of Jonah it was everybody in Nineveh who needed to repent: everybody from the king down to the beggar in the street. And it is *everybody* in Britain who needs to repent today, because it is everybody in Britain who will come under God's judgment. Oh that it might be said of us, the people of Britain, not just the Church, as it was said of the people of Nineveh:

> And God saw their works, that they *turned* from their evil way; and God repented of the evil, that he had said that he would do unto them: and he did it not (Jonah 3:10).

But is it going to happen? Is it? That is the question.

That, therefore, to an extent, is the national situation in Britain today viewed biblically and prophetically. I shall be returning to it later, as I proceed.

Note

On Wednesday 10th July 1990 Shropshire and the borders of Wales were again shaken by earth tremors. *The Daily Telegraph* of 11th July reported this on its front page: 'Police in Shrewsbury and Telford, Salop, were flooded by calls from people saying their houses had been shaken by an earth tremor early yesterday.'

That same day a report appeared on the same front page of *The Daily Telegraph* that, 'An asteroid sped past earth at a comparatively tiny distance of three million miles yesterday', scientists in Pasedena, California, announced. 'The asteroid, estimated at 300 feet to 1,000 feet in diameter, made one of the closest crossings of earth's orbit observed in 50 years,' the Jet Propulsion Laboratory said.

In view of what I have been preaching, and then writing along these lines, I am obliged to ask: Is God underlining what the preacher and writer is saying, by causing these two reports to appear on the same front page, and on the same day? It is a question that needs to be faced up to.

Chapter Three

The State of
the World Today
Viewed Biblically and
Prophetically

What of the state of the world today viewed biblically and prophetically? As we enter this last phase of human history?

There is no doubt whatsoever but that we live in a *world* which is ripe for judgment, just as we are living in a nation which is ripe for judgment. And so I would like to turn your attention once again to Haggai 2:6–7. There is a reason why I need to repeat it. It says:

> For thus saith the Lord of hosts; Yet once, it is a little while, and I will shake the heavens, and the earth, and the sea, and the dry land; and I will shake *all nations*, and the desire of all nations shall come.

Now, with those words still in your minds, look at Isaiah 2:10–19:

> Enter into the rock, and hide thee in the dust, *for fear of the Lord*.

I want you to note those words, 'for fear of the Lord'. It is important that you do. The verse continues:

> And for the glory of his majesty. The lofty looks of *man* shall be humbled, and the *haughtiness* of men shall be bowed down, and the Lord *alone* shall be exalted *in that day*.

In *what* day? The next verse, verse 12, begins to tell you. It is talking about the coming day of the Lord that I have been referring to, the great and terrible day of the Lord. It says:

> For *the day of the Lord of hosts* shall be upon every one that is *proud* and *lofty*.

I need to ask you, 'Are *you* proud? Are *you* lofty?' If so, you'd better watch it!

> The day of the Lord of hosts shall be upon every one that is proud and lofty, and upon every one that is lifted up; and he shall be brought low: and upon all the cedars of Lebanon, that are high and lifted up, and upon all the oaks of Bashan, and upon all the high mountains, and upon all the hills that are lifted up, and upon every high tower, and upon every fenced wall. And upon all the ships of Tarshish, and upon all pleasant pictures. And the loftiness of man shall be bowed down, and the haughtiness of men shall be made low: and the Lord alone shall be exalted in that day.

Notice, the words *in that day* have now been twice repeated thus far.

> And the idols he shall utterly abolish.

All false religions, all false gods, that means, because Almighty God, the True God, the Living God says in Jeremiah 10:11:

> Thus shall ye say unto them, The gods that have not made the heavens and the earth, even they shall perish from the earth, and from under these heavens.

That is what God says. There is therefore, no argument. *In that day* all false religions, and all false gods will *go* And why? Because the Lord *alone* will be exalted *in that day*.

> And they shall go into the holes of the rocks, and into the caves of the earth, *for fear of the Lord*, and for the glory of his majesty.

There are the words again: '*for fear of the Lord*, and for the glory of his majesty.'

When will this all happen? The last part of verse 19 tells you:

> When he ariseth *to shake terribly the earth*.

That is exactly what Haggai 2:6-7 was talking about, and why I need to repeat it. It connects with what the Prophet Isaiah is saying here. In fact, it is referring to the same 'shaking terribly of the earth' which God will do 'in that day'. And *that day* is still ahead of us.

Isaiah, in chapter 2 verse 20, goes on:

> *In that day* [in that day when God ariseth to shake terribly the earth] a man shall cast his idols of silver, and his idols of gold, which they made each one for himself to worship, to the moles and to the bats; to go into the clefts of the rocks, and into the tops of the ragged rocks, *for fear of the Lord*.

There the phrase is stated for the third time, please notice; this needs to be emphasised in a day, when there is no *fear of God* before our people's eyes. Men will go into these rocks, and into these caves *for fear of the Lord* and for the glory of His *majesty*. When? The last part of verse 21 tells you:

> When he ariseth to shake *terribly the earth*.

This teaching is twice repeated in this chapter.

Verse 22 says:

> Cease ye from *man*, whose breath is in his nostrils: for wherein is *he* to be accounted of?

This entire chapter is talking about the day of the Lord of Hosts that is coming when God arises to shake terribly the earth. Haggai 2:6-7 also speaks of this. So you see how basic this is to this whole series of addresses, and how basic it is as a background to these addresses. It is a theme which runs right

through Scripture, which, as I proceed, I will go on to show.
But when did you last hear it preached upon?

Now we shall consider Isaiah 24:1–6, and then verses 17–23.

> Behold, the Lord maketh the earth empty, and maketh it
> waste, and turneth it upside down, and scattereth abroad
> the inhabitants thereof. And it shall be, as with the
> people, so with the priest; as with the servant, so with his
> master; as with the maid, so with her mistress; as with the
> buyer, so with the seller; as with the lender, so with the
> borrower; as with the taker of usury, so with the
> giver of usury to him (vv 1–2).

A great 'levelling off' shall take place, in other words.
   The chapter goes on:

> The land shall be utterly emptied, and utterly spoiled:
> for the Lord hath spoken this word. The earth mourneth
> and fadeth away, the world languisheth and fadeth away,
> the *haughty* people of the earth do languish (vv 3–4).

Now notice this in verses 5 and 6:

> The earth also is *defiled* under the inhabitants thereof;
> because they have transgressed the laws, changed the
> ordinance, broken the everlasting covenant. Therefore
> hath the curse devoured the earth, and they that dwell
> therein are desolate.

We need to pause here for a moment and take note of what
these two verses are saying, before we pass on. 'The earth also
is *defiled* under the inhabitants thereof.' That speaks about
what is happening to the earth *today*, surely. The earth is
defiled, it is polluted. And who has done it? The inhabitants
thereof. If it were not for the inhabitants it would never have
happened!
   Why is the earth defiled? Verse 5 tells you: 'Because they
have transgressed the laws [God's laws], changed the ordinance, broken the everlasting covenant.'
   Is that why we have all this *pollution* everywhere today? In

the rivers, in the seas, in the soil, on the land, in the animals, in the fish, in the eggs, in the poultry, in the cows, in the sheep, in the cats even, in the things we eat, in the entire food chain, in the very water coming out of the taps that we drink, even in mineral water now? And the reason? It is because we have transgressed the laws—God's laws; we have changed God's ordinances, broken God's everlasting covenant. And all for human profit, human greed. All for the lust of filthy lucre. All to make more and more money! To get rich! Have you considered that *this* is the cause of all this pollution? You 'Friends of the Earth', and all you who have been going 'Green', but not because of sea-sickness! Have you considered that this is the cause?

God has set certain laws and ordinances which govern everything which has to do with the earth and the husbandry of it, such as in the realm of agriculture, farming, keeping livestock, and so on.

When He created cows, for instance, He created them to eat grass. That is a basic law of nature. That is His ordinance. He did not create them to eat each other in the form of offal fed to them as animal feed! But we have changed that law, that ordinance, that they should eat grass. So now we have 'mad cow' disease. And at the root was the desire to make more money.

When God created poultry, He created them to roam in the meadows, to enjoy what we now call 'free range'. He did not create them in order that they should be penned up, hundreds of them together, in terms of 'battery-farming'. But we changed that basic law of nature, that ordinance, in order to get more eggs out of them, and make more money. So now we have salmonella in the hens, and in the eggs!

When I was a boy I was brought up in the country with farms stretching for miles around. I well remember that in those days the farmers manured their fields with cow manure, horse manure, sheep manure, pig manure, chicken manure, all of which was mixed with the straw on which these animals had been bedded down. They also ploughed humus into some fields, which consisted of rotting vegetation. That was a basic law of the land in those days, a basic ordinance.

But then, because they thought they could get more out of the land, and so make more money, they changed that basic law—transgressed it, in other words—and began to feed the land with artificial fertilisers instead of *natural* fertilisers. So what happened? That fertiliser got into the streams, and from the streams it got into the rivers, and from the rivers it got into the sea, and from the sea it got into the oceans, and it wasn't long before we began to read newspaper reports that the eggs of penguins right up in the Arctic Circle were impregnated with this artificial fertiliser and with chemicals which had been used on the land! The fish, too, were affected. And we eat the fish! Now we are being told that certain of the shell fish are not safe to eat. In fact, the entire food-chain today has become polluted in one way or another, causing the Ministry of Health to issue one warning after another, sometimes almost daily, so that one begins to wonder what is safe to eat!

All these problems have arisen because we have transgressed the basic laws, changed God's ordinance, and broken His everlasting covenant, according to this Scripture. We need to take serious note of this. Parliaments do, too.

Furthermore, there is a consequence. Isaiah 24:6 says:

> Therefore hath the *curse* devoured the earth, and they that dwell therein are desolate.

There is no doubt but that *the curse of pollution*, with all its dire effects, has now spread *world-wide*. The entire earth has been devoured by it, and irretrievably so, I fear. That shows how true and relevant the previous verse is: 'The earth also is defiled.'

But now we will read on to verses 17 to 23 of Isaiah 24. Verse 17 says:

> Fear, and the pit, and the snare, are upon thee, *O inhabitant of the earth*.

I wish it was! There isn't much fear of the pit, today; or of the abyss! But there should be.

Verses 18 to 23 then go on to say:

> And it shall come to pass, that he who fleeth from the noise of the fear shall fall into the pit; and he that cometh up out of the midst of the pit shall be taken in the snare:

for, [because] that means, the windows from on high are
open, and *the foundations of the earth do shake*.

There is reference again to the day when God will *shake
terribly the earth*.

The earth is utterly broken down [in consequence], the
earth is clean dissolved, the earth is *moved exceedingly*
[note that, *exceedingly*!]. The earth shall *reel to and fro*
like a drunkard [can you picture that?!], and shall be
removed like a cabbage; and the *transgression* thereof
shall be heavy upon it; and it shall fall, and not rise
again.

And it shall come to pass *in that day*, that the Lord
shall *punish* [I repeat, *punish*] the host of the high ones
that are on high, and the kings of the earth upon the
earth.

And they shall be gathered together, as prisoners are
gathered in the pit, and shall be shut up in the prison,
and after many days shall they be visited.

Then the moon shall be confounded, and the sun
ashamed.

When?

When the Lord of hosts shall reign in Mount Zion, and
in Jerusalem, and before his ancients gloriously.

Notice! That last verse of Isaiah 24 takes us right beyond
the climax of this age, which is now very fast approaching, to
the time when the Lord shall be King over all the earth, in
fulfilment of Zechariah 14:9, which I shall be coming to later.

Now, in view of that fast-approaching climax of this age,
namely the Lord's return, what of the state of the world today
viewed biblically and prophetically, especially against the
background of these Scriptures that I have just quoted?

First we will look at the *United States*.
America today is being visited with God's judgments.

• Earthquakes: the San Francisco earthquake is the most
recent serious one.

- Hurricanes: Hurricane Gilbert, Hurricane Hugo, and so on, are recent examples. Scenes showing their devastating effect were shown on television.
- Tornadoes: some have occurred very recently.

And then there has been considerable turmoil, upheaval, violence, unrest and strife in El Salvador, Nicaragua, Costa Rica, Panama, Honduras, and Colombia—all countries comprising what is termed as Central America.

The United States is being visited with all kinds of judgments, I say, including *AIDS* on a frightening scale.

But I cannot speak from first-hand experience. I am not on the spot. Read David Wilkerson's books if you want to know more. He *is* on the spot in America and has been setting the trumpet to his mouth to sound out the warnings there. In a message published in leaflet form in June 1989, entitled 'The Last Days of America', he says:

> America is dying. The great empire is crumbling. It is now in the throes of a terminal disease. This country [America] is heading the way of all fallen empires.

He compares the state and condition of America today with all that God said in Deuteronomy chapter 28, which, incidentally, I myself also did in Chapter 10 of Volume 1 of *The Trumpet Sounds for Britain*, in answer to the question, 'What really is wrong with Britain?' What I was saying about Britain then is strikingly similar to what David Wilkerson is saying about America today.

David Wilkerson says, "America today is under a curse." He then lists twelve of the signs which are given in Deuteronomy chapter 28 which indicate that a nation is under a curse. He proceeds to show from these signs that America is under such a curse today.

I quote only seven of these signs.

1) *A curse is upon our cities*. 'A crime occurs every twenty seconds, a murder occurs every five hours. New York City is becoming unlivable. Now it is spreading even to our smallest towns.'
2) *A curse is upon our economy*. I will return to that in a moment.

3) *A curse is upon our future markets*. I will return to that also in a moment.

4) *A curse is upon our foreign negotiations*. 'United States foreign policy is in complete disarray. Our negotiators come home confused, upstaged by Russia, upstaged in China.' He could have added, 'Upstaged by Japan, and even by Saddam Hussein.' 'We appear befuddled before the whole world in our foreign policy,' he continues. That is certainly true of America's Middle East foreign policy, including their dealings with Israel.

5) *A curse is upon us in terms of incurable illnesses*. Deuteronomy 28 says that the Lord will smite thee with pestilence whereof thou canst not be healed. And AIDS is incurable.

6) *A curse of the loss of an entire generation of youth*. 'Today, in America,' he says, 'a nation of adults, supplied with all money and might, can merely stand by and watch in horror, as drugs, alcohol, and violence swallow up an entire population of youth.'

7) *The curse of becoming a debtor nation rather than a lender*. David Wilkerson quotes Deuteronomy 28:44:

> He shall lend to thee, and thou shalt not lend to him: he shall be the head, and thou shalt be the tail.

He then says, 'In the last five years, we [the United States] have become the world's biggest debtor nation. At this moment *we are now the tail*, and Japan is the head.'

Turning to other subjects David Wilkerson says, 'The *hospital system* in our cities has become unmanageable.' So it has over here, hasn't it? I am a regular hospital visitor, and am constantly in touch with patients, and I see all the mismanagement which goes on, and the appalling lack of cleanliness due to unsupervised cleaning staff.

He says, 'Our *jails* are overflowing, resulting in the release of many criminals.' So are ours over here, aren't they?

He says, 'Our *penal institutions* are horror houses of rape, violence, and hopelessness.' So are ours, aren't they?

He says, 'Our *courts* can't handle the case loads anymore.' That is true of ours, isn't it?

He says, 'Our *schools* are the shame of the whole world. Teachers live in fear. The schools are devoid of morality. Kids use knives, drugs, guns, violence, and indulge in promiscuous sex.' Much of that is true of our schools, too, isn't it? You ask any headmaster, or teacher!

He says, 'Our *welfare systems* are in total chaos.' Ours leave much to be desired, too, don't they?

He says, 'Nobody in the United States Government, in Congress, on Wall Street, or at the Federal Reserve can tell us what is happening to *our economy*. It is beyond us all. No one knows what is holding the system together.'

The more I see and read David Wilkerson's recent assessment of the state and condition of the United States of America, the more I see that it is strikingly similar to the state and condition of this nation of Britain today. For instance, teachers are leaving our schools in frightening numbers because they can no longer cope with the situation there. Who can deny it? We need to face up to *the truth*. And in February 1990 the Home Office was obliged to set up an Inquiry because of the high rate of suicides in our prisons. How horrific!

David Wilkerson also comments on how weak and spineless those in authority, or in any position of so-called leadership in the United States have become, completely fearful of making a bold stand about anything. He quotes Nahum 3:13, which says:

Behold, thy people in the midst of thee are *women*.

He says:
In other words, you have grown soft, and effeminate through your luxury. You have no will; no resolve. All dying empires become soft and effeminate, unwilling in the end to take a stand for anything. Like Belshazzar, the king of Babylon, who saw the writing on the wall, they end up giving the prophets their day in court, telling them, 'Yes, they are on target,' that what they are saying is all true. But then they go back to their parties, drunk, completely 'stoned', and are completely immune from all the warnings.

Concerning abominable filth, David Wilkerson says:

We, in America, have become the shame and disgrace of the world. America is now experiencing a veritable baptism of filth. We are literally drowning in pornography.

It is now a multi-million-dollar business. Ten years ago much of it was imported. But today the US is the biggest exporter of filth in all the world. Our nation has developed an appetite for perversion, for sadism, etc. Even day-time soap operas are full of smut, fornication and homosexuality. Television has become the open flood gate of this barrage of filth.

But it is very much the same over here, isn't it?

He adds:

The United States of America is now known as 'the nation where anything goes'. There are virtually no more restraints. Young eleven- and twelve-year-old boys are becoming rapists. Girls are getting pregnant at the age of twelve, and then have abortions.

The same has become true in Britain, hasn't it? British law has had to be altered recently because boys of ten to thirteen years of age are now guilty of rape. All this spells inevitable *judgment*.

David Wilkerson says:

God has every right to ask America, 'What is different about America from wicked Sodom?' Are we better than Noah's generation whom God wiped out in the judgment of The Flood? Or Lot's generation when God destroyed Sodom and Gomorrah by raining fire and brimstone upon them from heaven? Are we more deserving than Nineveh, which God eventually wiped out when they went back on their earlier repentance under Jonah's preaching? Considering what happened to all these people when God visited them in judgment, why should He spare us, since we, in the United States, are committing acts *seven times worse* than *any* of those wicked people?

The same questions could equally be put to us in Britain, surely.

But then David Wilkerson says:

Many in America don't like to hear about the coming economic collapse. It happened to every past society and empire when they were in the throes of Divine judgment. Don't believe it won't happen to us.

Rest assured that the day is not far off when Japan, Taiwan, Korea, and Germany will take their money from the United States and flee.

One day soon, Japan will quit buying our government bonds, as will all other nations. We will not be able to finance our massive national debt. It will tumble and fall.

The real estate market [property market] will crash as well.

To which I myself need to add that when all that happens, the whole world's economy will collapse like a pack of cards.

And it is going to happen, because it is prophesied in the Bible. Revelation chapter 18—whatever else it is about—describes a great trading system, a *world* trading system, which God is going to bring down *in judgment*, without warning. It says:

> In *one hour* so great riches is come to nought (Revelation 18:17).

It will all happen 'in one day' says Revelation 18:8. And the whole world will be shattered and shaken at the sight of it.

Revelation 18 says:

> And after these things, I [John] saw another angel come down from heaven, having great power; and the earth was lightened with his glory. And he cried mightily with a strong voice, saying, Babylon the great is fallen, is fallen, and is become the habitation of devils, and the hold of every foul spirit, and a cage of every unclean and hateful bird. For all nations have drunk of the wine of the wrath of her fornication, and the kings of the earth have committed fornication with her, and the merchants of the earth are waxed rich through the abundance of her delicacies (vv 1–3).

Notice that it says 'the merchants of the earth'. That is one piece of evidence that what is being referred to is some kind of trading system, or economic system—a *world* trading or economic system, in fact, since it embraces the merchants of the earth, not just merchants of one locality.

Then the chapter goes on:

> And I heard another voice from heaven, saying, Come out of her, my people, that ye be not partakers of her sins, and that ye receive not of her plagues. For her sins have reached unto heaven, and God hath remembered her iniquities. Reward her even as she rewarded you, and double unto her double according to her works: in the cup which she hath filled fill to her double. How much she hath glorified herself, and lived deliciously, so much torment and sorrow give her: for she saith in her heart, I sit a queen, and am no widow, and shall see no sorrow. Therefore shall her plagues come *in one day*, death, and mourning, and famine; and she shall be utterly burned with fire: for strong is the Lord God who judgeth her (vv 4–8).

Again, it says it will all happen *in one day*. And it says how it will happen: 'She shall be utterly burned with fire'—Babylon the great, that is.

Then verses 9 and 10 say:

> And the kings of the earth, who have committed fornication and lived deliciously with her, shall bewail her, and lament for her, when they shall see the smoke of her burning. Standing afar off for the fear of her torment, saying, Alas, alas, that great city Babylon, that mighty city! for *in one hour* is thy judgment come.

Once more we are told that it will all happen *in one hour*.

The following verses must be referring to some great trading system, a world trading system which is centred on this city, 'that great city Babylon', for they say:

> And the merchants of the earth shall weep and mourn over her; for no man buyeth their merchandise any more: the merchandise of gold, and silver, and precious

stones, and of pearls, and fine linen, and purple, and silk, and scarlet, and all thyine wood, and all manner vessels of ivory, and all manner vessels of most precious wood, and of brass, and iron, and marble, and cinnamon, and odours, and ointments, and frankincense, and wine, and oil, and fine flour, and wheat, and beasts, and sheep, and horses, and chariots, and slaves, and souls of men (vv 12–13).

The chapter continues:

And the fruits that thy soul lusted after are departed from thee, and all things which were dainty and goodly are departed from thee, and thou shalt find them no more (v 14).

It has all been brought down in judgment—God's judgment; with a snap of the fingers, as it were.

Then we get a description of how the whole world will be shattered and shaken at the sight of all this:

The merchants of these things, which were made rich by her, shall stand afar off for the fear of her torment, weeping and wailing. And saying, Alas, alas, that great city, that was clothed in fine linen, and purple, and scarlet, and decked with gold, and precious stones, and pearls! For *in one hour* so great riches is come to nought (vv 15–17a).

Yet again, it is mentioned that it will all happen *in one hour*.

The description of how shattered and shaken the whole world will be when this takes place then continues:

And every shipmaster, and all the company in ships, and sailors, and as many as trade by sea [another indication that reference is being made to a trading system], stood afar off, and cried when they saw the smoke of her burning, saying, What city is like unto this great city! And they cast dust on their heads, and cried, weeping and wailing, saying, Alas, alas, that great city, wherein were made rich all that had ships in the sea by reason of her costliness! for *in one hour* is she made desolate (vv 17b–19).

This is the *third* time this chapter has said it will all happen *in one hour*. Furthermore, the reference to 'all that had ships in the sea' being 'made rich' must unquestionably be referring to some great world trading system. It cannot possibly be referring to anything else. And it is a world trading system, or economic system, that was centred on 'this great city' until it was all brought down like a pack of cards *in one hour*.

The following verses read:

> Rejoice over her, thou heaven, and ye holy apostles and prophets; for God has avenged you on her. And a mighty angel took up a stone like a great millstone, and cast it into the sea, saying, Thus with violence shall that great city Babylon be thrown down, and shall be found no more at all (vv 20–21).

How total that destruction and desolation shall be is described in verses 22 and 23:

> And the voice of harpers, and musicians, and of pipers, and trumpeters, shall be heard no more at all in thee; and no craftsman, of whatsoever craft he be, shall be found any more in thee; and the sound of a millstone shall be heard no more at all in thee; and the light of a candle shall shine no more at all in thee; and the voice of the bridegroom and of the bride shall be heard no more at all in thee: for thy merchants were the great men of the earth.

Note that the reference to her merchants being the great men of the earth must, inevitably, once again, be referring to some kind of world trading or world economic system. And when it says 'thy merchants *were* the great men of the earth', it means they were, *no more*. The whole system had now crashed to the ground. It was totally finished.

The fact that the whole system was the height of deception and diabolical delusion is made plain by verse 23b, which says:

For by thy sorceries were all nations deceived.

They were all 'taken in', in other words. And by 'sorcery' it means, wizardry—the use of magic or deceptive arts, the activity of deceiving spirits, and so on.

Verse 24 concludes the chapter, when it says:

And in her was found the blood of prophets, and of saints, and of all that were slain upon the earth.

This gives those who have eyes to see a clue as to the identity of this great city, which is described in this chapter as, 'that great city Babylon', and 'Babylon the great' (vv 10, 21, and v 2). But I will make no comment on that here. Suffice it to say at this point that one of the principles which governs the interpretation of Bible prophecy is that you recognise what it is referring to when you see it happening. And we, ourselves, will recognise 'Babylon the great' when we see that awful judgment fall *in one hour* on a world trading, or world economic system that is already in existence, but which is not yet clearly identifiable—at least, not finally identifiable.

Then, very briefly, what about the Far East? Japan is the rising power in the world today, and has been since World War II. She is even fast outstripping America now. Furthermore, she is about to re-arm, even if she has not already started to re-arm. Japan stated publicly that when the new Emperor succeeded Emperor Hiro-hito, they would re-write their Constitution, which was drawn up under General MacArthur after Japan surrendered in 1945; they would then re-arm, and equip their armies ready to send them overseas. It is very ominous, indeed, if they intend to do that, or have even begun to do that!

A Tokyo correspondent, before the enthronement of the new Emperor in November 1990, drew attention to the disturbing implications of the Shinto ceremony:

In the Shinto initiation he will become a god. The Shinto religion marks the Japanese as a superior people and fires them with a mission to dominate the world.

Unfettered military expansion is another objective, this correspondent says.

Then China revealed its true nature on Tiananmen Square, and is showing it over the issue of Hong Kong. Recently she entered into an economic alliance with Japan. But supposing that is to be followed by a military alliance, and they both come together in that way also? If so, is this to be interpreted as God preparing 'the way of the kings of the east', when armies 200 million strong will come against the Middle East and against Israel at the time of Armaggedon, as is prophesied in Revelation 16:12–16, and 9:14–21? If so, that is yet another piece of end-day Bible prophecy falling into place.

And then we need to watch what is happening in India, which in Bible days was included among 'the kings of the East'. The Book of Esther begins with the words:

> Now it came to pass in the days of Ahasuerus [who ruled over the then Medo-Persian Empire], (this is Ahasuerus, which reigned, *from India* even unto Ethiopia, over an hundred and seven and twenty provinces).

So India was part of the Medo-Persian Empire in those days, and was included in the description 'the people of the east'.

India is in ferment just now. And I am being told that far from being pacifist she is very, very militant indeed and particularly in the north of India. Today she has nuclear weapons, as has Pakistan. We need to watch what is happening in India from a prophetic point of view.

Chapter Four

The Situation in Europe and in Eastern Europe Today

How, in the days of *glasnost* and *perestroika*, is this situation to be viewed biblically and prophetically?

I need to remind you that when the disciples asked Jesus what would be *the sign* of His coming and of the end of the world, or of the age, the first thing that He said in reply was, 'Take heed that no man *deceive* you' (Matthew 24:4). And that applies very much to what is going on in Europe today. Deception is an inbuilt ingredient of Communism.

In the first place, Gorbachev, in his speeches, has been saying that the world must become one. He said so in his United Nations speech in New York in December 1988. I studied that speech in minute detail. His speech was a call to *make the world one*.

Again, the speech he gave in London, on 7th April 1989, was shot through with *one-world* language. I studied it in detail. So much was it shot through with one-world language that I asked myself 'who was his speech-writer'! He talked about the need for one-world politics, one-world economy, a one-world concensus of opinion, a one-world security, a one-world unity, the *unification* of the world into one. 'We need to move forward to *a new world order*,' he said. He even used language that could only imply a *one-world government*, towards which he sees us moving rapidly. He had already stated all this in his book entitled *Perestroika*, which I have read. The subtitle is 'New Thinking for our Country and the World'.

Gorbachev occupies the centre stage in world affairs at the moment (February 1990). So much so, that, as somebody has commented, he only has to sneeze and the stockmarket is immediately affected, and Wall Street turns topsy-turvy for fear that he is going to die of a cold!

In his speeches Gorbachev has said, 'We must bring all this about,' that is, this unification of the world into one. Immediately after his United Nations speech in New York, Mrs Thatcher appeared on the steps of 10 Downing Street and faced the Press and the television cameras. When asked what she thought of his speech, she said with great enthusiasm, 'His speech was *marvellous*. He sees us all as *one world*.' This is 'New Age' language, whether the speakers realise it or not. Gorbachev has even said, 'We need to *humanise* the world.' In order to do that, you have to get rid of all religion, which is what the 'New Age' people intend to do anyway.

Let us look more closely at what this means. Gorbachev said emphatically, '*We* must do this.' '*We* must bring it about.' Do you see the implication of all this? *Man* is setting out to reverse what God did at the Tower of Babel. At the beginning of the account of what happened at the Tower of Babel we read:

> And the whole earth was of *one* language, and of *one* speech.... [Then they said] let us build us a city and a tower, whose top may reach unto heaven.... And the Lord came down to see the city and the tower, which the children of men builded. And the Lord said, Behold *the people is one* [notice, 'Behold *the people is one*] and they have all *one* language: and this they *begin* to do: and now nothing will be restrained from them, which they have imagined to do. Go to, let *us* [notice God said, 'Let *us*'; 'us' is plural—God the Father, God the Son, and God the Holy Spirit!] go down, and there confound their language, that they may not understand one another's speech.' So the Lord scattered them abroad from thence upon the face of all the earth: and they left off to build the city. Therefore is the name of it called Babel, because the Lord did there *confound* the language *of all the earth*: and from thence did the Lord scatter them abroad upon the face of all the earth (Genesis 11:1–9).

The previous chapter gives the genealogies of the sons of Noah, ie, Shem, Ham, and Japheth, and says in verse 25:

> And unto Eber were born two sons: the name of one was Peleg; for in his days *was the earth divided*.

Divided! Not *one* anymore.

So when Gorbachev, *who is a front man*, and is very cleverly stage-managed, with first-class public relations agents, and with carefully arranged world-wide television coverage, delivers two major speeches saying, 'We must make the world one', and when, in an *international* speech from New York he calls on *the whole world* to do it, that is *man* setting about to *reverse* and *undo* what God did at the Tower of Babel. That is the first thing that we need to see about it.

I noticed also that immediately after Gorbachev's United Nations speech in New York, Eduard Shevardnadze, with others, set out on a rapid 'global trot' tour, visiting India, China, Japan, and other countries, sparking off furious diplomatic activity, and saying to each country in turn that we must settle all our regional differences, *de-militarise* everywhere, and *make the world one*. That looked suspiciously like 'New Age' activity to me.

President Gorbachev's state visit to Italy to see the Pope between 29th November and 2nd December 1989 appeared to be a step in the same direction. Some sort of 'merging', or 'unification', surely, was taking place. Everywhere it was proclaimed that Gorbachev was making history. The Press said, when he and the Pope clasped hands and beamed at one another:

> The Kremlin and the Vatican are now at last *joined* in a common cause in this first meeting between a leader of the Roman Catholic Church and a leader of the avowedly atheist Soviet Union.

But what were they up to? What 'merger' was this? The question also needs to be asked, 'What is the common cause in which, at last, they became *joined*?'

In addition to all this, and no doubt connected with it all, there is something which we also need to see prophetically (I am speaking in 1990).

The Pope and the Archbishop of Canterbury, Dr Runcie, and others, Free Church leaders included, have been working hand in hand to bring about a one-world Church under the supremacy of the Bishop of Rome. They have been doing so for some time, and still are. This is the present trend. Not only that, they have been working hand in hand to merge all the faiths and religions of the world, including Christianity, into one, so as to bring into being a *one-world faith*, a one-world religion, in other words. And they still *are* doing that. Multi-faith services in our Cathedrals, including Canterbury, are but one example of this.

At the same time, Europe and the EEC have been working fast towards bringing about *one common currency* in Europe, with 1992 as a possible date line. But those who control the World Bank and the International Bankers,—the Rothschilds, the Rockerfellers, and others—are working fast towards bringing in a one-*world* currency, not just a common European currency. In fact, the *economic* forces on earth are moving relentlessly towards a *unified* world system. '*Unify* the world' is the cry. Economic forces are bringing this about, not just the world politicians.

The 'in' word, therefore, is 'merge'. Merge the world into one. Merge all religions and faiths into one, including Christianity. Merge all currencies into one. Merge all governments and parliaments into one. This is the very climate in which we are living today. This is the atmosphere, this is the *trend*, the world trend. Merge all peoples of the world into one is a trend that also is already well advanced.

What does all this add up to, prophetically? *Making the world one*, with a one-world currency, one-world politics, a one-world security system, a one-world concensus of opinion, a one-world religion, a one-world government or Parliament, merging all the peoples of the world into one, is all paving the way for a *one-world ruler*, who, according to the Book of the Revelation chapter 13, will ultimately be the Anti-Christ, the Beast, and the Man of Sin of 2 Thessalonians 2:3. Events are fast moving in the direction of bringing him on to the scene.

He could emerge at any moment. For instance, 2 Thessalonians 2:2–3 says:

> The day of Christ [meaning the day when our Lord Jesus Christ shall return]...shall not come, *except there come a falling away first*, and *that man of sin* be revealed, the son of perdition.

There certainly *has* come a falling away, an *alarming* falling away from the faith. It is going on all around us. So things are indeed fast moving in the direction of bringing this sinister person on to the scene.

Since all one-world activity is being done *without God*, and without any reference to God whatsoever, and in a completely God*less* way—in fact it is *anti*-God activity in every respect—then it must be the *spirit* of Anti-Christ which is bringing it about. It is the spirit of Anti-Christ mightily at work in the world. It is certainly not the *Holy* Spirit who is doing it all. We need to recognise it as the activity of the spirit of Anti-Christ, and must not be hoodwinked, or taken in by it.

Then what about all these mighty convulsions, upheavals, breath-taking changes that are so dramatically taking place all over Eastern Europe, and even beyond Europe now? It is early yet to comment. But Peregrine Worsthorn, the then editor of *The Sunday Telegraph*, said this, in print, on Sunday 19th November 1989, as he saw the changes taking place:

> *The making of peace*, that is what the world is now engaged upon.

Then he said:

> It can be as perilous a business as waging war.

To which I say, *Exactly!*

The world situation has, in fact, become extremely dangerous. *We need to be warned!* It is not a time to begin to sit back and relax. Never! Mrs Thatcher said on Saturday 10th February 1990:

> We must not let down our guard lest the dramatic

changes now taking place in Europe *do not lead to a period of co-operation and peace*.

She said the same thing at the NATO conference in London shortly after, warning that Russia's military might is very formidable.

I have a strong conviction as I watch all that is going on in the Soviet Union, in Eastern Europe, and so on; as I consider the negotiations that are going on in the Middle East concerning Israel's *need to trade land for peace*, and being pressurised to do so; as I heard President Bush, who is a *one-world man*, announce at the Malta summit in December 1989, 'We are now entering a period of *world peace* and co-operation'; with Mr de Klerk using the same language in his presidential address in South Africa on 2nd February 1990, when he talked about 'Breaking through to *peace*, reconstruction and reconciliation.' I can see very clearly that there are two end-day prophecies of the Bible which are extremely relevant concerning all this.

One is:

> When they shall say, *Peace* and *safety*; then sudden destruction cometh upon them, as travail upon a woman with child; and they shall not escape (1 Thessalonians 5:3).

This verse from the *more sure* Word of prophecy, the Bible, is a warning, against being *lulled into a false sense of security*. I hope you can see that.

The second prophecy is:

> God shall send them *strong delusion* that they should believe a lie (2 Thessalonians 2:11).

Again, this is from the *more sure* Word of prophecy, namely, the Bible! I say this verse sums up exactly where we are, in the world situation, *prophetically*, right at this very moment. We are right there!

If you want to know who the 'them' is to whom God shall send strong delusion, 2 Thessalonians 2:10 tells you.

> [It is to them] that perish: because they received not the love of the truth, that they might be saved.

Verse 11 of 2 Thessalonians 2 goes on to say:

> For *this cause* God shall send them strong delusion, that they should believe a lie: that they all might be damned who believe not the truth, but had pleasure in unrighteousness (2 Thessalonians 2:11–12).

In view of these two prophecies from the Bible, I want to issue a warning. Whatever it is that has been, and is, being brought about by Gorbachev and by those who are behind him in Eastern Europe, in Berlin, and in the Soviet Union, we should not be fooled by anything. We should not be taken in. We should not be hoodwinked. We should not be conned. We should not be *deceived*!

Gorbachev has been making all the running so far, you notice (said in February 1990). The Russians are the best chess players in the world! You need to realise that the Kremlin *is working to a strategy*, and has been all along, ever since the Russian Revolution in 1917, in fact, and even before then. *And that strategy has not changed*. The tactics might have done, but not the strategy. The chameleon may change the colour of its skin, but it does not change *its nature*!

Furthermore, in this game of chess, it is not the move on the chess-board that they are making now which counts. Discernment, spiritual discernment and perception is needed to perceive what they, and their Chiefs of Staff, have in mind five moves from now. Russia remains a mighty military power. Let us never forget that.

During the NATO conference held in London during the week ending 7th July 1990, Mrs Thatcher revealed that in 1989, Russia produced 6 new tanks *per day*, and 2 fighter aircraft *per day*, a nuclear submarine *every 6 weeks*, and, 100 tactical air-launched missiles *per week*! What's all *that* in aid of?

Furthermore, on 29th January 1990, the very day that the United States announced big cuts in its European forces, it was disclosed that the Soviet Union had deployed another of its giant Typhoon-class nuclear submarines from its Arctic base on the Kola Peninsula. This is the *sixth* of its class to be built. They are the biggest in the world—560 feet long and of 20,000 tons displacement. Its main weapon is the SS-N-20 missile, which can strike at *any* European or North American city from their own northern oceans, and is fitted with a titanium hull and fins to smash through Polar Arctic ice. They have also modernised their warships, which are fitted *for the attack*. And very recently they have launched another aircraft-carrier of immense size. What is all *that* for if they are out for peace? What *deception* is this?

I have quoted many times, in many parts of this country, that one of the Kremlin's chief spokesman has said:

> We'll strike the West when we have lulled them to sleep with the biggest peace propaganda campaign the world has ever known.

I repeat, 'When they shall say, Peace and Safety; then sudden destruction cometh upon them, as travail upon a woman with child; and they shall not escape.' And, 'God shall send them strong delusion, that they should believe a lie.'

I am so glad that Mrs Thatcher and the United States Defence Secretary have repeatedly reiterated, 'The West must not let down its guard.' It *still* mustn't!

Furthermore, I myself have been asking the question: Can the Soviet Union afford to dismantle their nuclear missiles because they have something far more lethal to put in their place? It is a question that needs to be asked. I understand the answer is: Yes. They hold the trump card! But then, how do we know that they are, indeed, dismantling their nuclear weapons?

Whatever else may be going on in the Soviet Union, there is something else that is clear, and which has prophetic significance: Russia is now prepared to release 100,000 Soviet Jews this year, 1990. In addition to which, Russian Jews are now very fearful of the growing anti-Semitism in the Soviet Union. An East European Jewish correspondent says this anti-Semitism was due to reach a climax on 5th May 1990, the date when a certain sinister nationalist movement, called Pamyat, and other extremist organisations, had called for a pogrom in Moscow and in Leningrad. It has been reported more recently that Pamyat has the support of the Russian military and the KGB. There has already been a blatant public expression of anti-Semitism in Leipzig, when neo-Nazi youths marched through the city, waving Nazi-like symbols, and shouting,

'Kick out the Jews.' 'To hell with the Jews.' This growing anti-Semitism is resulting in *more* Jews wanting to leave the Soviet Union. The Jews are being blamed for the failure of the Communist system and are therefore in danger of being made the scapegoats. This has been a feature of their history all down the centuries. They have always been used as scapegoats.

The release of so many Jews from the Soviet Union brings events into line with a further end day Bible prophecy, for God says in Isaiah 43:6:

> I will say to the north, Give up; and to the south, Keep not back: bring my sons from far, and my daughters from the ends of the earth.

And it is happening! Right now! As confirmation, Ethiopia, which is to Israel's south, is also releasing a considerable number of Jews. Russia is to Israel's far north, of course. And President Gorbachev is being urged to take prompt action for direct flights to be arranged from the USSR to Israel because of increasing anti-Semitism.

What else is there of prophetic significance in the European situation?

There is no doubt that the map of Europe is being re-drawn. The reunification of Germany is now being accelerated apace, and nothing is likely to prevent it. We don't know yet, in February 1990, what the result of this will be, but the effect of it on the whole of Europe will be considerable. There has been talk about a new Federal States of Europe. There has also been talk in the Press about the return of some of the European kings, whether or not this will materialise. We shall see!

Then more than just mention has been made of the scholarly Archduke Otto, or Dr Habsburg, as he prefers to be called, who is the son of the former Emperor of Austria. He is, significantly enough, a descendant of Emperor Charlemagne, who created the First Reich. He is a committed Member of the European Parliament and is said to have done more than anyone to bring such a new Federation of European States into the realms of possibility. He is, by descent, none other than the rightful Holy Roman Emperor himself and could no doubt claim that title if circumstances developed that way.

It might not be without significance that a certain Roman Catholic Father spoke for nearly half an hour at the European Parliament at the end of 1989 about the marvels of the Holy Roman Empire. What he said was then published in a long article in *The Financial Times*, in which he raised the question, 'Who was it who proposed the *re*-establishment of the Holy Roman Empire?' He claimed it was Otto von Habsburg. If, indeed, Otto von Habsburg did make such a proposal it is quite noteworthy. *The Financial Times* is never guilty of sensationalism! This Roman Catholic Father then added, 'And another Otto made the same proposal, Otto von Bismark.' So it seems there has been quite serious talk behind the scenes in European circles of the re-establishment of the Holy Roman Empire, or of that possibility! It has obviously been more than just mentioned.

This statement appeared in the 10th February 1990 issue of *The Telegraph Magazine*:

> There is a glorious irony as we approach the end of the 20th century that the *ideal person* to become the leader of a new Federal States of Europe is *none other* than the rightful Holy Roman Emperor himself, Dr Habsburg, that is, Archduke Otto.

By 'rightful', it means, *by descent*. All this means that there has been quite serious talk along these lines. Are we indeed going to see very soon the re-establishment of the Holy Roman Empire? They say, 'Where there is smoke there is fire'! We don't know. But we shall see. It happens to be a fact that many of the EEC countries are Roman Catholic countries. If we do see the re-establishment of the Holy Roman Empire, then that will have most profound prophetical significance indeed.

All this raises the further question: In all the shaking and upheaval that is going on, on the Continent, are we going to see the ten kingdoms of Nebuchadnezzar's vision in Daniel chapter 2 eventually emerge after all 'the dust' has settled? By that I mean, are we going to see the present twelve members of the EEC sorting themselves out into ten? It is a most interesting question, and has profound significance from a biblical point of view.

I say again, we should bear in mind that several of the present countries of Europe are Roman Catholic countries. It will be interesting to see if, after all the shaking and upheaval is over, and after 'the dust' has all settled, the present twelve members of the EEC sort themselves out into ten Roman Catholic member-countries, omitting those who are not. That would mean Britain, who is not a Roman Catholic country, but a Protestant one, would be among those who are omitted. That would be very significant indeed, especially as I myself believe it was never the will of God that we should have gone into the EEC in the first place; and never the will of God that we should have built the Channel tunnel.

All this also raises the question, 'Are we *then* going to see the False Prophet and the Anti-Christ, spoken of in the Book of the Revelation emerge on the human scene?' See Revelation chapter 13, Revelation chapter 17, and Revelation 19:11–21 in particular. We don't know. But again, we shall see! I believe many of us who are alive today *will see*. Everything is happening so quickly!

What we *do* know is that Daniel 2:44 says:

> In the days of *these kings* [these *ten kings* is what this passage in Daniel is talking about] shall the God of heaven set up a kingdom, which shall never be destroyed: and the kingdom shall not be left to other people, but it shall break in pieces and consume all these kingdoms, and it shall stand for ever.

In other words, all *other* kingdoms will be destroyed, but the one that the God of heaven sets up will not be. For then will be fulfilled that most glorious prophecy of the Bible:

> The kingdoms of this world are become the kingdoms of our Lord, and of his Christ; and he shall reign for ever and ever [Hallelujah!] (Revelation 11:15).

As we study Daniel 2:44, where it talks about, 'in the days of these kings shall the God of heaven set up a kingdom, which shall never be destroyed', we should look at the previous verse to see the context:

> They shall mingle themselves with the seed of men: but they shall not cleave one to another, even as iron is not mixed with clay.

If this is talking about the creation of multi-racial societies and multi-racial nations in the end days, as I believe it may well be, then we must be right there! We are living in such a multi-racial society here in Britain today. We see it all around us! And furthermore, in our big cities what do we see happening? Answer: the Asians live as a community in one part of a city, the West Indians in another part, the Chinese in another part, the Africans in another part, and so on. And they never mix! In other words, as this prophecy of Daniel 2:43 says, 'they shall not cleave, one to another, even as iron is not mixed with clay.' We see it happening, right before our eyes!

I say we must be *right there*, because the next part of this prophecy is about to be fulfilled:

> In the days of these kings shall the God of heaven set up a kingdom, which shall never be destroyed.

Already they are mingling themselves with the seed of men, mixing the races, and they are not cleaving one to another, even as iron is not mixed with clay. It is happening all around us! We must be within a hair's breadth of being there—of being right at the time when the God of heaven sets up His Kingdom and all these *other* kingdoms are destroyed, leaving only *His*!

If all that I have said previously about the re-establishment of the Holy Roman Empire and the emergence of the ten kingdoms which the prophetic Scriptures talk about proves to be true, then everything that we see happening on the Continent, in world events, and all around us, is heading up to this—the moment when the God of heaven will set up His Kingdom, having overthrown all *other* kingdoms and governments, those ten kingdoms included. We live in most breath-taking times, therefore. How near must we be to it all!

A passage of prophetical Scripture which is a key passage in helping us to interpret these times in which we live—what the Bible calls the end days—is Ezekiel 38:1-6. This whole chapter, and chapter 39 of Ezekiel, is about certain armies of the north coming against the land of Israel in the latter days. The two chapters together describe in detail what will happen to those armies. They should be read together as one; there should be no division between the two chapters. They describe what is often referred to as the Gog and Magog war. We need to see their extreme relevance today, especially to the events which, right now, are taking place in Europe. It all forms part of one big picture, one big *prophetic* picture, the Bible's revelation of all that is taking place.

Verses 1 to 6 of Ezekiel chapter 38 mention *Gomer* and *Togarmah* amongst those armies and regions who will come against the land of Israel in the latter days. The most ancient maps which are in existence show that Gomer equals the area of the present East Germany. In fact, when I checked this from a very ancient map in the London Map Room, Kensington, I found that the letters 'GO' were printed where present-day West Germany is, and the letters 'MER' were printed where present-day East Germany is. So you could say Gomer equals the two Germanies. And they are soon to be re-unified! This is very significant indeed, prophetically! They now *are*, at the time of going to print.

Then *Togarmah*, on the ancient maps, equals the area of present-day Armenia, Azerbaijan and the Caucasus, where the Cossacks and their famous horsemen and cavalry had their origin, and where, before them, the even more famous Mogul horsemen and cavalry had their origin. It is important, prophetically, to mention this, because horsemen and horses are mentioned in the prophesied invasion of Ezekiel 38:1-6. Togarmah also includes the area where present-day Turkey is situated, which, incidentally is *Islamic*, as also is Azerbaijan. Turkey, today, has the strongest army in the world next to the United States, but nobody realises it.

These areas are constantly being brought before us in the news these days, and it is important, prophetically, to take note of that.

You will no doubt know, also, that many regions of the Soviet Union *are Islamic* today. Central Asia is, in particular.

But how many will know, I wonder, that a sixth part of the Soviet land mass, with its 55 million inhabitants in Central Asia, is *mostly Islamic*? How many will know, I wonder, that by the end of this present century (that is, by the year 2000), between a third and a half of the 'Red Army's' recruits will be from an *Islamic* background? This is very significant indeed in view of the fact that Islam is anti-Israel, and always refers to Israel as 'Our enemy', even in the mildest of conversations. It is very significant, too, in view of the fact that that end-day invasion of Israel which is prophesied in Ezekiel chapters 38 and 39, is going to comprise of armies which come from these regions according to Ezekiel 38:1–6, many of which today are Islamic.

So in this respect also, events which are taking place on the Continent today are fast being brought into line with the fulfilment of Bible prophecies, and especially into line with the fulfilment of all that is laid before us in the prophecies of Ezekiel 38 and 39. Sooner or later these prophecies will unquestionably be fulfilled, and in absolute and minute detail. For, 'The thing that God has spoken *shall be done*.' There is no question about it. All the events which are taking place in the world today are fast shaping up that way, and in that direction, extremely fast, in fact. We need to watch world events very carefully, and with our eyes on all these prophecies of the Bible that I have been quoting.

But I believe the time has come to ask, 'Who exactly, is this man Gorbachev?' especially if he remains in power (said in February 1990), and especially as he has now greatly strengthened his power base and now has greater powers than he ever had before.

To begin with, he did not get what he wanted, but he did so in the end. He had already become extremely powerful prior to this, and particularly on the world stage. Furthermore, he has almost reached the stage where the whole world worships him. I even heard a leading evangelical preacher say in his sermon one Sunday morning in February 1990, 'My hero right now is Gorbachev'!

But we need to watch it because the Scriptures tell us that a certain person *is* going to emerge on the scene of human history who all the world will go after and worship. See the Book of the Revelation 13:8, which says:

And *all that dwell upon the earth* shall worship him ['all', it explains], whose names are not written in the book of life of the Lamb slain from the foundation of the world.

All true believers need to take heed that no man deceive them. *Jesus* taught that. And that applies to *this* man. 'Take heed that ye be not deceived' is what Jesus taught. That means, 'Do not be *taken in*.' 'Watch it!'

Now I am not saying that Gorbachev *is* that person who will appear on the human scene and who the whole world will go after. But we need to watch it.

My point is that he was already very powerful. And now that he has got *more* power he could become more powerful than Napoleon, more powerful than Alexander the Great ever was, more powerful even than Bismark, more powerful than Hitler, or Stalin, or Breznev. And that, despite setbacks. And if he does, who, then, is he likely to prove to be? He occupies the central place on the world stage at the moment (February 1990).

Whoever he may be at the moment, the fact of the matter is that the Soviet strategies which he has been pursuing ever since he came to power are placing him, right now, in history, as the second most adept *propagandist* of this century, next to Adolf Hitler. When I say that I am quoting strategic analysts.

And 'propagandist' is the right word. He is an actor, remember, and an expert at stage managing. And he has become *the* central figure on the world stage (in February 1990).

At the moment he is benevolent. All smiles! *But!!!*

Some even say that Gorbachev sees himself as potentially the greatest historical personality of all time. They say he sees himself as a genius whom no opposing nation or group of nations can outwit or outmatch. But now that he has strengthened his power base and has got more power, what would happen if he *was* opposed, or was in danger of being outwitted or outmatched? I guess we would see his true nature then!

One Continental was heard to say, 'Behind his smiling mask is the face of a snarling wolf'! We shall no doubt see. It is even said that he envisages himself as ending his days as the Master of the Third Rome, a system which he envisages would embrace all Europe, all Central Asia and the Middle East, a system to which all Africa would have to be in submission. Again, we shall see!

This is very significant indeed since, in December 1989, he entered into some kind of union with the Pope, and the Pope with him. Behind closed doors in the Vatican City in Rome, atheistic Communism and Rome were united in some way. It is very significant, also, that he has been mentioned more than once by the Press as a likely candidate to head up a new Federal States of Europe, and to become its first President, especially as it is he who has always talked about bringing into being 'a common European home'.

Furthermore, it has become plain that Gorbachev is siding with the Muslims—with Islam, in other words—who are against Israel. He is an avowed Communist, and has said so, and therefore is anti-God, anti-Christian and anti-Israel if he really showed himself in his true colours.

People are even asking, 'Is he going to turn out to be 'the Chief prince of Meshech and Tubal' who is mentioned in the prophecy of Ezekiel 38:2? This prince is a person—a person called 'Gog'. In Ezekiel 38:2, the Lord says to the Prophet Ezekiel:

> Son of man, set thy face *against Gog*, the land of Magog, *the chief prince of* Meshech and Tubal, and prophesy *against* him.

Now I am not saying that he *is* that person. But some are beginning to ask that question, and in print! Such a suggestion could sound very far-fetched at the moment. But so did a lot of things, until they suddenly began to happen, recently.

Let us consider for a moment what Gorbachev has achieved so far, since he came to power.

1) He has succeeded in practically neutralising Western Europe, and to a very large extent has successfully eliminated the strategic effectiveness of NATO. The NATO conference held in London during the week ending 7th July 1990, made that plain.

2) He has practically succeeded in getting the Americans out of Europe. The Soviet Union has tried in various ways to achieve that ever since victory in Europe was granted to us by

God's grace in 1945, but never succeeded in doing so. But this latest ploy seems to be doing the trick! And now he looks like doing it without having to fire a shot! It is only a matter of time now before they are all withdrawn. Watch events, and see! He must be laughing!

3) He has successfully pursued the well known *Leninist* policy of lulling the West to sleep to such an extent that the Soviet military might, which unquestionably still exists, can smash the West while its guard is down. For it is the intention now, of the USSR, to defeat the West *without any direct military conflict with the Western powers*. Instead, it intends to defeat them by other and more subtle means, and with that formidable military power still in the background.

4) He has effectively, and very cleverly, eliminated Western Europe as a *potential* military front, removing every threat of a Western attack, if ever there was such a threat, which there most certainly was not.

It should be noted that Gorbachev has been working for all these changes, and for all the other changes that have been taking place so dramatically, for a long time.

Meanwhile, we should never forget for one moment that the Soviet military might remains *massive*. Mrs Margaret Thatcher stressed that very strongly in mid-February 1990, when she was addressing the Board of Jewish Deputies in London. 'It is *really massive*,' she said with great emphasis. She repeated that warning at the NATO conference in London in the first week of July 1990 when she said, 'The Soviet forces remain *formidable*.'

'*Why* has Gorbachev been doing all this?' is what we should be asking. What lies behind it all? And what is it all leading up to?

There happen to be certain brilliant Intelligence agents in different parts of the world *who know*. The international Intelligence community has known for a long time what the Soviet plans are—their *military* plans. These plans even pre-date the Bolshevic Revolution of 1917. And we need to see things in that context in order to understand what is going on. Furthermore, it is the Russian military and their Chiefs of Staff that we need to keep our eyes on constantly, not whoever is the political leader at the Kremlin in any given time.

I have already said that the Soviet Union is working to a strategy, and has been doing so for a long time. We need to know that the Russian leadership, even before the Bolshevic Revolution of 1917, had ambitions which it regarded as *foundational*.

One of them was the ambition to rule the world. To have a one-world empire, in other words, was their ambition and their aim. And they have been manoeuvering events ever since to bring that aim about.

The BBC, for instance, revealed in a programme in mid-February 1990 that *glasnost* and *perestroika* have been tried before, *prior* to 1917, in the days of Emperor Nicholas I. But it backfired then because they tried to bring it about too fast. The Communists merely capitalised on that ambition to rule the world when they took over power.

Now one primary or first objective to achieve that ambition of world rulership has been to obtain a warm-water port to the south. The Soviet Union has built up her navy to enormous proportions, until now, it is the most powerful navy in the world, and with modern technology can now outmatch the United States fleets.

The earlier Gulf War in which Iran was defeated, brought her nearer to achieving that objective of a warm-water port than ever before.

Meanwhile, Russia is, at the moment, expanding her port facilities. In 1968 she began to use the Syrian port of Tartus in the Eastern Mediterranean, and she is expanding this port, at the very time when it was thought that she was interested in disengaging herself from expensive military moves! What is that for? Deception is a built-in ingredient in the whole Communist system, and we should never forget that. It cannot be repeated often enough.

Russia has also been arming Syria to the teeth for an attack on Israel, when the USSR regards the time to be right. Syrian military moves are controlled by Russia.

So what are Gorbachev and the Soviet leadership plus their Generals and their military planning to do? The answer is this, according to the printed international Intelligence community's reports, *which have nowhere been denied*:

After effectively neutralising and eliminating Western Europe *non-militarily* as a potential military front, thus removing the threat of a Western attack, the Soviet Union will soon be free to turn *all* her attention to the Middle East and open up another front there, and with no danger of a second front being opened against her in Western Europe.

Her major objectives would be the Middle East oil, control of the Gulf itself, plus the Eastern Mediterranean warm-water ports, and also control of the Suez Canal with its access to the Red Sea, the Indian Ocean, the Arabian Sea and the Pacific Ocean. (Far-Eastern Christians have told me that Russia is taking a lot of interest in the Pacific area nowadays.)

Gorbachev even asked President Bush at the Malta summit in December 1989 to withdraw the United States fleet from the Eastern Mediterranean! Whether President Bush was taken in or not, remains to be seen. If he falls for it he must have blinkers on!

But the Soviet Union has also promised to give the possession *of Jerusalem* to fundamentalist Islam so that Islam can fulfil its long-desired aim of making Jerusalem the Islamic capital of the Middle East. This means that Islam and the Soviet Union, *in conjunction with one another* would have to deal with Israel. Were that to happen, it would immediately bring events in the Middle East well into line with the fulfilment of many of the Bible's end-day Prophecies concerning Israel, and particularly into line with the fulfilment of all that is contained in Ezekiel chapters 38 and 39, and in Zechariah 14 and Joel chapter 3.

In any case, Israel stands in the way of the Soviet Union taking over the Suez Canal. It is also a fact that international Intelligence has known for a long time that in order to ensure total victory for themselves and for Islam, the Soviets have long planned a massive military strike against Israel. Israel has long since known this as well.

I therefore need to say this: in the things that have been happening in the *glasnost*, *perestroika* scenario—including the dismantling of the Berlin Wall and the other events that have been taking place in Eastern Europe—all of which, together, have brought about so much optimism and euphoria everywhere, there are clear evidences that this is all part of the Soviet policy of lulling the West to sleep and of giving it a false sense of security. By that I mean it is part of their policy of 'taking the West in', so that they can, with the West completely unprepared for it, make their massive strategic move against the Middle East, against Israel and Jerusalem, when they think the time is right. And they would do it very unexpectedly. Let us never forget that Jesus said, 'Let no man *deceive* you.' Would He add to that today by saying, 'Don't be taken in by one great subterfuge'?

Moreover, it needs to be realised that had Russia's Eastern European system of states remained intact, then when Russia makes her long-planned bid for the Eastern Mediterranean, every one of those countries armed forces would have mutinied, which would, of itself, have defeated Russia. But now they will all be neutral, and will cause no such problem, and will no doubt even supply Russia with resources, especially if by doing so, their economies are helped. The neutralisation of Europe was, therefore, necessary in order to bring about this taking of the Eastern Mediterranean.

As to the Soviet armies, if a very high percentage of their recruitment now stems from those who are of an Islamic background, there would be no problem of mutiny from them, because they would be anti-Israel anyway, and would regard this onslaught as being involved in their 'cause', in their Jihad, their 'holy' war, against Israel.

It would follow that, in the taking of the Eastern Mediterranean, the Suez Canal, and Israel, together with Jerusalem, the USSR and its forces would be assisted by Islamic Syria, Islamic Libya, the Islamic PLO, Islamic Iran, which is biblical Persia, Communist or Islamic Ethiopia, and no doubt Islamic Turkey, plus all the Islamic regions in the Soviet Union, and particularly in largely Islamic Central Asia. This is exactly what Ezekiel chapters 38 and 39 say will happen anyway! Do you see how everything is fast shaping up in that direction?

Now that Jordan has gone over at least 50 per cent to fundamentalist Islam as a result of their latest election, and has even more recently sought an alliance with Islamic Iraq, Jordan and Iraq together would also be involved against Israel.

Then we need to note this: if Israel were indeed to be destroyed, and the Suez Canal were indeed to be taken over by a Russian-Islamic military alliance, and all the Middle East oil were to be denied to Britain and the West, then British and Western European industry would grind to a halt *within weeks*. This is not very good news for Britain as a nation which is already under judgment!

Furthermore, if the powerful Soviet navy, including her submarines with their high technology, could effectively prevent the United States from obtaining strategic minerals from South Africa, whilst at the same time the United States were also deprived of Middle East oil, the United States industry would also slow to a point where resistance to the Soviet Union could not continue. The United States would find itself in 'a Book of Jeremiah situation', which means to be in a position where there is no alternative but to surrender, and she would fall like over-ripe fruit into Soviet hands *just as Lenin long since* envisaged. Russia has always said she could bring America down without having to fire a shot! Do you see what I mean when I say Russia and the Soviet Union and her military have been working to a strategy—to a *long-term* strategy? And they are still pursuing it!

So all the glowing optimism, all the euphoria in the West over what has been happening in the USSR and in Eastern Europe in recent months *is extremely dangerous*. I really must emphasise that. It is dangerous because it is lulling the West to sleep and is creating a false sense of security, *as is planned*, at a time when the West, and, indeed, America, are on the very brink of impending disaster. The clarion call, therefore, is: '*Set the trumpet to thy mouth*.' 'Sound the alarm!' And, 'Wake up the West. Wake up Britain. Wake up the United States of America, while there is still time!' says the Lord!

I need to repeat once again that Jesus said, you will remember, 'Let no man *deceive* you. *Take heed* that no man deceive you.' That dire warning of the Lord's is three times repeated in the Gospels: once in Matthew 24:4; again in Mark 13:5; and yet again in Luke 21:8. And it is thrice repeated because it is most urgent that it be *heeded*, especially in these last days. So I need to stress very strongly that the following New Testament prophecies could not be more relevant as end-day prophecies.

When they shall say, Peace and safety; then sudden destruction cometh upon them, as travail upon a woman with child, and they shall not escape (1 Thessalonians 5:3).

God shall send them strong delusion, that they should believe a lie (2 Thessalonians 2:11).

Let no man deceive you by any means (2 Thessalonians 2:3).

And they should be *shouted out from the housetops*!

If you don't believe all I have said, just watch events, and see it all happen!

Convulsions and upheavals and ferment have already been taking place at break-neck speed during these last few years and months all over Europe, and even beyond Europe now. Region after region on the Continent has been in ferment and turmoil. The whole of Europe has been, and is being violently shaken. Journalists are saying that the shock waves are being felt all over the world. Parts of Africa and the Caribbean are also being violently shaken. Meanwhile, the British Isles have been shaken by one deeply disturbing catastrophe after another, and have been severely battered and shaken by one hurricane-force gale after another.

But even all this violent shaking is *not*, repeat *not*, the shaking which Almighty God is talking about when He says in Haggai 2:6–7:

For thus saith the Lord of hosts; yet once, it is a little while, and I will shake the heavens, and the earth, and the sea, and the dry land; and I will shake *all* nations, and the desire of all nations shall come.

The shaking being talked about here will cause all these other shakings to pale into insignificance. So what *is* He talking about?

Chapter Five

Jerusalem To Be the Culminating Point in World Affairs

That brings me finally to the situation in the Middle East today seen biblically and prophetically and against the background of the fast approaching climax of the ages, and of the personal return of our Lord Jesus Christ. For whatever has to be said about the state of our nation today, whatever has to be said about the state of America, whatever has to be said about the state of the Far East, whatever has to be said about the state of Europe, or whatever has to be said about the state of the world today, or about any part of the world, the *real* point on which we should be focussing our attention in these latter days in which we are living is the *Middle East*.

Everything is going to culminate there. World history is going to culminate there. It is not going to culminate in the Western world. It is not going to culminate in Europe. It is not going to culminate in the United States of America, whether they like it or not! It is all going to culminate in the Middle East. History, *His* story—*God's* story—is all going to culminate in the Middle East.

And things are *fast coming to a head*, out there. For instance, one of the latest developments is that ancient Babylon is being rebuilt! I had seen various snippets of information about this during the past two or three years, but I could never get the information confirmed. And I never preach, teach, or write about anything until I have got my facts well and truly confirmed, and authenticated. But now, major write-ups, and coloured photographs have been appearing in the national Press and in their colour magazines. Several-page articles have been written about it. These articles and coloured photographs have been appearing since August 1989. Even the Hanging Gardens of Babylon, formerly one of the seven wonders of the world, are to be rebuilt when an engineer can be found who can work out the secret of how they were watered without the use of a pumping device.

President Saddam Hussein of Iraq apparently wants to go down in history as someone who is on the same level as King Nebuchadnezzar II, the King of Babylon who originally built ancient Babylon. See Daniel 4:30 where Nebuchadnezzar said:

> Is not this great Babylon, that I have built for the house of the kingdom by the might of my power, and for the honour of my majesty?

President Saddam Hussein has also been trying to resurrect the glory of the ancient Mesopotamian civilisation of Bible days.

I don't know what all this means, or whether it has any prophetic significance at the moment, except to mention, in passing, that Revelation chapter 18, as I said earlier, talks about a city called 'Babylon the great', or 'that great city Babylon', and then describes how it is going to be utterly destroyed by God in a terrible judgment 'in one hour', and 'in one day', by some kind of raging fire. But this is not the place to discuss whether what President Saddam Hussein has rebuilt, is 'that great city Babylon' referred to in Revelation chapter 18. His rebuilding of ancient Babylon *might* have prophetic significance. Perhaps it is too soon at the moment to know. But it is one of the *latest* developments in the Middle East. Photographs show that the rebuilding of ancient Babylon is almost completed.

However, there is another thing which has happened recently which I think does have real significance. Sheer consternation arose in Syria and Iraq in January 1990, when Turkey announced she was to stop the flow of the mighty River Euphrates for a month. To me it is significant because of what Revelation 16:12 says:

> And the sixth angel poured out his vial upon the great

river Euphrates; *and the water thereof was dried up, that the way of the kings of the east might be prepared*.

That should make some people sit up and take notice!

That Scripture then goes on to say that John the Beloved saw three unclean spirits like frogs come out of the mouth of the dragon (who is identified as Satan) and out of the mouth of the Beast (who is the Anti-Christ), and out of the mouth of the False Prophet. For, it says:

> They are *the Spirits of devils*, working miracles, which go forth unto the kings of the earth *and of the whole world*, to gather them to *the battle of that great day of God Almighty* [which is still ahead of us].... And he gathered them together into a place called in the Hebrew tongue Armageddon (Revelation 16:14, 16).

What the Book of the Revelation is talking about here, in the drying up of those waters, is something which is done by the sixth angel when he pours out his vial upon the great River Euphrates. But this decision of Turkey to stop the flow of that mighty river shows that it can even be done *by human means*. It shows that it is *possible* for those waters to be dried up, in other words. The Euphrates is a mighty river, flowing through country after country. It stretches for miles, from Turkey, through Syria, through Iraq, and out into the Persian Gulf. The significance of Turkey's action is that it makes us see how possible it is for that prophecy to be fulfilled. If *man* can do it, how much *more* can God?!

Turkey decided to stop the flow of the Euphrates in order to fill the Ataturle dam—one of the largest dams in the world—and it will take eight years to fill it! The report on 3rd January 1990, said:

> Turkey controls the source of most of the water from both the River Tigris *and* the River Euphrates, the cradle of the earliest civilisations. Some do not exclude the prospects of *war* over water, and that disputes over water will intensify in that region out there in the Middle East, where there is already a problem of water shortage.

The July 1990 issue of the *National Geographic* magazine, the monthly magazine of the Royal Geographical Society, has a major article about this possibility, entitled, 'Water Strife in The Middle East'. So there is a real flash-point there.

In any case, so far as *Iraq* is concerned, she is still a very formidable *military* power in the Middle East, despite her seeming defeat in the recent Gulf War. (Written in June 1991). And as a formidable military power she is a major threat to Israel, and is out for Israel's eventual extermination when she thinks the time is right. It has been revealed recently that she can still deploy extremely heavily armed troops at very short notice on any of her borders. It also became very apparent during the recent Gulf War that she had scud missile launchers deployed all along her borders with Jordan, aimed at Israel.

President Saddam Hussein is still unsubdued and very belligerent, and still has strong ambitions to become the leader of the entire Arab world. That, in itself, would constitute a formidable threat and menace to Israel if it materialised.

Syria is also a major threat to Israel, and is equally out for her extermination. Syria aims to occupy the whole of Lebanon in order to launch an attack from there, as well as over the Golan Heights. But again it would be when Syria felt that the time is right, and no doubt when she got the signal to attack from Moscow.

Islamic Turkey, too, would be against Israel. She comprises at least part of ancient Togarmah, as I have already pointed out.

And so, in fact, is *the Soviet Union* against Israel. So is Gadaffi's *Islamic Libya*. Fundamentalist *Islamic Iran*, the biblical Persia, is, also.

Let me remind you once again that the region now called East Germany, together with what is present West Germany, is the Gomer of Ezekiel 38:5–6, and that Togarmah, also mentioned in Ezekiel 38:6, as well as including Turkey, equals the area in Southern Russia, namely the Caucasus area, where the famous Cossack horsemen and their superior cavalry forces originated, and where, far earlier, the even more famous Mogul horsemen and their extremely superior cavalry forces originated. To see the significance of all this we need to read Ezekiel 38:1–9.

And the word of the Lord came unto me [Ezekiel], saying, Son of man, set thy face *against* Gog, the land of Ma-gog, the chief prince of Me-shech and Tu-bal, and prophesy *against* him, and say, Thus saith the Lord God; Behold, I am *against* thee, O Gog, the chief prince of Me-shech and Tu-bal: and I will turn thee back, and put hooks into thy jaws, and I will bring thee forth, and all thine army, *horses and horsemen* [note that!] all of them clothed with all sorts of *armour*, even a great company with bucklers and shields, all of them handling swords: *Persia* [present-day Iran], *Ethiopia* [which at the moment is Communist but could become Islamic], and *Lib-y-a* [that's Gadaffi's lot!] with them; all of them with shield and helmet. [The list continues:] *Gomer*, and all his bands [that's the two Germanies; and 'bands' means armies]; the house of To-gär-mah of the north quarters, and all his bands [armies]—[that is present-day Islamic Turkey, Islamic Azerbaijan and the region of the Caucasus]; and many people with thee. Be thou prepared, and prepare for thyself, thou, and all thy company that are assembled unto thee, and be thou a guard unto them (Ezekiel 38:1–7).

When will this happen? The next verse tells you.
After many days thou shalt be visited: *in the latter years*.
That is when! *In the latter years*.
And *where* will this happen? The same verse tells you.

Thou shalt come into the land that is brought back from the sword, and is gathered out of many people, *against the mountains of Israel*, which have been always waste: but it is brought forth out of the nations, and they shall dwell safely all of them (v 8).

That is where it will happen! In Israel and on the *mountains* of Israel—the land which has been 'brought forth out of the nations', and 'out of many people'. There is no question as to where it will happen. This is to be taken *literally*. It is Israel, the *land* of Israel, and the mountains of Israel. This is not to be spiritualised. One of the principles of interpreting Bible prophecy is never to spiritualise what God never intended to be spiritualised. This prophecy is to be taken literally, I say. Israel *means* Israel, just as Persia, Ethiopia, and Libya in verse 5 mean Persia, Ethiopia and Libya! It certainly doesn't mean the Church!

Verse 9 continues:

> Thou [Gog] shalt ascend and come like a storm, thou shalt be like a cloud to cover the land, thou, and all thy bands [armies], and many people with thee.

Things are fast shaping up towards the fulfilment of all this. In fact, things are coming to a head so fast in the Middle East that I believe we are living *far nearer than we realise* to the time when the Lord will gather *all nations* against Jerusalem to battle, in fulfilment of Zechariah 14:1–2 which says:

> Behold, *the day of the Lord* cometh, and thy spoil [Jerusalem] shall be divided in the midst of thee. *For I will gather all nations against Jerusalem to battle.*

Joel 3:2 will also be fulfilled at this time:

> I will *also* gather *all* nations, and will bring them down into the valley of Jehoshaphat, and will plead with them there for my people and for my heritage *Israel*, whom they have scattered among the nations, and parted my land.

Another prophecy that will be fulfilled is Daniel 11:40 right through to 12:1:

> And *at the time of the end* shall the king of the south push at him: and *the king of the north* [that's who we have been talking about] shall come against him like a whirlwind, with chariots, and *with horsemen* [note that!] and *with many ships*: and he shall enter into the countries, and shall overflow and pass over. He shall enter also into *the glorious land* [which is Israel], and many countries shall be overthrown: but *these* shall escape out of his hand, even Edom, and Moab, and the chief of the children of Ammon [all of which are in present-day Jordan].

He shall stretch forth his hand also upon the countries: and the land of Egypt shall not escape. But he shall have power over the treasures of gold and of silver, and over all the precious things of Egypt: and the Libyans and the Ethiopians shall be at his steps. [Egypt is the king of the south who was referred to earlier in verse 40. But the term 'king of the south' could also include Libya and Ethiopia with Egypt, in view of what certain other Scriptures say.]

But tidings out of the east and out of the north shall trouble him: therefore he shall go forth with great fury to destroy, and utterly to make away many [take them prisoner, that means]. And he shall plant the tabernacles of his palace between the seas [that means between the Dead Sea and the Sea of Galilee, or alternatively the Mediterranean] in the glorious holy mountain [Jerusalem]; yet he shall come to his end, and none shall help him.

And at that time shall Michael stand up, the great prince which standeth for the children of thy people [meaning Daniel's people, the people of Israel]: and there shall be a time of trouble, such as never was since there was a nation even to the same time: and at that time thy people shall be delivered ['thy people', meaning Daniel's people, Israel], every one that shall be found written in the book [of life].

Things in the Middle East are coming to a head so fast that I believe we are living far nearer than we realise to the fulfilment also of Haggai 2:21–22, which says:

I will shake the heavens and the earth…and I will destroy the strength of the kingdoms of the heathen; and I will overthrow the chariots, and those that ride in them; and the horses [note that!] and their riders shall come down, every one by the sword of his brother.

We are also close to the fulfilment of Isaiah 63:1–6 which says:

Who is this that cometh from Edom, with dyed garments

from Bozrah? this that is glorious in his apparel, travelling in the greatness of his strength? I that speak in righteousness, mighty to save. Wherefore art thou red in thine apparel, and thy garments like him that treadeth in the winefat?

I have trodden the winepress alone; and of the people there was none with me: for I will tread them in mine anger, and trample them in my fury; and their blood shall be sprinkled upon my garments, and I will stain all my raiment. For *the day of vengeance* is in mine heart, and *the year of my redeemed* is come.

And I looked, and there was none to help; and I wondered that there was none to uphold: therefore mine own arm brought salvation unto me: and my fury, it upheld me. And I will tread down the people in mine anger, and make them drunk in my fury, and I will bring down their strength to the earth.

I believe we are living far nearer to seeing the fulfilment of that prophecy than we realise; to what is referred to here by God Almighty, as (1) 'The Day of Vengeance' and (2) 'The Year of My Redeemed'.

I believe, too, that we are living far nearer than we realise to seeing Isaiah 66:15–16 being fulfilled. It says:

For, behold, the Lord will come with fire, and *with his chariots* like a whirlwind, to render his anger with fury, and his rebuke with flames of fire. For by fire and by his sword will the Lord plead with all flesh: and the slain of the Lord shall be many.

And to the fulfilment of Jeremiah 30:1–11, which says:

The word that came to Jeremiah from the Lord, saying, Thus speaketh the Lord God of Israel, saying, Write thee all the words that I have spoken unto thee in a book. For, lo, the days come, saith the Lord, that I will *bring again the captivity of my people Israel and Judah*, saith the Lord: and I will cause them to return to the land that I gave to their fathers, and they shall possess it (vv 1–3).

Notice God says, 'My people Israel and Judah'. He is referring to *both*: not just to Judah, but to *Israel* and Judah. Israel was the northern kingdom from the days of King Rehoboam, the son of Solomon, onwards. Judah was the southern kingdom from that time onwards. We need to realise, too, that the Jews stem from the tribe of Judah, plus the tribes of Benjamin and Levi. But there are the other *ten* tribes in existence somewhere, which comprised the northern kingdom of Israel. What God is saying in this passage of Scripture is, 'I will bring again the captivity of both My people Israel, *and* My people Judah.' He is referring to the *whole house of Israel*, in other words— to all twelve tribes. He is not just referring to Judah. And we need to be made aware of that. The restoration of the whole house of Israel to their land in the end days is emphasised time and time again, all through the end-day prophecies of the Bible.

Verses 4 to 9 of Jeremiah 30 go on to say:

> And these are the words that the Lord spake concerning Israel and concerning Judah [both are mentioned again]. For thus saith the Lord: We have heard a voice of trembling, of fear, and not of peace. Ask ye now, and see whether a man doth travail with child? wherefore do I see every man with his hands on his loins, as a woman in travail, and all faces are turned into paleness? Alas! for that day is great, so that none is like it: it is even *the time of Jacob's trouble*; but he shall be saved out of it.
>
> For it shall come to pass *in that day*, saith the Lord of hosts, that I will break his yoke from off thy neck, and will burst thy bonds, and strangers shall *no more* serve themselves of him: But they shall serve the Lord their God, and David their king, whom I will raise up unto them.

I believe we are living far nearer to the fulfilment of all that than we realise, and to the fulfilment of all that is contained in the two chapters, Ezekiel 38 and 39, and many similar Scriptures. This is this *more sure* Word of prophecy again. And so much that we see happening today is fast heading up to the fulfilment of it all.

These Scriptures, if we study them closely, ought to enable

us to see that what is being talked about in many places in them is *the time of Jacob's trouble*. That is what is being talked about in Jeremiah 30:4–9, which is why I have underlined those particular words. That is what is being talked about in Daniel 12:1. And that is what is being talked about in Isaiah 63:1–6 and in Isaiah 66:16. '*The time of Jacob's trouble*' means unregenerated Israel's trouble, because Jacob is the name for unregenerated Israel. Jacob, you will remember, was the name he had before he was regenerated. He wrestled with the angel all night, as his brother Esau was approaching with a great company (see Genesis 32:1–32). He thought Esau would be hostile and would attack him and his great company, and slaughter them. Then this angel of the Lord appeared, and Jacob wrestled with him all night, and prevailed. Then God said to him:

> Thy name shall be called no more Jacob, but *Israel*: for as a prince hast thou power with God and with men, and hast prevailed.

After that he was a changed man. He had become regenerated during that all-night wrestling. It transpired, in fact, that he had been wrestling *with God*, for in Genesis 32:30 he said:

> I have seen *God* face to face, and my life is preserved.

Jacob is the name for unregenerated Israel, therefore. And *the time of Jacob's trouble*, unregenerated Israel's trouble, is spoken of in all these Scriptures that I have quoted; in Jeremiah 30:7–9 and in Daniel 12:1 very specifically. But the Scripture says, 'But *he will be saved out of it*' (Jeremiah 30:7). Hellelujah!

And that will lead to his rebirth—his regeneration; that is, the nation of *Israel's* regeneration, their *spiritual* rebirth, their *spiritual* regeneration. That is why there is this strange reference to 'every man with his hands on his loins, as a woman in travail, and all faces are turned into paleness', and to the question, 'Ask ye now, and see whether a man doth travail with child?' It is a reference to a nation coming to birth, to *re*-birth, to regeneration—a reference to *the nation of Israel coming to rebirth*. This is one of the great prophecies, mentioned several times in Scripture. Israel's *spiritual* rebirth is going to take place. God has *covenanted* with them that it will. So it is bound to happen. But I will be taking up that point again, a little later.

If we are true believers, we should be familiarising ourselves with all these Scriptures, and particularly with these Old Testament Scriptures, in view of the most momentous days in which we are living. We must not be New Testament *only* Christians. This list of Scriptures to which I have just referred is included in '*all that the prophets have written*'—a phrase which was used emphatically by the Lord Jesus when He was conversing with His disciples about 'the things concerning himself'. And we should *know* them. They tell us *where we are* at this point of history—*His* story—His *unfolding* story, just as consulting a map tells us where we are.

Are we encouraging young Christians everywhere to do that? Are we? In our churches, in our fellowships, at Spring Harvest, or wherever they are, wherever they meet? We most certainly need to. They, of all people—the rising generation of Christians—need to know where we are at this vital moment of world history.

The next question that we need to come to is: What is the line-up with regard to Israel today? Or, to put it another way: What are the *major factors* concerning the present Middle East situation, and concerning Israel in particular? And *how close do they come into line with the prophecies of the Bible?* That is the crucial question.

On the one hand, as I think most people know by now, Yasser Arafat, and the PLO are demanding at this present time, an independent, *armed*, Palestinian state, *with Jerusalem as its capital*. And they are using the Interfada uprisings on the West Bank, in Jerusalem, and in the Gaza Strip as part of the means of bringing that about, fanned, of course, by outside forces. And this Palestinian-Israeli conflict, *in itself*, is likely to reach boiling-point at any moment. The PLO's demand that Jerusalem should be the capital of this armed Palestinian state would be the crunch-point. All that could be described as Israel's *enemy within*.

On the other hand, others are aiming at taking Jerusalem. For instance, it has been reported that as recently as 1989, an

Islamic-Russian alliance was quietly formed, which directly threatens the whole of the Middle East, but Israel in particular. Rafsanjani, the new President of Iran, visited Russia in June 1989 and is reported to have made certain proposals.

A pact, it was reported, was entered into which will undoubtedly prove to be of vast significance before long, certainly prophetically. It is reported that the deal which has been made has horrified both London and Washington. But they are keeping quiet about it at the moment.

Rafsanjani's proposal in Moscow was reported to be that by means of a Russian-Iranian axis, or alliance, Islam would obtain its great and long-standing aim to liberate Jerusalem and to make it the Islamic capital of the Middle East, with Soviet assistance, and 'kick Israel into the sea' whilst so doing. Rafsanjani, and certainly the Kremlin, are reckoning without Almighty God, *the God of Israel*, of course!

Moreover, *were*, indeed, this Islamic-Russian alliance to move *militarily* together through Iran to take over the whole of the Middle East, Russia herself would, if successful, have achieved what *for years* has been the aim of her military chiefs of staff and of her military, namely, hegemony over the Middle East, which would mean control over its vital oil wells, other energy supplies, mineral resources, and even more importantly, warm-water ports and outlets to the sea. The taking of the Suez Canal would be included in this aim, and would thus give Russia access to the Indian Ocean, the Arabian Sea and the Pacific Ocean, and so to the Far East, India, Australia and New Zealand. And if Gorbachev was still in power, he would have brought about a great personal achievement, and so would have enhanced his standing and stature as leader of the Soviet Union, particularly in the eyes of the Soviet military who are so important to him. And, remember, Gorbachev has already been asking President Bush for the withdrawal of the American fleets from the Eastern Mediterranean!

Then *if*, at the same time, the Soviet Union assisted Islamic Iran to capture Jerusalem for Islam, this would be a major means of stilling and quietening much of the Islamic unrest in the Islamic regions of the Soviet Union. This Islamic unrest is increasing the threat of the Soviet Union's break-up at the present time.

It is reported that this Islamic Iranian-Russian alliance has met with the approval of Syria and of Gadaffi's Libya.

Now *here is the crunch*. Islam, on the one hand, simply cannot give up its claim to Jerusalem. Muslims have been claiming that it is theirs for years, and are fully and irrevocably committed to taking it *when the time is ripe*.

Israel, on the other hand, simply will not give up Jerusalem or its claim to the city. It came back into their hands in 1967 for the first time in nearly 2,000 years, and they are never going to let it go. It is theirs *by Divine right, by right of God's covenant with them*. And so is their land, which God describes in many of the Bible prophecies as '*My* land'—*God's* land.

The United States is fully committed to stand by Israel in support of her claim, at least, she is *at the moment*.

The Soviet Union is anti-Israel and is committed to backing the Arabs, Iran, Syria, Libya, Egypt and all Israel's surrounding neighbours who are against her.

That is the line-up!

So right before our very eyes today, *Jerusalem* has become *the* central issue in world affairs. Jerusalem is the issue, of all issues, today, and will increasingly be so.

One single city, therefore—*Jerusalem*—will force all other issues on the world stage completely into the background, and will render them all totally insignificant. They will become as peanuts!

So how can all this be seen *prophetically*? Everything that is happening before our very eyes is happening precisely according to Bible prophecy—this *more sure* Word of prophecy. For it places us *right now*, straight into the situation described in the Book of the Prophet Zechariah 12:2–3, where God says:

> Behold I will make Jerusalem a cup of trembling unto all the people round about, when they shall be in the siege both against Judah and against Jerusalem. And *in that day* will I make Jerusalem *a burdensome stone* for all people: *all that burden themselves with it* shall be cut in pieces, though all the people of the earth be gathered together against it.

God says *He* will do that! And we are seeing it happen. It is actually taking place before our very eyes, in these days of the

1990s in which we are living. We see it, and hear about it, on our televisions so often. And *will* do, increasingly.

But what is happening out there in the Middle East, in Israel, and in Jerusalem, is also bringing us extremely near to the fulfilment of Zechariah chapter 14 as well, which is being addressed to *Jerusalem*. The first two verses say:

> Behold *the day of the Lord cometh*.

Notice it is again a warning about the day of the Lord that is coming. And maybe very soon. Maybe sooner than we think.

But it is a very *specific* Day of the Lord. These two verses tell you how specific it is:

> Behold, the day of the Lord cometh, and thy spoil [Jerusalem] shall be divided in the midst of thee. *For* I will *gather all nations against Jerusalem to battle*.

That is how specific it is. *That* is what is going to happen when that Day of the Lord which is mentioned here comes—that *great Day of God*!

It will be a fulfilment also of Ezekiel chapters 38 and 39— that *more sure* Word of prophecy—when the armies of the distant North, which must inevitably mean Soviet armies, and the armies of Persia (which is present-day Iran), and the armies of Libya and the armies of Ethiopia, and many others, will come against Israel and against Jerusalem: Gomer, Togarmah and so forth, horses and horsemen included. I say it must inevitably include all these, because they are specifically mentioned by name.

Now here is another crunch in view of all that I have been saying. It is reported that Gorbachev is now deeply sympathetic to the principles of Islam. It is even reported that one of his top aides or advisors is a Muslim. And the countries surrounding the land of Israel in the Middle East are mainly Islamic countries. So are many of the African countries. Gaddafi has been quietly seeing to that, right across Africa!

With the situation as it is in Europe right now, if that preconceived move towards the Middle East were, indeed, to be made, Gorbachev and the Soviet Union could *now* not only guarantee the neutrality of Germany, but he might also obtain her assistance, in the sense that no Atlantic military personnel, *nor weaponry* would be allowed to leave Germany to be used in any opposition to a Russo-Islamic strategic move in the Middle East. It would all be 'interned', in the sense of being neutralised. That is how things are shaping up!

The United States could not go to the assistance of Israel *without Britain* because the US would need the use of the United States air bases here, as was seen when the Reagan Administration decided to bomb Gadaffi's Tripoli in Libya a few years ago.

English public opinion, unfortunately, has become anti-Israel to a degree since the Interfada uprisings in Israel. This anti-Israel attitude continues to be manifest in any debates in Parliament on the Middle East situation, so any Prime Minister in future might find it difficult to get British support for America on behalf of Israel, especially as the British Foreign Office is very pro-Arab and has been for years.

On the other hand, Syria, Libya, Ethiopia, Egypt, Saudi-Arabia, Iraq, the Gulf States, Yemen and all the Islamic African countries would guarantee support for the Russo-Iranian Jerusalem cause, because of the long-term aim of fundamentalist Islam to take possession of Jerusalem and make it the Islamic capital of the Middle East.

Furthermore, it is authoritatively reported that since Rafsanjani's visit to Moscow in June 1989, and all that took place there, all this scenario which I have described was to be canvassed to all Islamic leaders in Russia and all over the Soviet Islamic Republics, and was to be made the prophetic talk of all the Islamic bazaars. Meanwhile, as this goes to press it is being reported that Iran is quietly building up her armies.

So the question I ask myself is: Is all that is happening in Eastern Europe and in the Soviet Union as a result of *glasnost* and *perestroika* being used to divert the West's attention from what is planned soon to take place in the Middle East? I don't know. But any Serviceman will tell you that when a Field Marshal (like Montgomery of Alamein, for instance), is planning to launch a major offensive, he always creates a diversion to draw attention away from where he plans to launch his offensive! And all the attention of the West has been concentrated on Europe in recent years, and away from the Middle East!

Meanwhile, the *Jerusalem Post* reported on its front page, on 18th November 1989, that Prime Minister Yitzhak Shamir of Israel told a political meeting that *up to a million* Jews would leave the Soviet Union in the next few years, and that many more would come from Ethiopia. He said, 'a great many of them may come to Israel.' Then that same week, the *Jewish Chronicle*, on 17th November 1989, reported on its front page that many of *Syria's* remaining 5,000 Jews may soon be able to emigrate. So the return of the Jews to their own land is accelerating apace. And Gorbachev is now being urged to arrange direct flights from the USSR to Israel because of the threatened pogroms in parts of the Soviet Union, as I have already mentioned.

What is the prophetic significance of this? It is very significant indeed, for what do the opening words of the Book of the prophecy of Joel chapter 3, say—this *more sure* Word of prophecy?

> For, behold, in those days, *and in that time, when* I shall bring again the captivity of Judah and Jerusalem, I will *also* gather *all nations*, and will bring them down into the valley of Jehoshaphat, and will plead with them there for my people and for my heritage Israel, whom they have scattered among the nations, *and parted my land.*

Notice carefully what this is saying: In those days, and in that time—*when* the return of the Jews is accelerating apace towards its final completion—*then*—at that time—*God will gather all nations* into the valley of Jehoshaphat to plead with them there; to *deal* with them there, that means, and *in judgment.*

We must be *almost there*! We must be almost within a hair's-breadth of being there!

And when all nations *are* gathered together against Jerusalem to battle, what will happen? Ezekiel 38:18–23 tells us—that *more sure* Word of prophecy:

> And it shall come to pass *at the same time when Gog shall come against the land of* Israel, saith the Lord God, that *my fury* shall come up in my face. For in my jealousy and

in the fire of my wrath have I spoken, Surely *in that day* there shall be *a great shaking* in the land of Israel; so that the fishes of the sea, and the fowls of the heaven, and the beasts of the field, and all creeping things that creep upon the earth, *and all men that are upon the face of the earth*, shall shake at my presence.

Notice that! 'And all men that are upon the face of the earth shall shake *at my presence*'! So that shaking will be felt *world-wide*! It will be felt here in Britain! It will be felt all over the British Isles, and in every part of the British Isles, however remote. The whole world will reverberate!

The passage goes on:

And the *mountains* shall be *thrown down*, and the steep places shall fall, and every wall shall fall to the ground. And I will call for a sword against him throughout all my mountains, saith the Lord God: every man's sword shall be against his brother. And I will plead against him *with pestilence*, and with blood.

That is how God will 'plead with them' (see Joel 3:2). He will deal with them in judgment, with that kind of judgment.

And I will *rain upon him*, and upon his bands [his armies], and upon the many people that are with him, an overflowing rain, and *great hailstones*, fire, and brimstone. *Thus* will I magnify myself, and sanctify myself, *and I will be known in the eyes of many nations*, and they shall know that I am the Lord.

That is what God is talking about in Haggai 2:6–7—that *more sure* Word of prophecy, when He says:

For thus saith the Lord of hosts; Yet once, it is a little while, and I will shake the heavens, and the earth, and the sea, and the dry land. And I will shake *all nations*.

That is what He is talking about in the Epistle to the Hebrews 12:26–29, when He says:

But *now* he hath *promised*, saying, Yet once more I shake not the earth only, but also heaven...that those things which cannot be shaken may remain.

That is what Isaiah chapter 2 is talking about when it says, 'When God shall arise *to shake terribly the earth*', twice over, in verse 19 and again in verse 21.

And it is what Isaiah 24:20 is talking about when it says, 'The earth shall *reel to and fro* like a drunkard.'

All of these Scriptures I quoted at the beginning of this series of addresses. So we have come full circle.

And it is a *literal* shaking that these Scriptures are talking about, not a metaphorical shaking—all false prophets and teachers please notice! It is literal, and should be taken literally. We must never spiritualise what God never intended to be spiritualised.

We read about it again in the Book of the Revelation 16:16–21:

And he gathered them together into a place called in the Hebrew tongue, Armageddon [that is in Israel]. And the seventh angel poured out his vial into the air; and there came a great voice out of the temple of heaven, from the throne, saying, It is done. And there were voices, and thunders, and lightnings; and *there was a great earthquake*, such as was not since men were upon the earth, so mighty an earthquake, and so great [the words 'since men were upon the earth' take us right back to the time of Adam!].

And the great city was divided into three parts [does that mean Jerusalem, or does it mean the great city Babylon? I am not sure], and the cities of the nations fell. [London is a city, Paris is a city, Moscow is a city, Washington DC is a city, Peking is a city, Tokyo is a city, and so I could go on]: I repeat. 'The cities of the nations fell'! and great Babylon came in remembrance before God, to give unto her the cup of the wine of the fierceness of his wrath. [the present-day Babylon which President Saddam Hussein has just rebuilt is in present-day Iraq in biblical Mesopotamia].

And every island fled away. [the British Isles are

islands! Ireland is an island, both North and South; the Outer Hebrides are islands; the Orkneys are islands; the Isle of Wight is an island; Malta is an island; Crete is an island; and so I could go on], and the mountains were not found [that's Everest vanished!].

And there fell upon men a great hail out of heaven, every stone about the weight of a talent [that's half a hundred weight, so if one of those fell on your head...I was going to say you would know all about it, but you wouldn't!]: and men blasphemed God because of the plague of the hail; for the plague thereof was exceeding great.

That *also* is what Haggai 2:6–7, and all those other Scriptures which I have quoted, are talking about.

But Haggai 2:7 goes on to say, 'And the desire of all nations shall come' as that mighty, world-reverberating shaking and convulsion is taking place. The desire of all nations is referring to the Lord Jesus Christ. And when He Himself, in Matthew chapter 24, was answering his disciples' question, 'What shall be the sign of this coming and of the end of the world,' He said, in Matthew 24:29–30:

The powers of heaven *shall be shaken*: and then shall appear the sign of the Son of man in heaven: and then shall all the tribes of the earth mourn, and they shall see the Son of man coming in the clouds of heaven with power and great glory.

This is also what Zechariah chapter 14 is all about. For after it says, 'For I will gather *all nations* against Jerusalem to battle', it goes on to say in verse 3:

Then shall the Lord go forth, and fight against those nations, as when he fought in the day of battle. And *His feet shall stand in that day upon the mount of Olives*, which is before Jerusalem on the east [meaning in front of Jerusalem looking towards the east], and the mount of Olives shall cleave in the midst thereof toward the east and toward the west, and there shall be a very great valley [opened up]; and half of the mountain shall

> remove toward the north, and half of it toward the
> south.

Only a mighty earthquake can do that surely, such as has
already been described in those other Scriptures—a mighty
world reverberating convulsion! Certainly, an earthquake is
mentioned in verse 5 of Zechariah chapter 14. Then it says:

> And the Lord my God shall come, and all the saints with
> thee [the desire of all nations!].

And verse 9 says:

> And the Lord shall be king over all the earth.

This is the *more sure* Word of prophecy! And when He *is*, He
will usher in His Messianic Kingdom and His Messianic Age:
the time when men 'shall beat their swords into ploughshares,
and their spears into pruninghooks; nation shall not lift up
sword against nation, neither shall they learn war any more',
in fulfilment of Isaiah 2:4.

The time when the wolf shall lie down with the lamb, and
the lion shall eat straw like the ox, and the leopard shall lie
down with the kid, in fulfilment of Isaiah 11:6−9.

It will usher in 'the times of restitution of all things, which
God hath spoken by the mouth of all his holy prophets since
the world began', to quote Acts 3:21.

It will be the time when 'the kingdoms of this world are
become the kingdoms of our Lord, and of his Christ; and he
shall reign for ever and ever', in fulfilment of Revelation 11:15.

It will be the time when 'the creature [animal creation] itself
also shall be delivered from the bondage of corruption into the
glorious liberty of the children of God', in fulfilment of
Romans 8:21. That means the whole created order: animals,
birds, insects, fish, and so on—the whole creation! 'Friends of
the Earth', 'Wild Life' enthusiasts, and 'Green' people should
read the Epistle to the Romans 8:21 to see what it says!

It will be the time when 'the earth shall be filled with the
knowledge of the glory of the Lord, as the waters cover the
sea', in fulfilment of Habakkuk 2:14. *This is the great culminating point towards which Almighty God is working.*

It is referred to again in Isaiah 66:15–16:

> For, behold, the Lord will come with fire, and *with his chariots* like a whirlwind, to render his anger with fury, and his rebuke with flames of fire. For by fire and by his sword will the Lord plead *with all flesh*: and the slain of the Lord shall be many.

It is referred to yet again in the Epistle of Jude, where it says:

> And Enoch also, the seventh from Adam, prophesied of these, saying, Behold, the Lord cometh with ten thousands of his saints, *to execute judgment upon all*, and to convince all that are *un*godly among them of all their *un*godly deeds which they have *un*godly committed, and of all their hard speeches which *un*godly sinners have spoken against him (Jude vv 14–15).

It is referred to even yet again in 2 Thessalonians 1:7–10, where it says:

> And to you who are troubled rest with us, when the Lord Jesus shall be revealed from heaven with his mighty angels, in flaming fire taking vengeance on them that know not God, and that obey not the gospel of our Lord Jesus Christ: who shall be punished with everlasting destruction from the presence of the Lord, and from the glory of his power; when he shall come to be glorified in his saints, *and to be admired in all them that believe . . . in that day*.

And it is referred to in countless other Scriptures, Old and New Testament alike.

This is no Kingdom *now* theology; it is Kingdom *then*! That is, *after* our Lord Jesus Christ has returned. Kingdom *now* theology is utterly false teaching. Let me make that quite plain. And they are totally false prophets and false teachers who teach, as some are doing, that *we* have to bring in God's Kingdom by taking over local governments, local institutions, schools, colleges, universities, Parliaments, industry, finance, countries, the world, and so forth; and that until we have, Jesus Christ cannot, and *will* not returnl They say that 'he is sitting up there in heaven, waiting until *we* have done it'! That is utterly false teaching. It is completely contrary to what the Bible says—this *more sure* Word of prophecy—and to what Jesus Himself said and taught. Those that are teaching this kind of thing, and who are leading others astray by so doing, should repent of being guilty of such false teaching, forthwith, and should correct what they have been teaching, by teaching what the Bible says. And those who have been under that kind of teaching should come out of it, right away, and go somewhere where the Bible is taught faithfully and accurately.

The Lord Jesus Christ is going to bring in His own Kingdom when He comes. *That* is what the Bible teaches. *That* is what *He* taught. And He won't need any assistance!

When He *has* brought in His Kingdom, all those who believe in Him and who *have* believed in Him all down the ages—all those who are, and have been born-again of the Holy Spirit of God all down the ages—will be joint heirs with Him in His Kingdom. That is what the Bible teaches also—this *more sure* Word of prophecy. This is *the inheritance*, the *promised inheritance*, that the Bible talks so much about. It is the inheritance which God has promised to *all true believers*, and *only* to all true believers, for only these are heirs of God, and joint heirs *with Christ* of His Kingdom (see Romans 8:16–17).

The question is: *How near are we to all this?* The answer is: Maybe far nearer than we think, *perilously* near for some, particularly for the unsaved.

So what is the message in view of all this? It is very clear.

First, to the people of the world, to all *unsaved* people everywhere, it is this:

> God…commandeth *all* men *everywhere* to *repent*: because he hath appointed *a day*, in the which he will judge the world in righteousness by that man whom he hath ordained; whereof he hath given assurance unto *all* men, in that he hath raised him from the dead (Acts 17:30–31). And 'that man' is The Lord Jesus!

Notice it says, 'All men, everywhere'. It does not say that it is *only the Church* that needs to repent, as some are erroneously teaching today. And when it says, 'all men everywhere', it *means* all men everywhere. It means, also, that we need to reach *the whole world* with this message *in view of the supreme urgency of the times*.

I only wish I could reach the whole world with this message through this book!

I only wish I could do it through the tape ministry.

I only wish I could do it over the radio, on television, by satellite broadcasting and by every modern form of communication that is available because the message is so urgent. The need for people to repent and be saved is so *urgent*.

God commands all men everywhere to *repent*. That is what God is saying to each and every one of the 56 million people who inhabit these British Isles, whether they be Scottish, English, Welsh, Irish, Muslim, Hindu, Budhist, Rastafarian, Shinto, Sikh, Freemasons, Satanists, Occultists, so-called 'New Age' people, 'Friends of the Earth' or whatever.

The message is the same who-ever you are. There is only *one way* of salvation, and that is: Repent towards God, the Creator of the universe, the *living* God, and put your faith in the Lord Jesus Christ for your personal, and eternal salvation. There is no other way.

This is what God, the *living* God, is saying to the *whole world* at this present time, and to each and every one who inhabits it, whatever their religion, or denomination or status, may be.

And this is what God, the *living* God, is saying to *you*. What matters supremely right now, is your own personal relationship with Almighty God, the Creator of the universe, in view of all that I have been saying.

The ultimate problem of every man and woman, every boy and girl, is his or her personal relationship to God. His or her *heart* needs to be right with God, and if it isn't, it needs to be put right.

Jesus died on the cross in order that you might be put right with God; in order that you might be *reconciled* to God, in other words.

For that to be applied to you personally right now, you need to *repent* of your sins; you need to *forsake* your sins; you need to *have done* with your sins. And you need to ask God to *have mercy* on you because of your sins. You need to say, 'God have *mercy* on me, a sinner.' And He will, if you really mean it, and if you are really repentant. The Apostle Paul's testimony after he had met the risen Lord in blinding light on the Damascus Road was, 'I obtained *mercy*.'

You need to ask the Lord Jesus Christ to *cleanse you* from your sins in His own blood and to *purge them all away*, for that was the reason why He shed His blood on the cross of Calvary.

You need to *trust* the Lord Jesus with your own personal salvation, and ask God to clothe you with *His own righteousness*, which is what makes you *acceptable* to Him. And you need to do it *now*, because *now* is the accepted time; *today* is *the day of salvation*.

When you have done that, *your* testimony, too, will be, 'I obtained mercy.' Then you will have become 'a new creature in Christ Jesus'. Old things will have passed away. All things will have become new. You will also find that you are now a person who has peace with God; that you are now in right relationship with Him; and that that peace of God will keep your heart and mind, now that you are in Christ Jesus, and now that you have been truly born again by the Holy Spirit of God.

That is the message to the people of the world, to all the unsaved people on the earth.

Second, the message to the true believer, and to *all* true believers is this:

> When these things begin to come to pass, then *look up*, and lift up your heads; for your *redemption* draweth nigh (Luke 21:28).

They have more than *begun* to come to pass. The question is: Are you *ready*? Am I?

Chapter Six

God is Working to a Plan, to a Purpose, and to a Timetable

I come now to the point where I need to say that the Bible clearly reveals that God is working to *a plan*, to *a purpose*, to *a timetable*, even to a specific timetable, and towards *a culminating point*. But *what is it*?

The Scripture I would like to draw your attention to at this point is Luke 21:5–28:

> And as some spake of the temple, how it was adorned with goodly stones and gifts, he [Jesus] said, As for these things which ye behold, the days will come, in the which there shall not be left one stone upon another, that shall not be thrown down.
>
> And they asked him, saying, Master, but *when* shall these things be? and what *sign* will there be *when* these things shall come to pass?
>
> And he said, Take heed that ye be not deceived: for many shall come in my name, saying, I am Christ; and the time draweth near: go ye not therefore after them. But when ye shall hear of wars and commotions, be not terrified: for these things must *first* come to pass; but *the end* is not by and by.
>
> Then said he unto them, Nation shall rise against nation, and kingdom against kingdom: and great earthquakes shall be in divers [various] places, and famines, and pestilences; and fearful sights and great signs shall there be from heaven.
>
> [Verse 12:] But *before* all these, they shall lay their hands on *you*, and persecute *you*, delivering you up to

the synagogues, and into prisons, being brought before kings and rulers for my name's sake. And it shall turn to you for a testimony. Settle it therefore in your hearts, not to meditate before what ye shall answer: for I will give you a mouth and wisdom, which all your adversaries shall not be able to gainsay nor resist. And ye shall be betrayed both by parents, and brethren, and kinsfolks, and friends; and some of you shall they cause to be put to death. And ye shall be hated of all men for my name's sake. But there shall not an hair of your head perish. In your patience possess ye your souls.

It should be noted that from verse 12 up to this point, what Jesus was saying referred to His disciples who were listening to Him at that very moment. What He was saying was that many of these things would happen to *them*. And it *did* happen to them, throughout the days of the Acts of the Apostles. For instance, they laid hands on some of them, namely Peter and John, after they had healed the lame man at the Beautiful Gate of the Temple; they persecuted many of them, they delivered them up to the synagogues, including Peter and John again, and later the Apostle Paul. They delivered them into prisons, Peter again included. Some of them were caused to be put to death. James the brother of John, Herod the king killed by the sword (see Acts 12:1–2). The Apostle Peter was later killed, and so on. Much, therefore, that Jesus was saying up to this point applied to His disciples who were listening to Him at that time.

Verses 20 to 24 also applied to His disciples:

And when *ye* shall see Jerusalem compassed with armies, then know that the desolation thereof is nigh [Jesus was referring to what would take place in AD 70 under Titus with his Roman armies]. Then let them which are in Judaea flee to the mountains; and let them which are in the midst of it depart out; and let not them that are in the countries enter there into. For these be *the days of vengeance*, that all things which are written may be fulfilled.

But woe unto them that are with child, and to them that give suck in those days! for there shall be great distress *in the land* [in the land of Israel, that means], and wrath upon *this* people [meaning the Jewish people who were living in the land of Israel at the time that Jesus was saying all this, and who were rejecting Him]. And they [the same Jewish people who lived in those days] shall fall by the edge of the sword [they did, in AD 70], and shall be led away captive into all nations [they were, in AD 70] and Jerusalem shall be trodden down of the Gentiles, *until* the times of the Gentiles be fulfilled. [It was, from AD 70 right up until 1967, when it came back into the hands of the Jews for the first time in nearly 2,000 years.]

So verses 20 to 24 contain what Jesus prophesied would happen in AD 70 to Jerusalem and to the Jewish people who were living in His day, as a result of Jerusalem being devastated by the Roman armies under Titus at that time. And it all happened exactly as Jesus had said it would, including the Jewish people of His day being led away captive into all nations, and Jerusalem being trodden down of the Gentiles (non-Jewish nations), until the times of the Gentiles be fulfilled.

All that needs to be pointed out because I am noticing that there are some today who are failing to see that Jesus, here, was speaking about what *He* knew would take place in AD 70. In consequence, they are getting the sequence of prophesied events all wrong. It is vitally important to get them right.

Then verses 25 to 28 begin to talk about things which are still future:

And there shall be signs in the sun, and in the moon, and in the stars; and upon the earth distress of nations, with perplexity; the sea and the waves roaring; men's hearts failing them for fear, and for looking after those things which are coming on the earth: for the powers of heaven shall be shaken.

And *then* shall they see the Son of man coming in a cloud with power and great glory. And when *these things* begin to come to pass, then look up, and lift up your heads; for your redemption draweth nigh.

It should be clear, from that reading of Scripture alone, that God is working to a plan, to a purpose, to a timetable—even to a *precise* timetable—and towards a clearly defined culminating point.

Here I want to stress that we need desperately to see the vital importance of getting to know the Bible and the *whole* of the Bible. The Bible is *one* book, and we need to see it as such. You cannot *begin* to understand much that is contained in the New Testament until you have got to know what is in the Old Testament. For instance, you cannot begin to understand the Book of the Revelation in the New Testament until you have obtained a thorough grasp of all that is in the Book of Daniel in the Old Testament, and particularly in the prophecies of Daniel, because much that is in the Book of the Revelation stems from there. Similarly, you cannot begin to understand what Jesus said, when so many times in His prophetic utterances He referred to Himself as the Son of man, until you have seen very clearly, and have understood, what Daniel's vision and prophecy in Daniel 7:9–14 is all about. In all such cases, the one throws light on the other.

Furthermore, in order to be able to see clearly that God is working to a plan, to a purpose, and towards a culminating point, and be able to see what that culminating point is, you need to read *all that the prophets have written*. You can't see it any other way. And by 'all that the prophets have written', I mean the Bible prophets, the Old Testament prophets in particular. What you need to understand is that God has spoken through the mouth of all His holy prophets since the world began (Acts 3:21). And what He has spoken is recorded *in detail* in the pages of the Old and New Testament. These prophets include Enoch, Noah, Abraham, Moses, Samuel, David, Isaiah, Jeremiah, Ezekiel, Daniel, Hosea, Joel, Amos, Obadiah, Jonah, Micah, Nahum, Habakkuk, Zephaniah, Haggai, Zechariah, Malachi, the utterances of King David—particularly in the Book of Psalms, but not only in the Psalms—and all the prophetic utterances of the Lord Jesus, because we must never forget that the Lord Jesus was, and *is*, a Prophet, as well as being the Son of God. They said of Him as He rode into Jerusalem, and as they waved their palm branches, 'This is Jesus, the *Prophet* of Nazareth.'

We need, therefore, to read and thoroughly familiarise

ourselves with *all of these prophecies*—'this *more sure* Word of prophecy'—if we want to know what God's plan, purpose, and culminating point is, and to be clear about it. We must *never*, *never*, regard the Old Testament as being out of date or redundant. It could not be *more* up-to-date.

I want to ask you: Are you a follower of the Lord Jesus? If you are, you should be able to do what Jesus did. As He walked along the Emmaus Road on the first Easter Day, for instance, He said to the two disciples who were bewildered about His crucifixion:

> O fools, and slow of heart to believe *all that the prophets have spoken*. Ought not Christ to have suffered these things, and to enter into His glory? And *beginning at Moses* [that's the first five books of the Bible] *and all the prophets, He expounded unto them in all the scriptures the things concerning himself* (Luke 24:25–27).

These were the *Old* Testament Scriptures. The *New* Testament Scriptures didn't even exist at that time!

That is where you get the truth from! That is where *Jesus* got it from. The *Old* Testament Scriptures were His Court of Appeal. He turned to 'all that the prophets have spoken' *in the Old* Testament Scriptures. He went through them all, from the first five books of Moses, and then, through all the prophets, expounded to them in all *these* Scriptures, the things concerning Himself. I ask again: Could *you* do that, as a follower of Jesus? We must never be New Testament *only* Christians. We are producing far too many New Testament only Christians, today.

Did you know that if you are a New Testament only Christian you are *unbalanced*? You are lopsided. And you will inevitably be unbalanced in your beliefs, unbalanced in your outlook, and unbalanced in your teaching, witness, and counselling.

Your Christian faith should be established four-square on the Word of God, and on the *whole* of the Word of God, from Genesis to the Book of the Revelation, with nothing excepted, if you are, indeed, a truly born-again believer, and a genuine follower of the Lord Jesus.

I ask again: Are you a follower of the Lord Jesus? 'Beginning at Moses, and all the prophets, he expounded unto them in all the Scriptures the things concerning himself.' I repeat: 'Could *you* do that? *Could* you? You should aim to be able to do so. And you should aim to be able to do so from this day onwards. I hope you will.

Or again, in the Upper Room on the same day, in the evening, we read:

> And [Jesus] said unto them, These are the words which I spake unto you, while I was yet with you, that all things must be fulfilled, which were written *in the law of Moses, and in the prophets, and in the psalms,* concerning me. Then opened he their understanding, that they might understand the scriptures [the *Old* Testament Scriptures—no other Scriptures existed at that time!], and said unto them, Thus *it is written*, and thus it behoved Christ to suffer, and to rise from the dead the third day: and that *repentance* and remission of sins should be preached in his name *among all nations*, beginning at Jerusalem. And ye are witnesses of these things (Luke 24:44–48).

And He might have added, 'And ye are witnesses of these things—that they have all happened *exactly in accordance with all these Old Testament Scriptures and prophecies*.'

May I point out that, 'all things which were written in the law of Moses', means all that is written in the first five books of the Bible, namely, Genesis, Exodus, Leviticus, Numbers and Deuteronomy; and that 'all things which were written in the prophets', includes what was written in that whole list of the prophets which I have already quoted. And the words, 'And in the psalms' includes everything which is written in the Book of 150 Psalms concerning Jesus.

Jesus was setting out to establish these early New Testament disciples (the Apostles), well and truly on all these Old Testament Scriptures. That was the *foundation* which He was laying in their lives. Everything had happened precisely according to all these Old Testament Scriptures, and He sought to ensure that their faith would be founded on that.

Are you a follower of the Lord Jesus? If so, you should

follow in His steps in this respect—that of seeking to lay a good, solid foundation in your life, namely on the *Old* Testament Scriptures and what they say concerning *Him*, *Jesus*, and *all* that they say concerning Him, and *all that the prophets* of the Bible have written. You should not be content with a constant diet of frothy choruses or of so-called 'songs' that contain no biblical teaching. Your church leaders, your church, fellowship, Christian centre, or house group should be setting out to do the same thing, getting everybody who comes, well-versed in the Scriptures, with emphasis on the *Old* Testament Scriptures. If they are not doing so you should ask them to.

Take also as your example the Apostle Paul. We read in Acts 28:17 that when he eventually arrived in Rome, he called the chief of the Jews together:

> And when they had appointed him a day, there came many to him into his lodging; to whom he expounded and testified the kingdom of God, persuading them concerning Jesus, *both out of the law of Moses* [the first five books of the Bible], *and out of the prophets, from morning till evening* (Acts 28:23).

That means, in the first place, that the Apostle Paul was extremely familiar with everything that was written in the Law of Moses and in *all the prophets*.

It raises the question: Are we?

It raises the question: Are the rising generation of Christians, the *young* Christians? What is being done to get them as familiar with all these Scriptures as was the Apostle Paul? But secondly, he was expounding and persuading them concerning Jesus and the Kingdom of God out of all these Scriptures *from morning until evening*. Just imagine! And again it was from the *Old* Testament Scriptures! And there isn't even so much as a suggestion that they had a tea-break!

It means, also, that it took him more than just the half an hour, or three-quarters of an hour which is about the limit any preacher is given for a Sunday morning or Sunday evening sermon!

'*From morning till evening*' he was expounding the Scriptures. That's all day! And why? Because there was a fantastic amount of the Scriptures to cover. He must have been completely engrossed in expounding all the Scriptures before them. And it would seem that there were no clock-watchers! No one looking at the clock or at his watch saying, 'It is time to go home now!' God is not a clock-watcher! Neither should we be. These Jews were having their own Scriptures expounded to them. And they were prepared to be there *all day*, listening to the Apostle Paul's exposition.

This was always his method with the Jews. He took them to *their* Scriptures, their *Old* Testament Scriptures, to the Law of Moses and the prophets, and the psalms.

When he was in Thessalonica that was his method also, for in Acts 17:2–3 we read:

> And Paul, as his manner was, went in unto them, and *three sabbath days* reasoned with them *out of the scriptures* [the *Old* Testament Scriptures—no other Scriptures existed then], opening and alleging, that Christ must needs have suffered, and risen again from the dead; and that *this Jesus*, whom I preach unto you, *is* Christ [*is* the Lord's Anointed One, in other words, this is the *Messiah*!].

If you read all through the Acts of the Apostles, you will find that it was always his method with the Jews. And this should always be our method with the Jews today. You *should not* start with the New Testament. If you do, their immediate reaction will be, 'We don't want any of that New Testament rubbish.' You start with *their* Scriptures, the *Old* Testament Scriptures, and lead them, from there, to where the Apostle Paul led them, to Christ, their Messiah, through the Old Testament.

By way of illustration may I relate the following. There was a certain Jewish doctor who became a great friend of mine. He was an orthodox Jew, and he told me that ever since he could remember, he had never once missed going to the synagogue or missed taking part in any Jewish Festival. He wanted to go for walks with me, so every Tuesday evening after his surgery we walked across Hampstead Heath and elsewhere. During those walks I began to talk about *his* Scriptures. I unfolded to him many of the things which the Prophet Daniel had said, which the Prophet Isaiah had said, which the Prophets

Jeremiah and Ezekiel had said, and much else which the Old Testament Scriptures said. Our times together continued for weeks. And he was obviously being *gripped* by it all. In the end he said to me, 'David, I have never missed going to a synagogue all my life, but these things that you have been telling me are entirely *new* to me. I have never heard them before!' His attention had obviously been riveted. You see. You start with *their* Scriptures as the Apostle Paul always did.

Then one evening, after a walk, we finished up in his own home where his wife, who told me she knew all about the Book of Daniel, gave me the opportunity to read Daniel chapter 9 to them both. Daniel chapter 9, of course, contains the prophecy concerning *when* the Messiah, the Prince, would come, and how He was to be 'cut off', but not for Himself. After I had read that chapter to them both, she said to me in absolute amazement, 'I have never heard *that* before; I didn't know *that* was in the Book of Daniel'! And yet she had told me that she knew all about the Book of Daniel! But I had already become aware that none of the Messianic chapters in the Old Testament are ever read in the synagogues today, whereas they always were in the Apostle Paul's day, and in Jesus' day.

I then asked the Jewish doctor to fetch me his own Bible, which he did. I opened it at Isaiah chapter 53, and said to him, 'I want you to read that. *All* of it.' He sat and read it. When he had finished reading, he looked up. So I said, 'Now who is Isaiah talking about?' He looked down at the chapter again, thought very deeply, then looked up and said, 'It must be talking about Jesus of Nazareth.' I asked, 'Why do you say that?' He said, 'Because it is talking about someone who had everybody's sins laid upon Him, and only Jesus of Nazareth did that'! So I said to him, 'Why then don't you accept Jesus of Nazareth as your Messiah?'

Do you see? When you are talking to Jews, you do what the Apostle Paul did, you start with *their* Scriptures, the *Old* Testament Scriptures, and you will *more* than *begin* to get somewhere with them! You *then* ask God to open their eyes, because only He can do that. But of course you need to *know* their Scriptures first. I say again, you must never be a New Testament *only* Christian.

As far as reaching the Jews for the Lord Jesus Christ today is concerned, you must *never, never* say, as some believers in

Israel and in this country are saying today, 'The time has not yet arrived when we should endeavour to reach them for the Lord Jesus Christ because the time is coming when the whole of Israel will be spiritually re-born, and we must wait until then, and not try to reach them for Jesus before then.' We must *never, never* say that. That is to *compromise*.

Did the Apostle Peter say anything like that on the original Day of Pentecost, when, after the Holy Spirit had come upon the 120 in the Upper Room, he went out into the streets of Jerusalem and preached? Was that his attitude then, when 'there were dwelling at Jerusalem Jews, devout men, *out of every nation under heaven*?' (see Acts 2:5). Was that the kind of attitude and outlook that resulted in, first, 3,000 of these Jews being converted, then 5,000, and then a great number of the priests coming to believe?

Did the Apostle Paul adopt that attitude after he met the risen Christ on the Damascus Road and was gloriously converted in consequence? Never! He did the exact opposite. He went straight into the synagogue at Damascus and preached *Christ*, that he is the Son of God (see Acts 9:20, for instance).

Furthermore, later, in the Epistle to the Romans, he laid it down that the preaching of the Gospel must be to the Jew *first* (see Romans 1:16). He would say the same today.

Then Jesus Himself said that all the things which had happened to Him, namely His suffering and so on, was, 'that repentance and remission of sins should be preached in his name among all nations, *beginning at Jerusalem*' (Luke 24:47). That meant, to *the Jews* at Jerusalem. How, then, can these people say today that the time has not yet arrived when we should endeavour to reach the Jews for the Lord Jesus? It *had* arrived in the day when Jesus issued His command, 'Begin at Jerusalem.' It *had* arrived on the Day of Pentecost when the Apostle Peter went out into the streets of Jerusalem and preached. It *had* arrived at the time of the Apostle Paul. And it *had* arrived before the days of the Acts of the Apostles. So how can they say that the time has not yet arrived, now?

Then as to their adopting the attitude that the time is coming when the whole of Israel will be spiritually reborn, and we must wait until then. Was that the Lord Jesus' attitude and outlook when He issued His command, 'Begin at Jerusalem'? Was that the Apostle Peter's attitude and outlook on the Day of Pentecost? Was it the attitude and outlook of the Apostle Paul?

How *false* can these false teachers be? And how *disobedient* can they be to the Lord Jesus' specific command? They should *repent* of their false teaching and outlook forthwith. They should correct it immediately, reverse their completely non-biblical outlook and policy, and get down to obeying the Lord's command, and encourage all those whom they have so tragically misled to do the same. And they should obey the Bible, the *whole* of the Bible.

Brethren! As I view the Christian situation today, I am obliged to say there is a crying need, a *desperate* need today for true believers who are completely steeped and saturated in the Word of God, and in the *whole* of the Word of God, and then who will uncompromisingly *obey* it. I need to say again, the Bible is *one* Book, and we should always regard it as such. We will never see what is the plan and purpose that God is working to, else, nor what is the culminating point towards which He is working.

Never was there a time, either, when it was so vitally important to stress that it is the *Bible* which is our *authority* and our *only* authority. And that it is the Bible plus *nothing*; not the Bible plus commentaries. Commentaries can be wrong. Some which deny what the Bible says most definitely are. They can also mislead.

Our authority is not the Bible plus tradition, either, whether it be Roman Catholic tradition, evangelical tradition, so-called 'Reformed' tradition, or any other tradition. During the last few years, for instance, there have been groups of believers who have said they wanted to 'come out of their tradition' and set up on their own. So they have set up on their own. But I have noticed that by now they have set up their own tradition! You can tell, week by week, exactly what is going to happen! No matter how they try to break with tradition, they always build up one of their own. Everybody does, before long!

So it is the Bible plus *nothing* which is our Court of Appeal, and our *only* Court of Appeal. And today, with many translations, or *mis*-translations of the Bible around, I need to say it is the Bible which has been translated from the Received

Text—the *Textus Receptus*—which is our authority. And we need to *preach* it, and *fearlessly proclaim it*, and uncompromisingly.

Do you know, this Bible which I have before me is a *hammer*? The Bible itself says so. It is a hammer which, when fearlessly and uncompromisingly proclaimed and forthrightly preached, smashes the hard rock in pieces. That is what it says of itself! And there are plenty of hard rocks around today! The Bible can do its own work of smashing them to smithereens when it is boldly and fearlessly preached and proclaimed.

Then we need to know that it is the Bible as interpreted to us by the Holy Spirit of God Himself which is our authority, and not as it is interpreted to us by some church's 'Magistarium', or by anybody's intellect or by anybody's human reasoning. It is not even the Bible as it is interpreted to us by some so-called self-appointed 'Shepherd', or by some self-appointed so-called 'Prophet', or so-called School of Prophets which take their name from some American city or another. Neither is it the Bible as interpreted by self-appointed so-called present-day 'Apostles'.

Jesus said, you will remember:

> When he, *the Spirit of truth*, is come, *he* will guide you into all truth (John 16:13).

He will do it, Jesus said. So let him!

Let me quote to you also the First Epistle of John 2:20, and then verse 27, in respect of what I have just said. Verse 20 reads:

> But ye have an *unction* from the Holy One, and ye know all things.

An *unction* is an *anointing*. It is an anointing of the Holy Spirit.

Then verse 27 says:

> But *the anointing* which ye have received of him abideth in you, and ye need not that any *man* teach you: but *as the same anointing teacheth you* of all things, and *is truth*,

and is no lie, and even as *it* hath taught you, ye shall abide in him.

This letter was written to *young* Christians. *They* didn't have any theological libraries. *They* didn't have any commentaries. But what they *did* have was the unction, the *anointing*, which they had received from Jesus. And that anointing is truth, says the Apostle John, and is no lie. So that anointing guided them into all truth. So let him guide *you*.

Then should there be any *unsaved* person, or people, reading this, I need to point out to you that you cannot understand the Bible *in your natural state and condition*. It is impossible. The Bible says:

> The *natural* man receiveth not the things of the Spirit of God: for they are foolishness unto him; neither can he know them, because they are *spiritually* discerned (1 Corinthians 2:14).

That means they are *spiritually* understood and *spiritually* perceived. That means, too, that in order to understand spiritual things you must become a spiritual person. And you are not born that way. You are born a *natural* person. As Jesus put it, 'You are born after the flesh.'

In order that you may become a spiritual person you must be born again by the operation of the Holy Spirit of God upon you. That is what the Bible teaches. That is what Jesus teaches, and taught. Jesus said to Nicodemus, who was a Master teacher in Israel:

> Except a man be born again, he cannot see [ie, understand] the kingdom of God.... Except a man be born of water and of the Spirit he cannot *enter into* the kingdom of God.... Ye *must* be born again [Nicodemus] (see John 3:1–7).

So being born again by God's Holy Spirit is *an absolute must*. That is what Jesus was saying. And why? Why! Because the Bible says:

> The god of this world [who is Satan] hath blinded the

minds of them which believe not, lest the light of the glorious gospel of Christ...should shine unto them (2 Corinthians 4:4).

What you need, if you are an unsaved person, is for the God who commanded the light to shine out of darkness on the first day of creation to shine *in your heart*, to give the light of the knowledge of the glory of God in the face of Jesus Christ (see 2 Corinthians 4:6).

And He does that when you are born again of God's Holy Spirit. When you *are* born again of God's Holy Spirit you will begin to understand *spiritual* things, because you have now become a spiritual person, and your eyes will have been opened to the truth. The Bible will become a *living book* to you in consequence, and you will hear God speak to you through it, as He lights up its pages to you.

If you want to know still further exactly *how* this can happen to you, the Bible tells you very clearly. You should read the Epistle to the Ephesians, in the New Testament, chapter 1, verses 13–14, where the Apostle Paul tells how it happened to him and to others, in order to understand what I am saying. In these verses he is talking about *the Person of Jesus*, and he says, 'In whom ye *trusted*.' So it is a matter of *trusting* in Jesus. That is the first thing that you need to know.

The Apostle Paul goes on: 'In whom ye trusted, *after* that ye heard the word of truth, the gospel of your salvation.' So that tells you *when* it happens.

But he goes on to explain still further:

In whom also *after that ye believed*, ye were sealed with that holy Spirit of promise, which is the earnest [or first 'down-payment'] of our inheritance *until* the redemption of the purchased possession.

So *what* is it to be born again by God's Holy Spirit? And *how* does it happen?

It is *trusting in the Person of Jesus*. That is the *first* thing.

The Apostle Paul, in verse 12 of Ephesians chapter 1, describes himself as amongst those who *first* trusted in Christ. And he did that *after* the Lord Jesus had appeared to him in

Person, in blinding light, on the Damascus Road. But then in verse 13 he refers to others who also *trusted*.

How did it happen? He tells you. *After* they had heard *the Word of truth*. Then he explains what *the Word of truth* is. He says, 'The gospel of your salvation.' So the Divine order is:

• You hear the Gospel preached.
• As a consequence, you *believe in Jesus*, that means, you *put your trust in him* to save you, and to save you *eternally*.
• *When* you do, you are sealed with God's Holy Spirit as one who now belongs to Him, and you are born again of the Holy Spirit of God, and in consequence you become an entirely new person in Christ Jesus, a *new creation*, in fact. Old things have passed away, all things become new.

That is how it happens. That is how the Bible says it happens. That is *the order* in which it happens. So it rules out entirely any possibility of it ever happening to a babe-in-arms! Infant baptismal regeneration is entirely ruled out here, and is a false doctrine. It, and all its implications, constitute another gospel, and cannot be upheld biblically—not if we are honest. Being spiritually regenerated, or born again by the Holy Spirit of God, happens by hearing the gospel preached; and then by believing in Jesus by way of personal response. It means *believing* that on the cross Jesus has done everything that is necessary to save you. And no babe-in-arms is capable of doing that. It requires being old enough to understand and then to respond, personally.

That was a message for any unsaved person, or persons, who might be reading this. But it is necessary for me to say, even to believers, that we need our eyes opened to understand what the Bible is saying, because our eyes can be holden. By that, I mean that it was said of the disciples in the Upper Room on the first Easter evening, 'Then opened he their understanding that they might understand the scriptures' (Luke 24:45). We need to ask Jesus to do that for *us*, also, as we ourselves turn to the Scriptures to read them. We need to pray, 'Lord that I might receive my sight', otherwise the truths of the Scriptures might be holden from us.

Now I want to lay down *certain vital principles* with regard to our approach to the Bible.

First, when referring to certain books of the Bible we should never say, '*Moses* said this', or '*Isaiah* said that', or '*King David* said so-and-so', and so on.

We should always do what the Apostle Peter did. He said, '*The Holy Ghost* by the mouth of David spake' (Acts 1:16). The Holy Ghost spoke, that is. Or again, in Peter's First Epistle he wrote *concerning the prophets*, the Old Testament prophets:

> *The Spirit of Christ* which was *in them* did signify, when *it* [the Spirit of Christ which was in them] testified *beforehand* the sufferings of Christ, and the glory that should follow (1 Peter 1:10–11).

This means, incidentally, that the Old Testament prophets often did not fully understand what it was that they were saying. In fact, 1 Peter 1:10–11 says exactly that:

> Of which salvation the prophets *have inquired and searched diligently*, who prophesied of the grace that should come unto you: *searching* what, or what manner of time the Spirit of Christ which was *in them* did signify, when *it* [the Spirit of Christ], testified beforehand the sufferings of Christ, and the glory that should follow.

That means they did not know or understand what it was all about. They didn't have to if it was the Spirit of Christ which was *in* them who was speaking, and not themselves. This gives the lie to the modern idea which is being put around by some evangelicals that they spoke according to their understanding of the times in which they lived and according to the thought-forms of their day. Rubbish! It was the Spirit of Christ which was *in* them who spoke, irrespective of the thought-forms of their day, or of their understanding of the times in which they lived.

So what we should be saying is, '*The Spirit of Christ* which was *in* these prophets said, so-and-so', or '*The Holy Ghost* said through Moses', '*The Holy Ghost* said through Isaiah', '*The Spirit of Christ* which was *in* Ezekiel said this and that', and '*The Holy Ghost* said through Jeremiah', and so on.

The Holy Ghost, the Spirit of Christ, cannot possibly be

wrong. What He spoke through the mouths of all these holy prophets since the world began was the *pure* Word of God. That is why I believe so strongly that this Bible is the infallible, inspired, God-breathed, and totally inerrant Word of God. And nobody, and no devil, will budge me from that belief.

The second vital principle is that when reading, studying, and interpreting the Bible, we should *never spiritualise what God never intended to be spiritualised.* And we should *always take literally what God intended to be taken literally.*

The third vital principle is that we must never *go beyond* what the Bible says, or *add* anything to it.

> Add thou not unto his words, lest he reprove thee, and thou be found a liar (Proverbs 30:6).

This is a very necessary command in some Christian circles today! There is a lot of adding to the Bible and twisting of the Scriptures too!

The fourth vital principle is that our constant, *uncom-promising* position should be: whatsoever I find written in the Bible I will accept. Whatsoever I cannot find written in the Bible, or supported by the Bible, I will *totally* and *utterly* reject.

The fifth vital principle is that we should be like the Bereans in the Acts of the Apostles and '*Search the Scriptures daily*' to see if those things that are being put to us from pulpits, from books, at conferences, and so on, are so, and we should do it *with a completely open mind*, not with a biased mind, or a mind that is already made up, or persuaded. In Acts 17:11 it says about the Bereans:

> These were more noble than those in Thessalonica, in that they received the word with all readiness of mind, *and searched the scriptures daily*, whether those things were so.

They checked it all out from their Scriptures, in other words. And incidentally, they were the *Old* Testament Scriptures! No other Scriptures existed at that time.

The sixth vital principle is that we should avoid like the plague the temptation to make the Bible say what we *want* it to say. You can easy do that. And some do! Neither should we tell ourselves and others that this particular verse, passage, chapter, or word, does not mean what it says, it means something else! We must *never* do that. *Never!*

The seventh vital principle is that we must constantly remember and bear in mind, also, that the Bible is *by revelation*. Therefore, we most certainly should not try to work out what it says with our own intellect, or reasoning, or according to *our own understanding*. The Bible itself says:

> Trust in the Lord with all thine heart; and lean *not* unto thine *own* understanding (Proverbs 3:5).

We should trust in the Lord with all our heart to reveal to us what the Bible is saying and meaning. These are seven vital principles that we should always adhere to.

To continue with the subject of God working to a plan, to a purpose, and towards a culminating point, what I need now to stress is that when we see the Bible as *one, interconnected*, and inter-related Book—when we see it as *one whole*—we see that this Bible clearly teaches that the history of the whole world is under God's control. The Bible takes in the whole of history—the history of the whole world, from start to finish. It tells us about the creation, about the final judgment and about everything else in between.

Many people are asking today: Whatever is happening in the world? Wherever is it all heading? Even in the supermarkets, in the pubs, in the restaurants and wine bars, or wherever people meet or congregate, that question is being asked. If ever there was a time to talk to people about prophecy—*Bible* prophecy—that time is *now*! You won't want for a hearing, or be without a listener—a *ready* listener—no matter what religion or faith your hearer may hold!

The Bible teaches that the history of the whole world is under God's control, and that it has been ever since the beginning.

The Bible tells us about the creation of this world, which, by the way, the Lord Jesus said *God* created! He said in Mark 13:19, 'From the beginning of the creation which *God* created.' And I believe Jesus! I also believe God. Not Darwin! It tells us about the Fall of man in The Garden of Eden when Adam and Eve disobeyed God and let sin into their lives, and how they have passed that sin into the life of everyone that has been born ever since. It tells us that *that* is the explanation of all the sin and gross wickedness that there is in the world today. All sin stems from the Fall in the Garden of Eden. And sin is the problem of every person's life.

The Bible tells us about the world's final Judgment Day when everyone will have to give an account of themselves to God, and of what they have done. It tells us about the coming new heaven and new earth which no sin will ever be allowed to enter. And it tells us a lot about other things, and other events that are due to take place in between.

History is, in fact, *His* story, *God's* story. From Genesis to the Book of the Revelation we find that *God* is in control.

What we need to see is that the Bible is a truly marvellous Book. The Bible is, in fact, history *prewritten*. By that, I mean history (or *His* story) written *thousands of years before it happened*, or *is due* to happen, and then it is seen to happen *precisely* as God said it would.

The Bible is also history *pre-spoken*. It was spoken thousands of years before it was due to take place, or *is due* to take place. The Bible is, therefore, a *Book of predictions*. And a Book of reliable, accurate predictions, extremely accurate predictions, in fact.

The Bible is also *that which has been revealed*. And furthermore, it is that which has been revealed *by God*. We should know nothing at all of what it contains had not God revealed it. Nor could we have discovered it, in any way, or found it out, or come to know it, not even with all our modern technology, computerisation, and so-called ingenuity, unless God had revealed it. No way! Let all those who rely on science, or look to science for their information, please take note of that; or those who look to their own intellect or reasoning to find out things!

What is more, we would not have a clue as to what is going on in the world today in these most momentous *end days* in which we are living had not God *revealed* it all, beforehand in the Bible. We would not even know that these are the end days, or that there was such a thing! So you see how much we depend on revelation—on *God's* revelation.

So the Bible is a Book of *Revelations*—all of it, not just its last book, commonly called the Book of the Revelation!

And furthermore, it is a Book of *Divine* revelations, so they are absolutely *reliable* and *trustworthy*—all of them.

What is revealed in the Bible is that *God is working to a plan*, to an *exact* plan. All history follows a Divine plan; His *own* plan. God is over it all—over *all* history.

There is no nation, for instance, or world power that is not ultimately controlled by Him, nor ever has been, since the history of man began. That is abundantly true of every nation or so-called superpower in the world today, whether it be the Soviet Union, the United States of America, China, Great Britain, Japan, India, the Arab States, Iran—even President Saddam Hussein of Iraq, and with him the whole Gulf and Middle East area, Kuwait, Saudi Arabia and Jordan included. They are all ultimately under God's control, and are *being* controlled and directed by Him, whether they are aware of it, or realise it, or not.

King Nebuchadnezzar, in the Prophet Daniel's day, had to learn that lesson—the lesson that:

> The living [should] know that *the most High* ruleth in the kingdom of men, and giveth it to whomsoever *he* will, and setteth up over it the basest of men (Daniel 4:17).

That truth needs to be realised in any country or state, as Presidential Elections approach. In West Germany, for instance; and in Israel, also, in any election that might be pending. It was the truth that governed the Revolutionary Plenum Session in the Soviet Union in 1990.

Nebuchadnezzar had to learn the lesson the hard way! God said that he must be 'put out to grass' *until* thou know that *the most High* ruleth in the kingdom of men, and giveth it to whomsoever *he* will' (Daniel 4:32). Our own government and Parliament need to realise that, whenever they decide to hold the next General Election. And so do the British people!

Daniel 2:21 says, 'He removeth kings, and setteth up kings.' And the same goes for governments! And for Prime Ministers!

The most High is in control. *God* most High. He is the governing factor, not the opinion polls! Not even the way people vote. In fact, He governs that!

King Belshazzar, Nebuchadnezzar's successor, had to learn about God being in control, to his cost. He hadn't *humbled* his *heart*; he had lifted up himself 'against the Lord of Heaven'. Woe betide *anybody* today who does that! He had 'praised the gods of silver, and gold, of brass, iron, wood, and stone'. And God had to say to him:

> The God in whose hand thy breath is, and whose are all thy ways, hast thou not glorified.... [Therefore] thou art weighed in the balances, and art found wanting. God has numbered thy kingdom, and *finished* it (Daniel 5:22–30).

And that very night, King Belshazzar was slain. God 'removeth kings, and setteth up kings' (Daniel 2:21). Just like that! With a flip of His fingers, so to speak.

That thought is a chilling one, indeed, for those who praise the gods of silver, and gold, and brass, and modern technological achievements, and North Sea oil, and so on, in Britain today, and the God in whose hands their breath is, and whose are all their ways have they not *glorified*!

I *fear* for them tremendously! They could be brought down in the twinkling of an eye. *Less* than overnight! I repeat: Every nation on earth is under the hand and control of Almighty God—the God that created the heavens and the earth—and is being *directed* by Him.

There is a purpose and plan in history; in *all* history—*His* story: *God's* purpose and plan. What we need to realise is that what is now happening in this twentieth century, and in this latter part of this twentieth century, is all part of that plan. This is true of Gorbachev's Soviet Union; of everything that is happening all over Eastern Europe; of the European Parliament and of everything connected with it; of the reunification of the two Germanies; of Britain; of the United States; of all the Middle East countries; of belligerent and brutal Iraq under President Saddam Hussein and his invasion of Kuwait, and of that crisis which is raging at this moment of writing; of everything to do with the Gulf and its oil; of China and Japan; of all the Far East countries and islands; of India and of all the States of Africa, South Africa included; and of whatever area you may like to mention. Whatever may be happening *anywhere* is all part of God's plan.

We need to see and *perceive* this, more and more, as certain most momentous and climactic events in different parts of the world take place. As the hymn says:

> God is working His *purpose* out,
> as year succeeds to year.
> Nearer and nearer draws the time—
> the time that shall surely be,
> when the earth will be filled
> with the *glory* of God,
> as the waters cover the sea.

And everything that we see happening in the world today is heading up to that.

Also, we need to realise, with confidence, that the Bible says, several times over, 'The thing which God has determined *shall be done*.' Nothing can stop it or stand in its way, whatever happens, or may happen.

So God is working to a plan; He is working to a purpose—a specific purpose, in fact. And it is all revealed and unfolded to us, here, in the Bible. The Bible, for instance, starts with the story of creation, and it looks *forward* to the time when the earth will be filled with the glory of God as the waters cover the sea (Isaiah 11:9 and Habakkuk 2:14). that is one of the major culminating points to which God is working.

We, ourselves, need to have this *full-orbed view* that the Bible has. That is one reason why all these things have been revealed to us.

The Bible is God's full-orbed view of everything, and He wants it to become ours. He wants us to have in mind this vast eternal span of the Bible's message.

Or to put it another way. The story of the Bible—His story—begins in a garden—the Garden of Eden. It ends in a city—Jerusalem, *new* Jerusalem, coming *down* from God out of heaven (Revelation 21:2); *not* going up from earth unto God, please notice, but coming down from God, out of heaven. In Genesis we see Paradise *lost*. In the Book of the Revelation we see Paradise *restored* and *regained*. That is *the* culminating point to which God is working. The Bible sets before us this wide sweep; it 'paints' a large canvas.

Furthermore, you need to know, believe it or not, that in the midst of all the turmoil, trouble, riots, upheavals, floods, hurricanes, brutal invasions, and other events that we see taking place throughout the whole world today, God Almighty is working towards what the Bible describes as '*The times of restitution of all things*' (Acts 3:21). That means, the restoring of everything to its original state. It means the time when God puts everything right. That's another major culminating point to which God is working.

As you look at the world, and all that is happening in it today, you may not think this is the case. But He *is*! The Bible even calls these things 'the birth-pangs'!

The Bible says:

> Heaven must receive [Jesus] until the times of restitution of all things, which God hath spoken by the mouth of all his holy prophets since the world began (Acts 3:21).

It goes *on* to say:

> Yea, and all the prophets *from Samuel* and those that came after, as many as have spoken, have *likewise* foretold of these days (Acts 3:24).

And that is all part of the Gospel!

Yet people have come to me after I have preached along these lines and have said to me, 'I have never heard anybody preach on "The times of restitution of all things" before.' 'Why not?' I ask!

According to Acts 3:21 this is the message which has been proclaimed by the biblical prophets ever since God brought the world into being! So Adam knew about it! Enoch did! Noah did! Abraham did! Moses did! Samuel did! King David did! But what do *we* know about it, today?

I say to all true believers everywhere: It is vitally important that we *know 'all that the prophets have written'*. I am talking about the *Bible* prophets, not the Kansas City prophets! Preachers everywhere should be preaching all that the prophets have written. Their congregations everywhere should know all that the prophets have written. Bible Colleges and Theological Colleges everywhere should be teaching their students all that the prophets have written because everyone of their students should be well versed in all that the prophets have written. This applies to all universities, everywhere, too. It certainly applies to all university and college Christian Unions everywhere, and to each and every one of their members. It goes for General Synods as well! And for Scottish Assemblies.

And *why*? Why! Because all history—*His* story—is fast heading up to a *great* and *marvellous climax*. And it is all unfolding, in detail, exactly and precisely in accordance with all that God has declared and spoken through the mouth of all His holy prophets since the world began.

I repeat: Teaching what the prophets have written is precisely what *Jesus* did, isn't it? When walking down the Emmaus Road on the first Easter Day after His resurrection, He said to those two puzzled and bewildered disciples:

> O fools, and slow of heart to believe *all that the prophets have spoken*.... And beginning at Moses and all the prophets, he expounded unto them in all the scriptures the things concerning himself (Luke 24:25–27).

I am never tired of repeating this.

This is what Jesus did again in the Upper Room in Jerusalem that same Easter evening, isn't it? He said:

> These are the words which I spake unto you, while I was yet with you, that all things must be fulfilled, *which were written in the law of Moses, and in the prophets, and in the psalms* concerning me. Then opened he their understanding (Luke 24:44).

I never tire of quoting that, either!

The Apostle Peter did the same thing when preaching in the streets of Jerusalem after the healing of the lame man at the Beautiful Gate of the Temple. He said in his preaching:

> Those things, which God *before* had shewed *by the mouth of all his prophets*, that Christ should suffer, *he*

hath so fulfilled. Repent ye therefore, and be converted, that your sins may be blotted out, when the times of refreshing shall come from the presence of the Lord; and he shall send Jesus Christ, which before was preached unto you: whom the heaven must receive *until the times of restitution of all things*, which God hath spoken by the mouth of all his holy prophets since the world began (Acts 3:18–21).

The Apostle Paul made the same approach when he was on trial before King Agrippa. He explained that what the prophets have written was the very *basis* of *all* his preaching, for he said:

Having therefore obtained help of God, I continue unto this day, witnessing both to small and great, *saying none other things than those which the prophets and Moses did say should come*: that Christ should suffer, and that he should be the *first* that should rise from the dead, and should shew *light* unto the people [meaning the Jewish people], *and* to the Gentiles (Acts 26:22–23).

What a revolution in preaching there would be today if every preacher did what the Apostle Paul did: 'say none other things than those which the prophets and Moses did say should come'!

Previously, in his defence before Felix, the Apostle Paul had said:

I believe all things which are written in the law and in the prophets (Acts 22:14).

He could not have believed in all these things that are written in the Law and in the prophets unless he first *knew* them, and was *extremely well versed* in them. Neither can any preacher today, or any true believer, for that matter.

Then, in his later defence before King Agrippa in Acts 26, the Apostle Paul asked Agrippa, 'Believest thou *the prophets?*', which meant that Paul realised that King Agrippa not only knew them, but was well versed in them. People were well versed in them in those days. They would be appalled at our ignorance of them, today.

Paul was even able to say to King Agrippa, 'Believest thou the prophets? I *know* that thou believest.' This meant that he realised that King Agrippa not only knew them, and was well versed in them, but that he also *believed* them—so much so that King Agrippa felt compelled to reply, 'Almost thou persuadest me to be a Christian' (Acts 26:27–28).

This was *always* Paul's method, to say 'none other things than those which the prophets and Moses did say should come'. It was the basis of all his preaching. He always appealed to '*all that the prophets have written*'. Do we?

Let us recall again what happened when eventually he arrived at Rome, as recorded in Acts 28:23. On arrival at Rome, Paul called all the chief of the Jews together:

> To whom he expounded and testified *the kingdom of God*, persuading them *concerning Jesus*!

How?

> Persuading them concerning Jesus, *both out of the law of Moses, and out of the prophets*, from morning till evening.

Paul persuaded his hearers *not* from his own intellect, you will notice! And certainly not from commentaries!

I say again, that is where you need to start, with the Jews. You never start with the New Testament. You do what Paul the Apostle did—he persuaded them concerning Jesus both out of the Law of Moses and out of the prophets. That means Paul went through the whole of the Old Testament with them. Could *you* do that, using the Law of Moses and the prophets? He did so, from morning until evening! Not just in a mere hour at some prophetic convention! So he must have covered a lot of Old Testament ground!

To emphasise once again how extremely important this method is, just take a look at 2 Peter 3:1–2, where the Apostle Peter says:

> This *second* epistle, beloved, I now write unto you; in

both which I stir up your pure minds by way of remembrance: that ye may be mindful *of the words which were spoken before by the holy prophets*.

It was vital to the Apostle Peter, therefore, that these Christians to whom he was writing should *remember* (stir up their minds) in order to be mindful of the words which were spoken before (in former times) *by the holy prophets*, by which he meant, the Old Testament prophets.

But you can't recall to mind what isn't there! That is why I say it is so vitally important that we know all those things which the prophets have written. These early Christians to whom the Apostle Peter was writing obviously *did* know all these things, otherwise he would not have written to them to tell them to call all these things back to mind.

Christians today, however, do not know all those things which the prophets have written. They haven't a clue as to what they are. Most certainly the rising generation of young Christians are unaware of them. So there has obviously been some very defective teaching somewhere! Or no teaching at all! We had better get down to studying 'these things', therefore, because as a result of studying them it will be revealed to us from them what tremendously momentous events are *yet* due to happen in these latter days in which we are living, and the glorious culminating point that they are heading up to. For the writings of the prophets reveal that God is working to a plan, as I have already said, to an exact plan; that He is working to a purpose, a specific purpose. But they *also* reveal that God is working to a timetable, and to a precise timetable.

I will give a few examples, but only in outline.

The *first major* example is Genesis chapter 15, where, in verses 13 and 16, God told Abraham that his seed (his descendants, none of whom had so far even been born) would be:

A stranger in a land *that is not theirs* [we now know that God was referring to Egypt, but Abraham didn't!], and shall serve them; and they shall afflict them *four hundred years*; and also that nation, whom they shall serve [again meaning Egypt], will I judge: and *afterward* shall they come out with great substance.... But in the *fourth generation* they shall come hither again [meaning to where Abraham then was, in the land of Canaan] (vv 13–14, 16).

God was working to a timetable, a stated timetable. He had even worked out precisely, and beforehand, the number of years that were going to be involved!

Then in Exodus 12:40, just after the account of the Passover night, immediately after which the children of Israel came out from under their bondage in Egypt, it says:

Now the sojourning of the children of Israel, who dwelt in Egypt, was *four hundred and thirty years*...even *the selfsame* day it came to pass, that all the hosts of the Lord went out from the land of Egypt.

That was the fulfilment of what God had prophesied to Abraham when as yet there was not a single descendant born! 'Even that selfsame day', it says. It all worked out precisely as God had said it would, and to the exact time. God had said to Abraham, 'In the fourth generation they shall come hither again.' It would seem that a generation in *this* particular case, in God's mind, was 100 years, not forty, as in some other cases. 'In the fourth generation they shall come hither again.' And they *did*, 400 years later to the exact day!

My second major example is the case of the southern kingdom of Judah being taken into captivity by Nebuchadnezzar, King of Babylon, in the Prophet Jeremiah's day, as a severe judgment of God for all their sin and iniquity. In Jeremiah 25:11–12 God says (and I abbreviate):

[They] shall serve the king of Babylon *seventy years*. And it shall come to pass, *when seventy years are accomplished*, that I will punish the king of Babylon.

Then in Jeremiah 29:10 it says:

For thus saith the Lord, That *after seventy years be accomplished* at Babylon, I will visit you, and perform my good word toward you, *in causing you to return to this* place ['this place' meaning Jerusalem].

This same truth was revealed to the Prophet Daniel, who by this time had been taken into captivity to Babylon along with other captives from the southern kingdom of Judah. He said in Daniel 9:2:

I, Daniel, understood by books the number of the years, whereof the word of the Lord came to Jeremiah the prophet, that he [God] would accomplish *seventy years* in the desolations of Jerusalem.

In 2 Chronicles 36:20 there is a further reference to their being carried away captive to Babylon by Nebuchadnezzar '*until the reign of the kingdom of* Persia'. Then it continues:

To fulfil the word of the Lord by the mouth of Jeremiah, *until* the land had enjoyed her sabbaths: for as long as she lay desolate she kept sabbath ['she' meaning the land of Israel], to fulfil *threescore and ten years* [that is, seventy years].

Then it says in verse 22 of 2 Chronicles 36:

Now in the *first* year of Cyrus king of Persia, *that the word of the Lord spoken by the mouth of Jeremiah might be accomplished*, the Lord stirred up the spirit of Cyrus king of Persia, that he made a proclamation throughout all his kingdom [to the effect that] the Lord God of heaven...hath charged me to build him an house in Jerusalem.

And so the return from captivity in Babylon began. And it happened at the *precise time* that God had said it would— after exactly seventy years! Once again God had worked out the number of years that were to be involved, long before the captivity in Babylon was due to begin. Then He brought about the fulfilment of what He had prophesied would happen, in precisely the number of years that He had said He would bring about that fulfilment, namely after seventy years. Again God was working to a timetable, and again to a precise timetable.

My next, and brief example is to show how the destiny and eventual fate of great world empires is determined by a timetable, and sometimes by a precise timetable that is being worked out by God Almighty. Their destiny and the length of their existence as world empires is not governed or determined by anything that they do themselves.

For instance, at the time of the Prophet Daniel, and leading up to the time of the Prophet Daniel, the greatest world empire that existed, certainly in the Middle East area, was the Babylonian Empire, with King Nebuchadnezzar at its head, and with the ancient city of Babylon, situated in present-day Iraq, as its capital. Under King Nebuchadnezzar, the armies of the Babylonian Empire had overrun country after country. By Daniel's day, those armies had overrun Israel, destroyed Jerusalem, and taken many captives, including the Prophet Daniel, from the kingdom of Judah to Babylon. As Daniel interpreted the vision which King Nebuchadnezzar had had of a great image which had stood before him in his dream, the form of which was terrible, he could say:

> Thou, O king, art a king of kings: for the God of heaven hath given thee a kingdom, power, and strength, and glory. And wheresoever the children of men dwell, the beasts of the field and the fowls of the heaven hath he given into thine hand, *and hath made thee ruler* over them all (Daniel 2:37–38).

So King Nebuchadnezzar was by this time ruling the greatest empire that then existed. It dominated all the Middle East countries and beyond; it was still growing and expanding, and was a terrible threat and a menace.

But then God spoke, through the Prophet Jeremiah, and He said:

> I have made the earth, the man and the beast that are upon the ground, by my great power and by my out-stretched arm, and have given it unto whom it seemed meet unto me. And *now have I given all these lands into the hand of Nebuchadnezzar the king of Babylon, my servant*; and the beasts of the field have I given him also to serve him. And all nations shall serve him, and his son, and his son's son, *until* the very time of his land

come: and then many nations and great kings shall serve
themselves of him (Jeremiah 27:5–7).

So it was God who gave Nebuchadnezzar this great Empire.
It was God who had given all these lands into his hands and
who had caused *all nations* to serve him.

But it was to be only for a time, for a *God-prescribed* time.
It was also for a *God-stated* time. That God-stated time was
put in this way: 'All nations shall serve him, and his son, and
his son's son.' That was how long it was to be for. God had set
the timetable long beforehand, and He stated what it was,
through Jeremiah, even long before it began to be worked out
in terms of the eventual fulfilment of that time-scale.

Nebuchadnezzar had been given his world empire by God,
but only for a time. It was to be 'until the very time of his land
come'. And then, God said, it would be given to others. That
is what 'And then many nations and great kings shall serve
themselves of him', means.

What God was saying here is further elaborated in
Jeremiah 25:11–13. Speaking of the land of Judah, which had
already been overrun by Nebuchadnezzar and his armies, and
the majority of whose inhabitants had already been taken
captive to Babylon, God said:

> And this whole land shall be a desolation, and an
> astonishment; and these nations shall serve the king of
> Babylon seventy years. And it shall come to pass, *when
> seventy years are accomplished*, that *I will punish the king
> of Babylon, and that nation*, saith the Lord, for their
> iniquity, *and the land of the Chaldeans*, and will make it
> perpetual desolations. And I will bring upon that land all
> my words which I have pronounced against it, even all
> that is written in this book, which Jeremiah hath proph-
> esied against all the nations.

There *God's* stated timetable is elaborated—the God-prescribed timetable—and is stated by Almighty God as a *precise*
timetable. 'All nations shall serve him [Nebuchadnezzar], and
his son, and his son's son' is now seen to be for a period of
seventy years. And it all happened precisely as God said it
would—even to the exact year.

This is another example of how God is working to a time-table, to a stated timetable, and to a precise timetable.

The words, 'until the very time of his land come', in Jeremiah 27:7, mean, until the very time come when God takes Nebuchadnezzar's Empire away; until He takes it away in judgment. And that time came when the Babylonian Empire was taken over by Cyrus, king of the Medes and Persians, and later by the Greek Empire, and then after that by the Roman Empire.

We should realise at this point that there was a time in the history of all the great world empires when the very time of their land came. It was true of the great Assyrian Empire; we have seen it was true of the great Babylonian Empire; it became true of the great Persian Empire; it was true of the great Greek Empire and of the great Roman Empire. We have to confess that it has become true of the great British Empire. It now seems to be happening of a great Russian Empire, in terms of what is now happening in the Soviet Union. It looks as if the very time of the Soviet Union's land has come.

The question which disturbs my heart and my mind at this moment of writing is: Do those words 'until the very time of his land come' have a particular significance for the land of Britain today? Are we about to see the very time of *our* land come? Not just of our Empire in judgment, awful judgment? I fear it may well be. We shall see. And what of the United States of America? It is a question that needs to be asked.

My fourth major example of God working to a timetable—to a stated and to a precise timetable—is to be found in Daniel chapter 9 from verse 25 onwards. The angel Gabriel appeared to Daniel in answer to Daniel's prayer, and said:

> Know therefore and understand, that *from the going forth of the commandment to restore and to build Jerusalem* [to which I referred when I mentioned Cyrus's proclamation] unto the Messiah the Prince shall be *seven weeks, and threescore and two weeks.*

In prophetic terms that's a total of sixty-nine weeks. Experts could tell you what they think that means in terms of prophetic weeks or years, but I am not going to attempt to do that here. All I am doing at the moment is demonstrating to you that God is working to a timetable, and to His own stated timetable.

Daniel 9:25 and the following verses go on to say:

> The street shall be built again, and the wall [the wall of Jerusalem, that means], even in troublous times.

And it was!

Then it says:

> And *after* threescore and two weeks [62 weeks, in other words] shall *Messiah* be *cut off*, but not for himself [that refers to the crucifixion of Jesus, when His life was cut off from the earth]: and the people of the prince that shall come shall destroy the city [of Jerusalem, that means] and *the sanctuary* [meaning the Temple in Jerusalem].

'The people of the prince that shall come' means the Roman people, the armies of Rome. And 'the prince that shall come' means the Roman Emperor, or Caesar. Jerusalem and the sanctuary, namely the Temple, were destroyed in AD 70 at the hands of the Roman armies led by Titus. We know that, *now*.

The passage continues:

> And the end thereof [meaning of Jerusalem and the Temple] shall be with a flood [that must mean with a flood of armies when you compare the use of the term 'flood' with other of Daniel's prophecies where it definitely refers to armies], and unto the end of the war *desolations* are determined [desolations of Jerusalem and of the Temple, that means].

The phrase 'are determined' is a very strong phrase indeed. It means desolations are determined by God, in terms of terrible judgment. Jesus said to His disciples, you will remember, when they came to Him to show Him the buildings of the Temple:

> See ye not all these things? Verily I say unto you, There

> shall not be left here one stone upon another, that shall
> not be thrown down (Matthew 24:2).

And it happened! It happened exactly as God had told Daniel
that it would happen. And it happened at *the precise time* that
God had told Daniel it would happen. It happened in AD 70.

In fact, *all* that the angel Gabriel had revealed to Daniel as
recorded in Daniel 9:25 and following, which I have quoted
and explained, is yet another clear example of how God is
working to a timetable, to a precise timetable, and to a pre-
stated timetable. He outlined well beforehand how the time-
scale would work out, plus the number of years that would be
involved, and it worked out precisely in the way God said it
would work out, and exactly according to the time-scale that
He had long before outlined.

My fifth major example is from Luke 2:20 and following.
Jesus is speaking to His disciples, and referring to that devastation and desolation of Jerusalem and of the Temple which
the prophecy in Daniel chapter 9 was talking about, and which
was *yet* to take place just over thirty years from the time Jesus
was speaking:

> And when ye [My disciples] shall see Jerusalem com-
> passed with armies, then *know* that the desolation
> thereof is nigh [He was prophesying in the ears of His
> disciples who were at that moment listening to Him,
> about what He *knew* would happen in AD 70].
>
> Then let them which are in Judaea flee to the moun-
> tains: and let them which are in the midst of it depart
> out; and let not them that are in the countries enter
> thereinto. For these be *the days of vengeance*, that *all
> things which are written* may be fulfilled [note that!].
>
> But woe unto them that are with child, and to them
> that give suck, in those days! For there shall be great
> distress in the land, and *wrath* upon *this* people ['this
> people' meaning the Jewish people who were living at
> the time that He was speaking]. And they shall fall by
> the edge of the sword [they *did*, in AD 70], and shall be
> led away captive *into all nations* [they *were*, from AD 70
> onwards]: and Jerusalem shall be trodden down of the
> Gentiles, *until* the times of the Gentiles be fulfilled.

God is working to a timetable *again*; to a precise and to a stated timetable; to a pre-stated timetable, in fact.

Furthermore, all these events which the Lord Jesus so accurately prophesied and predicted over thirty years before they began to take place, were accurately and precisely fulfilled, namely, His disciples seeing Jerusalem compassed with armies; the desolation of Jerusalem and of the Temple; those Jewish people that were then living falling by the edge of the sword, and being led away captive into all nations; and Jerusalem being trodden down by the Gentiles (by non-Jewish nations). That fulfilment is a fact of history. It is indisputable. It all happened. And it all happened precisely as the Lord Jesus said it would.

And so we must come to His statement, 'Jerusalem shall be trodden down of the Gentiles *until* the times of the Gentiles be fulfilled', and consider it once again. For this *also* has been precisely and accurately fulfilled: Jerusalem *has been* trodden down of the Gentiles (non-Jewish nations) right up until 1967.

But no longer! For the first time in nearly 2,000 years, Jerusalem came back into the hands of the Jews in 1967, and it is in their hands right now, in the 1990s. And they mean to keep it that way.

So God's precise and pre-stated timetable has been most accurately and precisely fulfilled, and in every detail, right up to this very moment. It follows, therefore, that it will continue to be so fulfilled.

In a three-page article, which appeared in a special fortieth anniversary edition of *The Jerusalem Post* magazine on Jewish Independence Day, 20th April 1988, a leading Jewish Rabbi said that as a result of the Six-Day War in 1967, when Jerusalem, *including the Temple Mount*, came back into Israel's hands with great rejoicing, they had been brought to the very threshold of the Messianic Age!

He then devotes the whole of his article to the subject of *the third Temple* in Jerusalem being built, now that Israel has been brought so far. He calls this present era of Israel's long history, the era of the third Temple.

In the article he says, 'The period of the third Temple has five basic requirements.' He then puts in brackets, significantly enough, 'We are not including the coming of the Messiah personally. His arrival entails *changes in the natural order*, major topographical changes.'

That is a very significant comment indeed, in view of all the Bible prophecies that talk about the whole area around Jerusalem being flattened by some mighty convulsion or earthquake, which causes the mountain of the Lord's house to be established in the top of the mountains, and *to be exalted above the hills* (see Isaiah 2:2, and Micah 4:1). And Zechariah 14:4 says that the Lord's feet shall stand *in that day* upon the Mount of Olives, which is in front of Jerusalem on the east, when the Mount of Olives shall cleave in the midst thereof toward the east and toward the west, *and there shall be a very great valley*; and half of the mountain shall remove toward the north, and half of it toward the south.

The verse from Zechariah is certainly talking about major topographical changes, and changes in the natural order taking place. This leading Jewish Rabbi obviously knows his Messianic prophetic Scriptures, and that what they say will happen at 'the coming of the Messiah personally', as he put it, or, as we would put it, at the *return* of the Messiah personally.

According to this Rabbi, the five basic *requirements of the period of the third Temple* are:

1) That the land of Israel be delivered from foreign domination.
2) That a sovereign Jewish government be established.
3) That there should be an ingathering of exiles which results in a Jewish majority in the land and the settlement of most of the land by Jews, although the majority of the Jewish people might remain in the Diaspora or Dispersion.
4) That there should be the establishment of the Sanhedrin—the Supreme Court which is prescribed—'without which,' he says, 'certain states of the Messianic Age cannot be fulfilled'.
5) The building of the Temple.

All these requirements remind me immediately of the prophecy of Hosea 3:4–5 which says:

> For the children of Israel shall abide many days *without a king*, and *without a prince*, and *without a sacrifice*, and *without an image*, and *without an ephod*, and *without teraphim*.

And they *have* abided without all these things, not only for many days, but for all these centuries—for over 2,000 years! But not for much longer, I think.

In his article the Rabbi goes on to say that at least three out of the five of those basic requirements have been partially or completely fulfilled. He writes:

> First, we have liberated the land. *Most* of the Holy Land is under Jewish control *for the first time since the destruction of the second Temple in AD 70.* It happened during the Six-Day War, when Bethlehem, Hebron, Shilo, Shechem, Jerusalem's *Old* City, the Temple Mount, the Western Wall [that is, the Wailing Wall], and the rest of the Holy Cities of biblical Israel came back into our hands.
>
> Secondly, an independent Jewish government was established between 1948 and 1967 *as a valid substitute for the Israelite kingdom.*

He says this because of the basic Principle that when a Jewish leader is appointed to deal with all the nation's needs, and he rules in a sovereign manner, *according to the will of the people and of the courts*, he is certainly *a valid substitute for a king*. If the leaders are *freely elected*, and do not *illegally* seize power, their government is tantamount to an Israelite *monarchy*. He claimed that principle was laid down by the first Ashkenazi Chief Rabbi of the Holy Land, Rabbi Auraham Yitzhak Hacohen Kook.

> Thirdly, the ingathering of the Jewish exiles from the Diaspora has been achieved to a very great measure.

He reckons 3.5 million Jews have, to date, returned to Israel. He then says:

> This may be considered *a real ingathering from the biblical standpoint.*

But I myself would add, it had accellerated a lot since he said that in April 1988!

He continues:

Of the two remaining requirements, we have not set up a Sanhedrin, because the contemporary concensus *prevents the appointment of 71 Jewish sages to act as such a body*.

As for the fifth Messianic basic requirement, the rebuilding of the Temple, it is clear that that has not been carried out.

But he devotes a great deal of his article to discussing the subject.

I can report, however, that even more recently, after a foundation stone was laid at the end of 1989, in the near vicinity of the Temple Mount in Jerusalem, the Chief Rabbinat in Israel, who was present at that ceremony, said: 'All the signs point to the rebuilding of the third Temple *in our day*.'

To all those points I would add that there has been a *partial* return of the Jewish people to their land, in fulfilment of many of the Bible prophecies, *since the Balfour Declaration of 1917*, which provided for a national Jewish home in Palestine for the Jewish people. And there is now a *State* of Israel, with Jerusalem as its capital.

And everything has been happening *according to God's precise*, specifically *pre-stated* timetable. And it will *continue* to happen that way. Jerusalem has, indeed, been trodden down of the Gentiles just as the Lord Jesus said it would be, right up to 1967 when it was liberated. And the remainder of what God has said will happen, will happen in the same way, and exactly according to His pre-stated timetable.

With regard to the rebuilding of the Temple, which is one of the requirements which have yet to take place, I am reminded of a conversation which I had a few years ago with Sir Barnett Janner, who, at that time, was the Member of Parliament for Leicester. He was an Orthodox Jew. A foreign affairs debate on the Middle East had been taking place in the House of Commons, to which I had been invited to listen. At a certain point during this debate one MP stood up and said, 'Israel should be dispossessed. What right has she to be there?' The great big, burly, Churchillian-like Sir Barnett Janner, stood up and said, 'Does he ask what right she has to be there? Does he not know his Bible? Does he not know that her right to be there is a Divine right?' And he proceeded to give what really amounted to a biblical exposition of the early history of Israel from the time of Abraham!

I was so deeply impressed that I expressed a wish to meet him. This resulted in him inviting me to have tea and a chat with him in the members' dining room. I congratulated him on his forthright outspokenness on behalf of Israel. He then said to me, 'I know that you are an evangelical Christian. I am an Orthodox Jew, and I believe that the things which are happening in the Middle East and in Israel right now are paving the way for the return of our Messiah.' I said 'You say *the return* of your Messiah?' He replied with a twinkle in his eyes, 'The return of *our* Messiah, yours and mine,' which indicated to me that he *could* be a secret believer in Jesus, as his Messiah, as well as mine.

However that might be, I said to him, 'What about the rebuilding of the Temple in Jerusalem? Do you see it ever taking place?' To which he replied, 'We now have the nation of Israel. You cannot have a nation of Israel without also having its central place of worship, and that central place of worship must be in Jerusalem. As you yourself will know, the Jew is required to go up to Jerusalem as his central place of worship at least three times each year. So it is inevitable that the Temple in Jerusalem will be rebuilt.'

I asked, 'So how do you envisage it happening?' To which he replied, 'You can rest assured that Israel will never do anything to upset the Arabs.' To which I replied in return, 'So how do you envisage it taking place, with the Mosque of Omar or the Dome of The Rock standing now on the Temple site?' He looked at me with that same twinkle in his eyes, and he said, 'There are such things as earthquakes!' From that encounter onwards he became a very dear and close friend.

But right at this very moment, Israel is surrounded by her enemies, who publicly declare that they are out for Israel's extinction, just as the Bible has prophesied that they would. The Israelis have, what they themselves describe as the *inner circle* of their enemies. By that they mean their neighbouring *Arab* enemies, such as Syria, Iraq, Saudia Arabia, the Arab Emirates, Egypt, and so on—I hope not Jordan. They also have what they describe as the *outer circle* of their enemies, namely, the Soviet Union, Iran (which is biblical Persia),

Communist Ethiopia, Gadaffi's Libya, and the other countries which are named in Ezekiel chapters 38 and 39.

It is interesting to see from the Bible prophecies, that when the final, biblically prophesied attack against Israel comes, it will be from that *outer circle* of her enemies, exactly as God, in His Word, the Bible, has said they would. And it will all happen precisely in accordance with God's pre-stated and predetermined and Divinely revealed timetable.

The question is: *When* will that be?

The answer is: We don't know. Jesus Himself said that even *He* did not know the time. Only His Father in heaven.

But I will tell you this. Not long before Dr Martyn Lloyd Jones, the former minister of Westminster Chapel in London, who was regarded by many as being the last of the great preachers, went to be with His Lord in heaven, he was interviewed. After his interviewer had asked him several questions and had received his answers, the interviewer said, 'What then do you consider should be the policy of the Christian Church during the next twenty years?'

Dr Martyn Lloyd Jones replied, 'I don't think we have twenty years to go.'

His interviewer said, 'Why do you say *that*?'

Dr Martyn Lloyd Jones replied, 'Because the most significant prophecy of the Bible was fulfilled in 1967.'

His interviewer said, 'Which of the Bible prophecies is that?'

Dr Martyn Lloyd Jones replied, 'The prophecy of the Lord Jesus, when He said, "Jerusalem shall be trodden down of the Gentiles until the times of the Gentiles be fulfilled." ' Then he said, 'Jerusalem is no longer trodden down by the Gentiles. It came back into the hands of the Jews in 1967 for the first time in nearly 2,000 years. Therefore I don't think we have twenty years to go.'

I find that a most challenging statement, because Dr Martyn Lloyd Jones never, *never*, made a statement until he had very carefully considered and weighed what he was about to pronounce.

It was on St David's Day, 1981, that he departed this life and went to be with Jesus. That is now ten years ago. If he was right, have we *less* than ten years to go before the Lord Jesus Christ returns?

We urgently need to face up to this question. We also need to prepare for, and to prepare others for, Jesus' return, in the time that we have left.

Chapter Seven

What Does the Bible Prophesy About Israel and About Its Future?

I come now to the question: What does the future hold in store for Israel—if anything—when viewed biblically and prophetically?

With Jerusalem fast becoming *the* crucial world issue of *all* issues today, what has God promised Israel in the future (if He has indeed promised anything), as seen from the Bible prophecies? This is a question which needs to be faced in all honesty in view of the teaching that is being spread around by some, today, that all references to Israel in the prophecies of the Bible should now be interpreted to mean the Church.

Now I have already said that whatever has to be said about the state of our own nation today, whatever has to be said about the state of the world, whatever has to be said about the state of Europe including Eastern Europe, whatever has to be said about the state of America today, the *real* point on which we should be focusing our attention in these latter days in which we are living is the Middle East, because everything is going to culminate *there*, everything is going to *come to a head* out there.

It has become even more true that the real point on which we should be focusing our attention is the Middle East since the Gulf War to drive Saddam Hussein out of Kuwait has come to an end, or *seems* to have come to an end. This part of the message is being written after the Gulf War against Saddam Hussein and his forces has been concluded. And the conclusion of that war has immediately brought more clearly into focus once again the fact that Jerusalem is becoming the central issue in world affairs today. It also raises the question once again as to the future of Israel, and has emphasised the fact that we are indeed fast approaching the climax of this age. Things are once again fast coming to a head in Israel and in the Middle East, even as this book is going to print.

Let me, at the outset, say, 'Let nobody dare to say that God has no future plan for Israel; that He has finished with them; that all He is interested in now is calling out His Church.' Such a statement is nonsense! Furthermore it is heresy! And it is utterly false teaching, the teaching of false prophets. People who say that kind of thing just do not know their Bibles. They do not know their Old Testament. And they certainly don't know all that the prophets have written, the Old Testament prophets in particular. And I need to emphasise this, because the 1991 May/June issue of a glossy Christian magazine carried no less than six main articles, all of which teach and uphold this false doctrine.

This erroneous teaching is by no means new. Augustine of Hippo was one of the first of the early Church Fathers to teach that all the references to Israel in the prophetic Scriptures now refer only to the Church. Later, Martin Luther followed the same line. So also did many of the other Reformers. So did some of the Puritans. The same line of teaching is found in many commentaries. The headings at the top of the pages in many translations of the Bible, including the King James version, unfortunately, imply that Israel now means the Church.

I want to utterly refute this doctrine and blow this false teaching sky high. In the first place, God has not only a future plan for Israel; He has a future plan for the Lord Jesus to be King of Israel, and a future plan concerning His future throne.

To establish that fact, may I remind you of how it is recorded in the first chapter of John's Gospel, verse 45 onwards, that:

> Philip findeth Nathanael, and saith unto him, We have found him, of whom Moses in the law, and the prophets, did write, Jesus of Nazareth, the son of Joseph.

Then a little later, in verse 47 it says:

> Jesus saw Nathanael coming to him, and saith of him,

Behold an Israelite indeed, in whom is no guile! Nathanael saith unto him, Whence knowest thou me? Jesus answered and said unto him, Before that Philip called thee, when thou wast under the fig tree, I saw thee. Nathanael answered and saith unto him, Rabbi, thou art the Son of God; thou art *the King of Israel* (vv 47–49).

You will also remember that the wise men who came from the East said to King Herod when they arrived in Jerusalem:

Where is he that is born *King of the Jews*? for we have seen his star in the east, and are come to worship him (Matthew 2:1–2).

But Jesus has never been the King of Israel yet, has He! Not so far. You will remember, too, that when they crucified Him, Pilate wrote His title, and put it on the cross: 'JESUS OF NAZARETH THE KING OF THE JEWS' (John 19:19). But He has never yet been the King of the Jews because the Jews and the Pharisees and the Sadducees and their High Priest had rejected Him as such, and had said, 'We have no king but Caesar' (John 19:15).

Jesus has *yet* to be the King of the Jews and *also* the King of Israel. How do we know that? Why, because the angel Gabriel, the messenger sent from God, said to Mary before His birth:

The Lord God shall give unto him the throne of his father David: and he shall reign over the house of Jacob for ever (Luke 1:32–33).

The House of Jacob means Israel, and all of its twelve tribes, as I will explain more fully later.

And Jesus hasn't reigned over the House of Jacob for ever yet. But He *will* do, in the future. That is God's plan. His reign is also part of God's future plan for Israel.

Furthermore Micah's prophecy, which the chief priests and scribes quoted to King Herod when Herod had demanded of them where Christ should be born, said, concerning Bethlehem:

Out of thee shall he come forth unto me that is to be ruler in Israel; whose goings forth have been from of old, from everlasting (Micah 5:2).

Or, as Matthew 2:6 has it:

Out of thee [Bethlehem] shall come a Governor, that shall rule my people Israel.

Notice that God says He 'shall rule my people *Israel*'. He did not say He would rule just *the Jews*, but *Israel*. And He has not ruled God's people Israel yet. But He *will* do, some time in the future. I repeat, that is God's plan, part of God's future plan for Israel.

I presume that all those who accept Replacement Theology believe in the personal return of our Lord Jesus Christ. But if they do, and if at the same time they still believe that God has no future plan for Israel, what have they to say about this? Isaiah 66:15 says:

For, behold, the Lord will come with fire, and with his chariots like a whirlwind, to render his anger with fury, and his rebuke with flames of fire.

That verse is talking about His Second Coming, isn't it? I will have reason to quote it again, later on.

First, let us look at it more closely in its context. It says, 'The Lord will come.' What to do? Two things in the main according to the context.

1) 'To render his anger with fury, and his rebuke with flames of fire.' Jude says something similar in his Epistle in verses 14 and 15: 'Behold, the Lord cometh with ten thousands of his saints, to execute judgment upon all....' That is the *first* thing that He is coming to do.

2) Isaiah 66 states the second thing He will do. Verses 15 to 18 speak of the judgment, then verses 19 to 21 go on to say:

And I will set a sign among them [meaning among Israel], and I will send those that escape of them unto the nations, to Tarshish, Pul, and Lud, that draw the bow, to Tubal, and Javan, to the isles afar off, that have not heard my fame, neither have seen my glory; and they shall declare my glory among the Gentiles. And they shall bring *all your brethren* for an offering unto the Lord *out of all nations* upon horses, and in chariots, and in litters, and upon mules, and upon swift beasts, *to my holy mountain Jerusalem*, saith the Lord, as the children of Israel bring an offering in a clean vessel into the house of the Lord. And I will also take of them for priests and for Levites, saith the Lord.

That is the second thing that He is going to do. 'Bring all your brethren [Israel and Jerusalem are being addressed] out of all nations...to my holy mountain Jerusalem' for an offering to the Lord.

These two things are going to happen when the Lord comes with fire—when He comes the second time, that means. They are going to happen together. They are going to coincide with one another, in other words—the judgment when He renders His anger with fury, and His rebuke with flames of fire on the one hand, and the bringing of all Israel's brethren out of all the nations to God's holy mountain, Jerusalem, as an offering unto the Lord on the other hand.

In view of all that, how can advocates of Replacement Theology possibly say that God has no future plan for Israel; that He's finished with them?!! What is more, God addresses Israel and Jerusalem in verse 22 of Isaiah 66, and says:

For as the new heavens and the new earth, which I will make, shall remain before me, saith the Lord, so shall your seed and your name remain.

What stronger argument can you have than that, that God has by no means finished with Israel?

But God not only has a future plan for the Lord Jesus to be King of Israel, and a future plan concerning His future throne, He has a future plan *for Jerusalem* also.

The first part of Isaiah 2:2–4, for instance, says:

And it shall come to pass *in the last days* [note that—we are living in them!], that the mountain of the Lord's *house* shall be established in the top of the mountains, and shall be exalted *above* the hills; and *all nations* shall flow unto it. And many people shall go and say, Come ye, and let us go up to the mountain of the Lord, to the *house* of the God of Jacob; and he will teach us of his ways, and we will walk in his paths: for out of Zion shall go forth the law, and the word of the Lord *from Jerusalem*. And he shall judge among the nations.

Micah 4:1–2 says the same thing.

Yasser Arafat may have his plan for Jerusalem; the Soviet Union and the Kremlin and their military and Chiefs of Staff may have their plan. Fundamentalist Islam may have *its* plan. But the God of all the earth, the God of Israel, the living God, the *only* living God, has *His* plan, and this is *it*, or part of it! And He will cause their plans to come to nothing, as we shall see later, and fulfil *His*!

God's plan for Jerusalem not only includes the mountain of the Lord's House being lifted up higher than the mountains. It also includes there being a *cloud of glory over it*, as Isaiah 4:5 states:

> And the Lord will create upon every dwelling place of mount Zion [which is part of Jerusalem], and upon her assemblies, a *cloud* and *smoke* by day, and *the shining of a flaming fire* by night.

That immediately reminds me of the pillar of cloud by day and the pillar of fire by night that went ahead of the children of Israel in the wilderness in Moses' day. It was the sign that God's presence was there. And it still *is*. The only difference between what happened then, when they were going through the wilderness, and what will be true of Jerusalem at the time that Isaiah is talking about, is that the pillar of cloud, and the pillar of fire moved on ahead of the children of Israel in the wilderness to show them the way they were to go, whereas in Jerusalem, and *over* Jerusalem, the cloud by day, and the shining of a flaming fire by night will be *stationary*. Jerusalem's inhabitants won't be travelling any more! What a wonderful sight that cloud and smoke by day and that shining of a flaming fire by night will be. How awe inspiring!

There is more about this in Isaiah 60:1-2. Speaking *of Jerusalem* it says:

> The *Lord* shall arise upon thee [Jerusalem], and his *glory* shall be *seen* upon thee.

Note that His glory will be *seen*! For miles! Jerusalem will be very high and lifted up, by then, higher than any of the surrounding mountains!

Furthermore, the prophecies of the Bible reveal that God's plan for Jerusalem also includes Jerusalem eventually being the *central place of worship for the whole world*. Did you know that? Isaiah 60:14-15 says:

> The sons [descendants] also of them that afflicted thee [Jerusalem, that means] shall come bending unto thee [Jerusalem, again, is being addressed]; and all they that despised thee shall bow themselves down at the soles of thy feet; and they shall call thee, The city of the Lord, the Zion of the Holy One of Israel. Whereas thou *hast* been forsaken *and hated*, so that no man went through thee, I will make thee an *eternal excellency*, a joy of many generations.

Then Isaiah 66:23 says:

> And it shall come to pass, that from one new moon to another, and from one sabbath to another, *shall all flesh come to worship before me*, saith the Lord.

'All flesh' will come to worship before the Lord at Jerusalem, from the one sabbath to another! That's every week! And 'from one new moon to another' is every month!
Zechariah 14:16 says:

> And it shall come to pass, that every one that is left [the survivors] of all the nations which come against Jerusalem shall even *go* up *from year to year to worship the King*, the Lord of hosts, and to keep the feast of tabernacles.

Jerusalem is the city of the Great King, as says Psalm 48:2, which Jesus Himself quoted in Matthew 5:35. And when it says, 'And it shall come to pass'—*it shall come to pass*! That is what *God* says! And I believe God!

God says again to Jerusalem in Isaiah 55:5:

> Behold, thou shalt call a nation that thou knowest not, and *nations* [in the plural] that knew not thee shall *run* unto thee [Jerusalem].

Why?

> Because of the Lord thy God, and for the Holy One of Israel; for he hath *glorified* thee.

Nations who did not know Jerusalem shall *run* to Jerusalem because *God* is there! How wonderful! And no poster campaigns will be necessary to bring it about, either!

I add that no *other* city in the whole wide world is ever going to be glorified. London isn't going to be! Glasgow or Edinburgh are not going to be! New York City isn't going to be! Washington DC, whether they like it or not, isn't going to be! Paris, Berlin, Moscow, Peking, Tokyo, New Dehli, Rome even—none of these is going to be! But *Jerusalem* is going to be! The time will come, saith the Lord, when it will be said of Jerusalem, 'God hath glorified thee.'

I could quote many other prophetic Scriptures which testify that *Jerusalem is eventually going to be the central place of worship for the whole world*. It is all part of *God's Divine plan*, of His Divinely revealed plan. In addition, it is God's predetermined plan to have *His sanctuary* in Jerusalem.

Ezekiel 37:26–28 includes the end of a prophecy which is unquestionably about the latter days. In it, God says:

> Moreover I will make a covenant of peace with them [meaning Israel]; it shall be an *everlasting covenant* with them: and I will *place them*, and multiply them, and will *set my sanctuary* in the midst of them *for evermore*. My tabernacle also shall be with them: yea, I will be their God, and they shall be *my* people. And *the heathen* shall know that I the Lord do sanctify Israel.

When?

> When *my sanctuary* shall be in the midst of them, *for evermore*.

That should give a lot of people a lot of room for thought! That is what *God* says. I am quoting the Word of God, the *pure* Word of God, this *more sure* Word of prophecy!

Did you notice what verse 26 of Ezekiel 37 said about *the peace settlement*? Various nations have been striving for years now to bring about an international peace conference, with the object of bringing *peace* to the Middle East. But their intention is that it would be peace *at Israel's expense*. 'Land for peace' has been the stated deal or requirement. Israel must give up Land. 'Trade land for peace' is the cry of the nations to Israel!

But the United States is not going to bring about a peace settlement. The United Nations is not going to do it. The Soviet Union is not going to do it. Yasser Arafat and the Intafada are certainly not going to do it. *God* is going to do it! He states this in Ezekiel 37:26:

> Moreover *I* will make *a covenant of peace* with them [Israel]; it shall be *an everlasting covenant* with them.

'*I* will,' He says. So when *God* makes that peace settlement, it will be *for keeps*! And it will be sure, and certain. It is an *everlasting* covenant with Israel that He will make. And so it will hold—for all time.

But even that is not all that God has included in His stated plan for Jerusalem! All the prophecies of the Bible say that the Lord is going to *reign* from there!

Micah 4:7–8 says, for instance:

> And the Lord shall *reign over them in mount Zion* from henceforth, even for ever. And thou, O tower of the flock, the stronghold of the daughter of Zion, *unto thee* shall it come, even *the first dominion*; *the kingdom* shall come to the daughter of *Jerusalem*.

The angel Gabriel said to Mary as I have already mentioned:

> The Lord God shall give unto him [Jesus] the throne of
> his father David: and he shall reign over the house of
> Jacob for ever: and of his kingdom there shall be no end
> (Luke 1:32–33).

That utterance of the angel Gabriel has not yet been
fulfilled. But it is going to be. And then no doubt the Micah 4
prophecy will be fulfilled also: 'And the Lord shall reign over
them in mount Zion.'

And may I point out that mount Zion is in Jerusalem. It
should never be interpreted as the Church. I need to say that
because I have heard a leading Keswick Convention speaker
say, 'Zion, of course, is the Church.' It isn't. It is Jerusalem.
And it is Jerusalem that is being referred to in Micah 4:7–8.

Then God calls Jerusalem '*My* city' in Isaiah 43:13. And
Zechariah 8:3 says, 'And Jerusalem shall be called *a city of
truth*.'

But over and above all this, the last verse of Ezekiel chapter
48 says:

> And the name of the city *from that day* shall be, *the Lord
> is there*.

Oh! How I love that! That city Jerusalem from that day shall
be called 'The Lord is there', because He *is*! Or *will* be!

How dare anybody say that God has no future plan for
Israel when He has all *that* in store for Jerusalem, and for the
inhabitants of it also?

So what is God's Divinely revealed plan and pre-stated purpose *for Israel itself*, not just for Jerusalem?

That there is such a plan is beyond question. The books of
the prophets reveal that there most definitely *is*. Furthermore,
it is a very *determined* plan so far as God is concerned, and a
most *definite* one.

For instance, God says in Jeremiah 30:10–11:

> Therefore fear thou not, O my servant Jacob, saith the

Lord; neither be dismayed, O *Israel*.... For I am with thee, saith the Lord, to save thee: *Though I make a full end of all nations whither I have scattered thee, yet will I not make a full end of thee*.

Look at that! Nothing could be more clear. The nations where God has scattered the people of Israel are quite numerous. What God is saying here is that He *could* make a full end of them all. He does not say He *will*. He is saying He could do. But even though He were to make a full end of them all, He will not make a full end of Israel. That is what God is saying.

How can anybody ever say that God has no further plan for Israel when He has pledged Himself to keep them in existence? How can they say God has finished with them!

Furthermore, the Bible says this, in Jeremiah 33:23–26:

Moreover, the word of the Lord came to Jeremiah, saying, Considerest thou not what this people have spoken, saying, The *two families* which the Lord hath chosen, he hath even cast them off? thus they have despised my people, that they should be no more a nation before them.

The *two families* 'which the Lord hath chosen' which are referred to here, are the northern kingdom of Israel and the southern kingdom of Judah. Israel became divided into these two families early in the reign of King Rehoboam, the son of Solomon. And they remained divided during the rest of their Old and New Testament history. I will come back to this matter of their being divided into these two kingdoms, or two families, later.

What 'this people' were saying in Jeremiah 33:24 was that God had even cast off these 'two families' that He had chosen. So God, in verse 25, proceeds to refute that. He says:

Thus saith the *Lord*; If my covenant be not with day and night, and if I have not appointed the ordinances of heaven and earth; then will I cast away the seed of Jacob, and David my servant, so that I will not take any of his seed to be rulers over the seed of Abraham, Isaac, and Jacob: for I will cause their captivity to return, and have mercy on them.

Nothing could be more definite. God would not have said 'I will cause their captivity to return' if He had even cast them off, as they were saying He had. Neither would He have pledged Himself so strongly that He would not cast away the seed of David His servant to be rulers over the seed of Abraham, Isaac, and Jacob if there was going to be none of that seed of Abraham, Isaac and Jacob left for the seed of David to rule over!

What is more, since God's covenant with day and night is bound to continue to remain, and since He *has*, indeed, appointed the ordinances of heaven and earth, then it follows that His people, Israel, are bound to remain, and to continue in being, also. That is the argument! *God's* argument!

God says yet again, in Jeremiah 31:35–37:

> Thus saith the Lord, which giveth the sun for a light by day, and the ordinances of the moon and of the stars for a light by night, which divideth the sea when the waves thereof roar; The Lord of hosts is his name; if *those* ordinances depart from before me, saith the Lord, *then* the seed of Israel also shall cease from being a nation before me for ever. Thus saith the Lord; *If* heaven above can be measured, and the foundations of the earth searched out beneath, I will also cast off all the seed of Israel for all that they have done, saith the Lord.

Again I say that nothing could be more definite. Nothing could be more impossible, either, than for the heavens above to be measured and for the ordinances of the sun as a light by day and the ordinances of the moon and the stars as a light by night to depart from before the Lord. So nothing could be more impossible than for the seed of Israel to cease from being a nation, or for the Lord to cast off that self-same seed of Israel. The position with regard to Israel is as strong as that, and as sure as that—no matter what they have done. That is what God is saying.

God puts their position even more strongly in Jeremiah 46:28, where He says:

> Fear thou not, O Jacob my servant, saith the Lord: for I am with thee; for I *will* make a full end of all the nations whither I have driven thee: but I will not make a full end of thee.

This is even more strong than what God said previously in Jeremiah 30:10–11, which I have already quoted, for in that passage of Scripture God said, '*Though* I make a full end of all the nations whither I have scattered thee, yet will I not make a full end of thee.' But in this passage, in Jeremiah 46:28, God says, 'For I *will* make a full end of all the nations whither I have driven thee.' That is a very chilling statement indeed, and extremely sobering.

But it should be emphasised that what God is saying is that despite whatever happens to all these nations to which God has driven them, *His* people, the people of Israel, will *remain*.

Nothing could be more clear, therefore, than that the first point about God's Divinely revealed plan and pre-stated purpose for Israel itself is that they should unquestionably continue to remain in existence and be inviolate as a people.

The *second* point about God's Divinely revealed plan and pre-stated purpose for Israel itself is that God intends to bring all of them out of all the nations where he has scattered them, and bring them back to their own land.

He says, for instance, in Jeremiah 31:10:

> Hear the word of the Lord, O ye nations, and declare it in the isles afar off, and say, He that scattered Israel will gather him.

That is a definite statement, so it is for sure. God is saying that.

I have already said that a partial return of the Jewish people to Israel has taken place, and that that return is now accelerating apace, especially as Russia is likely to release as many as 1 million Jews within a year, and especially as Ethiopia has now released most of the Ethiopian Jews that were in that country, and Syria is soon likely to do the same.

However, the prophecies of the Bible clearly reveal that there is far more to take place than has yet happened, and which has still to take place.

To quote one example, Isaiah 11:11 and onwards says:

> And it shall come to pass *in that day*, that the *Lord* shall set his hand again *the second time* to recover the remnant of his people, which shall be left, from Assyria, and from Egypt, and from Pathros, and from Cush, and from Elam, and from Shinar, and from Hamath, and from the islands of the sea. And he shall set up an ensign for the nations, and shall assemble *the outcasts of Israel* [notice—that refers to the northern kingdom of Israel], and gather together the dispersed of Judah [that refers to the southern kingdom of Judah] from the four corners of the earth (vv 11–12).

When it says in verse 11 that the Lord shall set His hand again '*the second time* to recover the remnant of his people', this cannot in any sense refer to the time of their being in captivity in Babylon. That was their *first* captivity, and they, the people of *Judah* returned from that captivity under leaders such as Nehemiah and Ezra. That was their first return. The Lord is referring in Isaiah 11:11–12 to a second time when they will be brought back but not *only* the people of Judah at that time, but the people of the northern kingdom also. From the time of the rebellion early in King Rehoboam's reign, the northern kingdom was referred to in the Old Testament Scriptures as Israel, whereas the southern kingdom, after that rebellion, was referred to in those same Scriptures as Judah. But I will be returning to that point later.

Then Isaiah 11:15–16 says:

> And the Lord shall utterly destroy the tongue of the Egyptian sea [the Red Sea]; and with his mighty wind shall he shake his hand over the river [the Nile, or it might mean the Euphrates River], and shall smite it in the seven streams, and make men go over dryshod. And there shall be an highway for the remnant of his people, which shall be left, from Assyria: like as it was to Israel in the day that he came up out of the land of Egypt.

None of *that* has happened yet! It has *yet* to happen, and it *will* happen.

As to all those place names which are mentioned in verse 11:

- *Assyria* is the region just north of present-day Iraq and is just south of present-day Armenia. It was where the ancient city of Nineveh, the capital of the ancient Assyrian Empire, was situated.
- *Pathros* equals Upper Egypt, the area which includes the present-day Asswan Dam.
- *Cush* equals present-day Ethiopia and Abyssinia.
- *Elam* equals ancient Persia or present-day Iran.
- *Shina* is the area which included all of ancient Babylonia, part of which is present-day Iraq.
- *Hamath* equals Upper Syria in the valley of the Orontes River, and includes the region of Baalbek.
- *The islands of the sea* could mean all the islands in the Mediterranean Sea, such as Malta, Crete, Cyprus, Sicily, and so forth. But it could also refer to more distant islands of the sea, not excluding the Pacific Islands.

What God is saying here is that the day is coming when He will recover the remnant of His people which is left from all these regions, all of which are very much in the news today, and that that will include gathering them from the four corners of the earth. And I stress that this will include not only the Jews who stem from the tribe of Judah, but it will also include assembling the outcasts of Israel who stem from the northern kingdom of Israel.

This seems to be something far greater and more widespread than anything that has happened yet. It will involve a mighty miracle of God which we have yet to see take place, namely God dividing the Red Sea like He did for Israel in the day that they came up out of the land of Egypt. It will also involve God smiting the Nile in its seven streams so as to make men go over dryshod. However, when it says the river whose seven streams God will smite, it could mean the River Euphrates.

A second example of what has yet to take place, is found in Isaiah 43:5–7, which is addressed to Israel:

> Fear not: for I am with thee: I will bring thy seed *from the east*, and gather thee *from the west*: I will say to *the*

north, Give up; and *to the south*, Keep not back: bring my sons *from far* and my daughters *from the ends of the earth*; even every one that is called by my name: for I have created him for my glory, I have formed him; yea, I have made him.

It is true that God has *begun* to say to the North, 'Give up', and to the South, 'Keep not back', as I mentioned in an earlier chapter, but what God is talking about here is bringing His people from all four points of the compass—east, west, north, and south—from far, and from the ends of the earth, which unquestionably means *from everywhere*! Much of this particular prophecy has not been fulfilled yet. Some of it has, but by no means all of it.

A third example of what has yet to take place is found in Isaiah 49:22 onwards, which says:

Thus saith the Lord God, Behold, I will lift up mine hand to the Gentiles, and set up my standard to the people: and they shall bring thy sons in their arms, and thy daughters shall be carried upon their shoulders. And kings shall be thy nursing fathers, and their queens thy nursing mothers: they shall bow down to thee with their face toward the earth, and lick up the dust of thy feet; and thou shalt know that I am the Lord: for they shall not be ashamed that wait for me.

Nothing like this has happened yet. Furthermore, the majority of Jewish people who have returned to Israel made their own way there. They were not brought there by all the Gentile people mentioned here. And kings and queens, or heads of state have not been involved. Furthermore, nothing has happened in such a way as to cause them to *know* that God is the Lord. A high percentage of the Jewish people who have, so far, returned, are extremely materialistic, and some are atheistic. There is no widespread attitude of *knowing the Lord* as a result of their being brought back. So this particular prophecy must still be related to the future. But it *will* be fulfilled.

However, it will not be without a struggle, for Isaiah 49:24, and following, goes on to say:

Shall the prey [meaning Israel] be taken from the mighty, or the lawful captive delivered? But thus saith the Lord, Even the captives of the mighty shall be taken away, and the prey of the terrible shall be delivered: *for I will contend with him that contendeth with thee, and I will save thy children.* . . . And all flesh shall know that I the *Lord* am thy Saviour and thy Redeemer, the mighty One of Jacob.

A fourth example of what has yet to take place is to be found in Jeremiah 16:14–17, which says:

Therefore, behold, the days come, saith the Lord, that it shall no more be said, The Lord liveth, that brought up the children of Israel out of the land of Egypt: but The Lord liveth, that brought up the children of Israel from the land of the north, and from all the lands whither he had driven them; and I will bring them again into their land that I gave unto their Fathers (Jeremiah 16:14–15).

This is not being said yet. But it *will* be said. And notice, the passage prophesies that it will be said that the Lord liveth that 'brought up *the children of Israel* from the land of the north, and from all the lands whither he had driven them'. It says 'the children of Israel', not just the Jews. I will come back to that later.

Verses 16 and 17 then go on to say:

Behold, I will send for many fishers, saith the Lord, and they shall fish them; and *after* will I send for many hunters, and they shall hunt them from every mountain, and from every hill, and out of the holes of the rocks. For mine eyes are upon all their ways: they are not hid from my face.

It would seem that God is not going to leave any stone unturned in order to find each one, and to bring them back. This has still to take place in the future.

A fifth example of what has yet to happen is to be found in Jeremiah 23:3–8. Here again God says:

> And I will gather the remnant of my flock *out of all countries whither I have driven them*, and will bring them again to their folds; and they shall be fruitful and increase. And I will set up shepherds over them which shall feed them: *and they shall fear no more, nor be dismayed*, neither shall they be lacking, saith the Lord (vv 3–4).

There are two points to notice here before we look at the rest of this passage.

1) This cannot possibly refer to the *first* captivity of the southern kingdom of Judah to Babylon because it says, 'I will gather the remnant of my flock *out of all the countries whither I have driven them*.' That first captivity of the southern kingdom of Judah was only to Babylon, and the captives returned from there.

2) It says, 'And they shall *fear no more*, nor be *dismayed*.' That certainly hasn't happened yet, not in all their history right up to the present day. But it is *going* to happen. So what is being referred to must still be future.

Then verses 5 to 6 go on to say:

> Behold, the days come, saith the Lord, that I will raise unto David a righteous Branch, and a *King* shall *reign* and prosper, and shall execute judgment and justice *in the earth*. In *his* days Judah shall be saved, and Israel shall dwell safely: and this is his name whereby he shall be called, THE LORD OUR RIGHTEOUSNESS.

All this must unquestionably be referring to the future. And why? Because the righteous Branch that God will raise unto David, and the *King*, is referring to the Lord Jesus Christ. But He has not reigned *as King*, yet. He did not, when He came the *first* time. In fact the people *rejected* Him and said, 'We will not have this man to reign over us.' But He *will* reign when He comes the *second* time. That is what the prophecies say which I have already quoted earlier. Neither has He *yet* executed 'judgment and justice *in the earth*'. What He did when He came the *first* time was restricted and limited within the confines of the Holy Land. But He *will* do. He *will* execute judgment and justice *in the earth*, not just in the Holy Land, when He comes the second time, when He is reigning *as King*. So all this must still be future.

But another point mentioned here is important. It says in verse 6, 'In *his* days *Judah* shall be saved, and *Israel* shall dwell safely.' Judah refers to the people who stem from the southern kingdom of Judah, as I have previously pointed out. And Israel refers to the people who stem from the northern kingdom of Israel. What verse 6 is saying, is that when He comes the second time, as King, something quite wonderful is going to happen to the *both of them*. This will be very revealing, since nobody knows at this present time what happened to the people of the northern kingdom of Israel after they were taken into captivity into Assyria, long before the people of the southern kingdom of Judah were taken into captivity to Babylon! And nobody knows where the people of the northern kingdom of Israel *are* at the present moment! But I will return to that, later.

Verses 7 and 8 of Jeremiah chapter 23 repeat what has already been said in Jeremiah 16:14–17:

> Therefore, behold, the days come, saith the Lord, that they shall no more say, The Lord liveth, which brought up the children of Israel out of the land of Egypt; but, The Lord liveth, which brought up and *which led* the seed of the house of Israel out of the north country, and from all countries whither I had driven them: and they shall dwell in their own land.

The word 'therefore' in verse 7, is there to indicate *when* this is going to happen. It is 'in *his* days', to quote verse 6, because the word 'therefore' is always used to refer back to what has preceded it. And since what has been stated in verses 7 and 8 did not happen when Jesus came the first time, it means it will happen when He comes the second time, as King, to reign, or near to the time of His Second Coming.

Furthermore, when the Lord brought the children of Israel out of the land of Egypt, it was all twelve tribes that He brought out. Similarly, when they shall say, 'The Lord liveth, which brought up and which led the seed of *the house of Israel* out of the north country, and from all countries whither I had driven them', *the house of Israel* means *all twelve tribes*, not *just Judah*! But I shall return to that subject later.

Then there is a sixth example of what has not happened yet, but which has yet to happen with regard to Israel. Jeremiah 31:31 onwards says:

> Behold, the days come, saith the Lord, that I will make a new covenant *with the house of Israel*, and *with the house of Judah*: not according to the covenant that I made with their fathers in the day that I took them by the hand to bring them out of the land of Egypt; *which my covenant they broke*, although I was an husband unto them, saith the Lord: but this shall be the covenant that I will make *with the house of Israel*; After those days, saith the Lord, I will put my law in their inward parts, and write it in their hearts; and will be their God, and they shall be my people. And they shall teach no more every man his neighbour, and every man his brother, saying, Know the Lord: for they shall *all* know me, from the least of them unto the greatest of them, saith the Lord: for I will forgive their iniquity, and I will remember their sin no more (vv 31–34).

There is really no need for me to point out that the Lord has not done that yet, not to the house of Israel and to the house of Judah. He has not put His Law in their inward parts and written it in their hearts. Neither is it true at this present time that they *all* know Him, from the least of them to the greatest of them. All this has *yet* to happen.

And may I point out most strongly that when God says, 'Behold, the days come, saith the Lord, that I will make a new covenant with the house of Israel, and with the house of Judah', He *means* the house of Israel and the house of Judah; He does not mean the Church.

In no way can 'the house of Israel and the house of Judah', which is referred to here, be the Church. It was not with the Church that God made a covenant when He took people out of the land of Egypt! It was with Israel—with *all the twelve tribes* of Israel. Neither did God take the Church 'by the hand to bring them out of the land of Egypt'! It was Moses and the children of Israel that He took by the hand, to bring them out!

Neither can it be said of the Church 'which my covenant they broke'!

I have to emphasise that very strongly because of those who say and teach that God has no further plan for Israel, that all that He is interested in now is calling out His Church. They take such a passage of Scripture as this, and say it refers to the Church. In no way does this passage refer to the Church. It refers specifically to the house of Israel and the house of Judah. And these prophecies are all going to be fulfilled in *the future*. God has not done so yet. But He *will* do. Let no one be guilty of twisting this Scripture to make it mean the Church. God will deal with him if he does, I warn you.

The last part of Jeremiah 31 refers to something else which is still to happen in the future. It says:

> Behold, the days come, saith the Lord, that the city [Jerusalem] shall be built to the Lord (v 38).

And after giving its measurements in verses 38–40 it says:

> It shall not be plucked up, nor thrown down *any more for ever* (v 40).

Jerusalem *was* plucked up, and thrown down in AD 70, by Titus and his armies. So this is talking about a future Jerusalem which shall *not* be plucked up, nor thrown down any more—not for ever! And that hasn't happened yet!

So *all* examples listed are of things regarding Israel which have not happened *yet*, but which are yet to happen, *in the future*. And because God has decreed them, they are bound to happen. Nothing can stop them. 'The thing that God hath spoken *shall be done*.' And they will each happen *according to God's appointed time*, according to His pre-stated time. They are all part of His future, Divinely revealed, pre-stated plan for Israel. So who can say He has no such future plan for Israel? That plan is clearly outlined and set out for us here, in these prophecies of the Bible.

But I now turn to the Book of the Prophet Ezekiel. In Ezekiel 11:13, the Prophet Ezekiel fell down upon his face, and cried with a loud voice, and asked this question:

Ah Lord God! wilt thou make a full end of the remnant of Israel?

The advocates of Replacement Theology would say to Ezekiel, 'He has'!

By way of answer, God said to him in verse 16:

> Thus saith the Lord God: *Although* I have cast them far off among the heathen, and *although* I have scattered them among the countries, yet will I be to them as a little sanctuary in the countries where they shall come. *Therefore* say, Thus saith the Lord God; I will *even* gather you from the people, and assemble you out of the countries where ye have been scattered, and I will give you the land of Israel. And they shall come thither, and they shall take away all the detestable things thereof...from thence. And I will give them one heart, and I will put a new spirit within you; and I will take the stony heart out of their flesh, and will give them an heart of flesh: that they may walk in my statutes, and keep mine ordinances, and do them: and they shall be my people, and I will be their God (vv 16–20).

In no sense can God be referring here to the return from the *first* captivity to Babylon, because it did not happen then that God gave them one heart, and put a new spirit within them, and took the stony heart out of their flesh, and gave them an heart of flesh in order that they might walk in His statutes, and keep His ordinances, and do them. This has not happened yet to the house of Israel. So God must be talking here about somethng which has *still* to happen in the future, after He has gathered them from the people, and assembled them out of the countries where they have been scattered and given them the land of Israel. God must be talking here about a *future* return.

Then, in Ezekiel chapter 20, God makes some most remarkable statements. In verse 33, for instance, He says:

> As I live, saith the Lord God, surely with a mighty hand, and with a stretched out arm, and with fury poured out, will I rule over you: and I will bring you out from the

people, and will gather you out of the countries wherein ye are scattered, with a mighty hand, and with a stretched out arm, and with fury poured out. And I will bring you *into the wilderness of the people*, and there will I plead with you face to face. *Like as* I pleaded with your fathers in the wilderness of the land of Egypt, *so* will I plead with *you*, saith the Lord God. And I will cause you to pass under the rod [of chastisement and judgment, that means], and I will bring you into the bond of the covenant: and I will *purge out from among you the rebels, and them that transgress against me*: I will bring them forth out of the country where they sojourn, and *they* [meaning 'the rebels, and them that transgress against me'] shall not enter into the land of Israel: and ye shall know that I am the Lord (vv 33–38).

God is speaking here about 'a great sifting' and 'shaking out' that He will cause to happen in this place that He calls 'the wilderness of the people'.

But then in verse 40 and onwards, God goes on to say:

For in mine holy mountain, in the mountain of the height of Israel, saith the Lord God, *there* shall *all* the house of Israel, *all* of them in the land, serve me: *there* will I accept them, and *there* will I require your offerings, and the first fruits of your oblations, with all your holy things. *I will accept you* with your sweet savour, *when* I bring you out from the people, and gather you out of the countries wherein ye have been scattered; and I will be sanctified in you before the heathen. And ye shall know that I am the Lord, *when* I shall bring you into the land of Israel, into the country for the which I lifted up mine hand to give it to your fathers. And *there* shall ye remember your ways, and all your doings, wherein ye have been defiled; and ye shall lothe yourselves in your own sight for all your evils that ye have committed. And ye shall know that I am the Lord, *when* I have wrought with you *for my name's sake*, not according to your wicked ways, nor according to your corrupt doings, O ye house of Israel, saith the Lord God (vv 40–44).

It is important to notice who is being referred to here. Verse 40 makes it unquestionably plain. It is 'all the house of Israel, all of them', not just Judah. It is *all the house of Israel*—all twelve tribes! It is important to notice that. It cannot possibly be referring to the Church.

Also, what God is referring to here has not happened yet. At no time yet have they remembered their ways, and all their doings, wherein they have been defiled, and lothed themselves in their own sight for all their evils that they have committed. In no way!

But they are going to do it. And the passage tells you *when*. It is when God has brought all these people that He is referring to, ie, *all* the house of Israel (not just Judah) out from the people, and has gathered them out of the countries wherein they have been scattered; it is when He has brought them into the land of Israel; and it is when He has wrought with them *for His Name's sake*.

So what God is talking about here is unquestionably still future. And it will include *all* the house of Israel. I repeat, not just Judah! So God is making a series of most remarkable statements here in Ezekiel 20:33–44.

Now I will turn your attention to Ezekiel 36:8 and following, where the mountains of Israel are being addressed. Here God is saying:

> But ye, O mountains of Israel, ye shall shoot forth your branches, and yield your fruit to my people of Israel; for they are at hand to come. For, behold, I am for you, and I will turn unto you, and ye shall be tilled and sown: and I will multiply men upon you, *all* the house of Israel, *even all of it* (vv 8–10).

Again it is most important to notice who it is that God is referring to. It is 'all the house of Israel, *even all of it*'. Nothing could be more emphatic. 'All the house of Israel even all of it' means all twelve tribes. It does not just mean Judah. Not in any way. That is, it does not just mean the Jews.

Then God makes statements in verses 10 to 15 which make it abundantly clear that what He is referring to is *still future*, despite what is happening in Israel today, and despite what has happened in Israel since 1948.

He first says:

> And the cities shall be inhabited, and the wastes shall be builded: and I will multiply upon you man and beast; and they shall increase and bring fruit: and I will settle you after your old estates, and will do better unto you than at your beginning (vv 10–11).

Up to this point it could be claimed that all that has been happening since 1948, and some of it ever since the Balfour Declaration. But then God goes on at the end of verse 11, and says:

> And ye shall know that I am the Lord.

That certainly has not taken place yet, not where the whole of Israel is concerned. The land of Israel at this time is very materialistic, even God*less*, in outlook. I have to repeat that. I've been there and seen that it is.

Then in verses 12 to 15 God goes on:

> Yea, I will cause men to walk upon you, even *my people Israel* [not just Judah]; and they shall possess thee, and thou shalt be their inheritance, and thou shalt *no more henceforth* bereave them of men.
>   Thus saith the Lord God; Because they say unto you, Thou land devourest up men, and hast bereaved thy nations; *therefore* thou shalt devour men *no more*, neither bereave thy nations *any more*, saith the Lord God. Neither will I cause men to hear in thee the shame of the heathen *any more*, neither shalt thou bear the reproach of the people *any more*, neither shalt thou cause thy nations to fall *any more*, saith the Lord God.

Not by any stretch of the imagination can anyone say that all that has taken place in Israel since 1948. It just hasn't happened. But it *will* happen. All of it. In *the future*. That part of this passage, at any rate, has yet to be fulfilled.

From verse 16 to verse 21 God rehearses part of the House of Israel's past history. And notice it is *the House* of Israel's past history, not just Judah's, for verse 16 and following says:

Moreover the word of the Lord came unto me, saying, Son of man, when *the house of Israel* dwelt in their own land, they defiled it by their own way and by their doings: their way was before me as the uncleanness of a removed woman. *Wherefore* I poured my fury upon them for the blood that they had shed upon the land, and for their idols wherewith they had polluted it; and I scattered them among the heathen, and they were dispersed through the countries: according to their way and according to their doings I judged them. And when they entered unto the heathen, whither they went, they profaned my holy name, when they said to them, These are the people of the Lord, and are gone forth out of his land.

Then from verse 21 onwards, God begins to relate what He intended to do with them, *despite* all that. But notice, He is still referring to *the House of Israel*, not just to Judah, not just to the Jews. He says:

But I had pity for mine holy name, which *the house of Israel* [not just Judah] had profaned among the heathen, whither they went. Therefore say unto *the house of Israel* [not just Judah], Thus saith the Lord God; I do not this for your sakes, O *house of Israel* [not O house of Judah, notice, but O *house of Israel*], but for mine holy name's sake, which ye have profaned among the heathen, whither ye went. And I will sanctify my great name, which was profaned among the heathen, which *ye* have profaned in the midst of them; and the heathen shall know that I am the Lord, saith the Lord God, when I shall be sanctified in you before their eyes. For [and here comes a promise of their return] I will take you from among the heathen, and gather you out of *all* countries, and will bring you into your own land (vv 21–24).

Then comes something which most certainly has not happened yet:

Then will I sprinkle clean water upon you, and ye shall be clean: from all your filthiness, and from all your idols, will I cleanse you. *A new heart* also will I give you, and *a new spirit* will I put within you: and I will take away the stony heart out of your flesh, and I will give you an heart of flesh. And I will put my spirit within you, and cause you to walk in my statutes, and ye shall keep my judgments, and do them. And ye shall dwell in the land that I gave to your fathers; and ye shall be my people, and I will be your God. I will also save you from all your uncleannesses (vv 25–29).

In no sense whatsoever did that take place after the return from the *first* captivity to Babylon. So God cannot possibly be referring to that first return from captivity. In no sense whatsoever, either, has anything like that, or even approaching that, taken place in Israel since 1948. Nor is it taking place in Israel today, at this present time.

So God is unquestionably referring to something which has *still* to take place in *the future*; and furthermore, to the *house of Israel*, not just to Judah, not just to the Jews.

Then God goes on in verse 29 and following to say:

And I will call for the corn, and will increase it, and lay no famine upon you. And I will multiply the fruit of the tree, and the increase of the field, that ye shall receive *no more reproach of famine among the heathen*. Then shall ye remember your own evil ways, and your doings that were not good, and shall lothe yourselves in your own sight for your iniquities and for your abominations. Not for your sakes do I this, saith the Lord, be it known unto you: be ashamed and confounded for your own ways, *O house of Israel* (vv 29–32).

Once again we just *have* to say that nothing like their remembering their own past evil ways, and their doings that were not good, and loathing themselves in their own sight for their iniquities and for their abominations, has ever taken place since 1948. Neither did it take place after their *first* return from captivity to Babylon. And it is not taking place in Israel *now*.

Again, God is referring to something which inevitably relates to the future. But it is all going to happen. It is bound to. This is God's prophesied declaration. So it is bound to be fulfilled, sooner or later; and perhaps *sooner* rather than later. And verse 32 makes it plain, once more, that it is *the house of Israel* God is referring to, not just Judah.

Then notice what God goes on to say in verse 33 and following.

> Thus saith the Lord God; *in the day that I shall have cleansed you from all your iniquities*. [He has not done that yet, so what follows in the next verse is what God says will happen *after* that; it does not refer to what is happening in Israel *now*, or to what *has* been happening in Israel since 1948.] I will *also* cause you to dwell in the cities, and the wastes shall be builded. And the desolate land shall be tilled, whereas it lay desolate in the sight of all that passed by. And they shall say, this land that was desolate is become like the garden of Eden; and the waste and desolate and ruined cities are become fenced, and are inhabited. Then the heathen that are left round about you [meaning the survivors] shall know that I the Lord build the ruined places, and plant that that was desolate: I the Lord have spoken it, and I will do it. Thus saith the Lord God; I will yet for this be inquired of by the *house of Israel*, to do it for them; I will increase them with men like a flock. As the holy flock, as the flock of Jerusalem in her solemn feasts; so shall the waste cities be filled with flocks of men: and they shall know that I am the Lord (vv 33–38).

What God is saying here is that He Himself will cause all this to take place, '*in the day that I shall have cleansed you from all your iniquities*'. And since He has not done that yet, it means that He will cause all this to happen *after* He has cleansed them, and that, despite everything of the nature of which we see has happened in Israel today, and which has been happening since 1948, and even since the Balfour Declaration. This is clearly something which God says *He* will do. He says, 'I the Lord have spoken it, and *I* will do it' (v 36). And He will do it in such a way, and cause it to happen in such a way that not only will the *House of Israel* know that He is the Lord, but the heathen that are left round about them the survivors, shall know that it is He that has done it. Furthermore, the fact that He says, 'I will yet for this be inquired of *by the house of Israel*, to do it for them' means that He is referring to something which has *still* to take place, *in the future*, because *the House of Israel* has never done anything like that so far.

I want to turn your attention now to a most remarkable passage in Ezekiel 37:15–28 concerning all this. It says:

> The word of the Lord came *again* unto me, saying, Moreover, thou son of man, take thee one stick, and write upon it, For *Judah*, and for the children of Israel his companions [that refers to what, in Old Testament days, after the rebellion under Rehoboam, the son of Solomon, became the southern kingdom of Judah]: then take another stick, and write upon it, For Joseph, the stick of *Ephraim*, and for *all the house of* Israel his companions (vv 15–16).

Ephraim was the name given to the *northern* kingdom of Israel after that rebellion in King Rehoboam's day. Notice also that when God refers here to *all the house of Israel*, He is referring to the *ten tribes* of which that northern kingdom was comprised. That northern kingdom was always referred to as Israel, after the rebellion under Rehoboam; and the southern kingdom thereafter was always referred to as Judah. We need to be clear about this, especially in view of what follows.

God said, take the one stick which represents Judah, and take the other stick which represents Ephraim:

> And join them one to another into one stick; and they shall become one in thine hand (v 17).

Then God proceeds to give the explanation:

> And when the children of thy people shall speak unto thee, saying, Wilt thou not shew us what thou meanest by these? Say unto them, Thus saith the Lord God; Behold, I will take the stick of Joseph, *which is in the hand of Ephraim*, and the tribes of *Israel* his fellows [that means the ten tribes of the northern kingdom of Israel

which the Scripture refer to so many times as Ephraim], and will put them with him, even with the stick of Judah [representing the southern kingdom], and make them one stick, and they shall be one in mine hand. And the sticks whereon thou writest shall be in thine hand before their eyes.

And say unto them, Thus saith the Lord God; Behold, I will take the children of Israel from among the heathen, whither they be gone, and will gather them on every side, and bring them into their own land: and I will make them *one nation* in the land upon the mountains of Israel; and *one king* shall be king *to them all*: and they shall be *no more* two nations, neither shall they be divided into two kingdoms *any more at all* (vv 15–22).

How remarkable! I say straight away, this has not happened yet! These two kingdoms, the northern kingdom of Israel and the southern kingdom of Judah, had always been at loggerheads one with the other, even fighting one another, until the northern kingdom of Israel with its ten tribes was taken away captive by the armies of the then king of Assyria. But no more. As God prophesied in Isaiah 11:13

The envy also of Ephraim [that is the northern kingdom of Israel] shall depart, and the adversaries of Judah [that is the southern kingdom of Judah] shall be cut off. Ephraim [the northern kingdom] shall not envy Judah [the southern kingdom], and Judah [the southern kingdom] shall not vex Ephraim [the northern kingdom].

When will this happen? Put verse 13 of Isaiah chapter 11 in the context of the rest of that chapter and it tells you. I need to quote Isaiah chapter 11 from verse 11 onwards. I have already quoted it earlier on, but it is good to quote it again. It is part of 'all that the prophets have written'! And it is extremely relevant in view of what has yet to happen to Israel in terms of God's future plan for her.

And it shall come to pass *in that day*, that the Lord shall set his hand again *the second time* to recover the remnant of his people, *which shall be left*, from Assyria, and from

Egypt, and from Pathros, and from Cush, and from Elam, and from Shinar, and from Hamath, and from the islands of the sea [I have already pointed out where all these places are].

And He shall set up an ensign for the nations, and shall assemble the outcasts *of Israel* [that's the ten tribes of the northern kingdom, wherever they are] and gather together the dispersed of *Judah* from the four corners of the earth [that's the two tribes of the southern kingdom of Judah, namely, Judah and Benjamin, plus Levites].

The envy also of Ephraim shall depart, and the adversaries of Judah shall be cut off: Ephraim shall not envy Judah, and Judah shall not vex Ephraim [there it is in its context; *this* is *when* it will happen!].

But they shall fly upon the shoulders of the Philistines [the present-day Gaza Strip] toward the west; they shall spoil *them of the east* together: they shall lay their hand upon Edom and Moab [they are in present day Jordan]; and the children of Ammon shall obey them [which is also in present-day Jordan].

And the Lord shall utterly destroy the tongue of the Egyptian sea [the Red Sea]; and with his mighty wind shall he shake his hand over the river [the Nile, or the Euphrates], and shall smite it in the seven streams, and make men go over dryshod.

And there shall be an highway for the remnant of his people, which shall be left, from Assyria; like as it was to Israel in the day that he came up out of the land of Egypt (Isaiah 11:11–16).

That puts Ezekiel 37:15–22 in its context. It is against the background of the fulfilment of all that, that God will make those two nations to become *one nation* in the land of Israel, because it is clear from Isaiah 11:11–16, and from other similar prophecies of Scripture, that all twelve tribes are to be brought back to their land in the return that God is speaking about there.

This is the reason why, when the phrase '*the house of Israel*', and '*all the house of Israel, even all of it*', has repeatedly occurred in many of the prophetic Scriptures which I have already quoted, I have said that I will come back to the subject later. By now it should be abundantly clear that 'the house of Israel', and 'all the house of Israel, even all of it', is referring to *all twelve tribes of Israel*, not just the tribe of Judah. And it should certainly be abundantly clear by now that all this cannot possibly be referring to the Church.

From all these prophetic Scriptures, it is apparent that a far greater return is prophesied by Almighty God than any that has yet taken place. This is a part of God's Divinely revealed, pre-stated plan and purpose for Israel, when His appointed time has come. What has taken place up to now is a return of *the Jews* to their native land, and is always referred to, and is always discussed as, the return of the Jews. But it should again be pointed out that the Jews stem from the tribe of *Judah*, plus Benjamin. But there are another ten tribes somewhere, who are referred to in the Scriptures as the ten tribes *of Israel*. These also have yet to return from wherever they are. And that is what God is talking about in Isaiah 11:11–16 and in Ezekiel 37:15–22 which I have just quoted.

In view of all this, I need to say also that the debate which has been going on for years now in Israel, and in the Jewish Press, has been on the question: Who is a Jew? The debate that now needs to take place, considering this far larger return which Almighty God has prophesied in these Scriptures that I have quoted, is: Who is a member of each one of all these other ten tribes?

Moreover, after Ezekiel 37:22 has stated, 'And I will make them *one* nation in the land upon the mountains of Israel; and *one king* shall be king to them all [meaning to all twelve tribes]: and they shall be *no more* two nations, neither shall they be divided into two kingdoms *any more at all*', and after He has stated in verse 23, 'Neither shall they defile themselves any more with their idols, nor with their detestable things, nor with any of their transgressions: but I will save them out of all their dwelling places, wherein they have sinned, and will cleanse them: so shall they be my people, and I will be their God'—*after* all that, God goes on to say in Ezekiel 37:24 and following:

> And David my servant shall be king over them; and they *all* [the twelve tribes] shall have *one* shepherd: they shall also walk in my judgments, and observe my statutes, and

do them. And they shall dwell in the land that I have given unto Jacob my servant, wherein your fathers have dwelt; and they shall dwell therein, even they, and their children, and their children's children *for ever*: and my servant David shall be their prince *for ever* (vv 24–25).

All that, agrees with what God had already said in Ezekiel 34:23–24:

And I will set up *one* shepherd over them, and he shall feed them, even my servant David; and he shall feed them, and he shall be their shepherd. And I the Lord will be their God, and my servant David a prince among them; I the Lord have spoken it.

It is obvious that none of that has happened yet. So there is much more that has *yet* to be fulfilled.

Furthermore, God goes on to say, in Ezekiel 37:26:

Moreover I will make *a covenant of peace with them*; it shall be *an everlasting covenant* with them [I have referred to that earlier]: and I will place them, and multiply them, and will set *my sanctuary* in the midst of them *for evermore*. My *tabernacle* also shall be with them: yea, I will be their God, and they shall be my people. And *the heathen* shall know that I the Lord do sanctify Israel, *when* my sanctuary shall be *in the midst of them* for evermore (vv 26–28).

None of that, most certainly, has *yet* been fulfilled. But it *will* be. It is all part of God's pre-determined, Divinely revealed, and pre-stated plan for Israel. And it will include Ezekiel 34:25b–27a also being fulfilled, where it says:

And [I] will cause the evil beasts to cease out of the land: and they shall dwell *safely* in the wilderness, and sleep in the woods. *And I will make them* and the places round about my hill *a blessing*; and I will cause the shower to come down in his season; there shall be showers of blessing. And the tree of the field shall yield her fruit, and the earth shall yield her increase, and they shall be *safe* in their land [which they have never been, so far], and shall know that I am the Lord, *when* [I repeat the word 'when' because that tells you *when* all this is going to happen] *when* I have broken the bands of their yoke [that means their enemies' yoke, which is a subject I shall deal with quite fully a little later], and delivered them out of the hand of those that served themselves of them. And they shall *no more* be a prey to the heathen, neither shall the beast of the land devour them; but they shall dwell *safely* [this is twice repeated; they never have, yet, dwelt safely, but they *will* do], and none shall make them afraid. And I will raise up for them a plant of renown, and they shall be *no more* consumed with hunger in the land, neither bear the shame of the heathen *any more*. *Thus* shall they know that I the Lord their God am with them, and that they, even *the house of Israel* [all the twelve tribes that means, not just Judah, not just the Jews!] are my people, saith the Lord God (Ezekiel 34:25b–30).

In view of all that I have stated and unfolded in the last few pages, and in view of the multitude of prophetic Scriptures and Divine utterances that I have quoted, how can anyone, ever, possibly say, if they are honest with themselves, and honest with Holy Scripture, that God has no future plan for Israel, that He has finished with her? According to all these Scriptures to which I have drawn your attention, God's future plan for Israel is even far more glorious than any man has ever yet dared to imagine. And how can anyone ever dare to say that all these Scriptures about Israel now apply to the Christian Church? I trust that by bringing all these prophetic Scriptures to the fore, I have entirely, and completely, and for all time, totally refuted that idea, and utterly demolished it.

Chapter Eight

What of Israel Now *Seen Prophetically?*

All that I have been quoting in the previous chapter still lies *in the future*. It has not happened yet. Not by any means. But it is *going* to happen. *All* of it. God Himself says so. So it is *bound* to happen. But what about the position with regard to Israel and with regard to Jerusalem today? We need to get back to that.

The first thing that needs to be said in answer to that question is that we need to keep our eyes on the Fundamentalist Islamic world and on what they are doing at this present time.

I have already said earlier that Fundamentalist Islam's plan always has been, and still is, the conquest of Jerusalem, with the object, and publicly declared aim of making Jerusalem the Islamic capital of the Middle East. In recent years they have been talking about 'the liberation of the whole of Palestine', to quote their own language, with that object in mind. And their aim would result in the destruction of Israel in the process.

The second thing that needs to be said in answer to the same question is that at the same time we need to keep our eyes on what God Almighty has said He will do. In that respect we should turn our attention to the Book of the Prophet Zephaniah 3:8 where God says in the second half of the verse:

> *My determination is* to gather the nations, that I may assemble the kingdoms, to pour upon them mine indignation, even all my fierce anger: for all the earth shall be devoured with the fire of my jealousy.

That language is very strong. God Almighty says, '*My determination is*' to do all that. He is determined to do it—'to gather the nations, that I may assemble the kingdoms.' What for? 'To pour upon them mine indignation, even all my fierce anger.'

God says something very similar in Zechariah 14:2:

> For I will gather all nations against Jerusalem to battle....

He says almost the same thing in Joel 3:2:

> I will also gather all nations, and will bring them down into the valley of Jehoshaphat, and will plead with them there for my people and for my heritage Israel, whom they have scattered among the nations, and parted my land.

So at least three times God has said He will do this. And the Scriptures say that 'out of the mouth of two or three witnesses shall a thing be established.'

In view of what God Almighty has said He will do, the third thing that needs to be said in answer to our question is that twice over in the last few years we have been brought to almost a hairsbreadth of seeing that prophecy fulfilled, namely, God gathering 'all nations against Jerusalem to battle' to quote Zechariah 14:2 once again.

For instance, there have been two Gulf Wars in the last few years: the Gulf War when the Ayotolla Khomeini of Iran was involved in a war with Saddam Hussein and Iraq, and the more recent Gulf War, with the coalition forces involved in driving Saddam Hussein's forces out of Kuwait.

Take Ayotolla Khomeinis' Gulf War against Iraq first, and what almost happened then. In that Gulf War the Ayotolla had five times publicly declared that his aim was not to take Basra. He declared that his aim was to defeat the Iraqi armies, and when once he had done that, to make straight for Jerusalem with its Islamic conquest in mind.

Supposing he had done that. Then what would have happened? First, the United States is committed to going to the aid of Israel. So one superpower would have been drawn in.

All the Arabs States would have had to decide what they were going to do. Syria would inevitably have had to be involved against Israel. The Soviet Union is committed to giving support to Syria, and to the Arab countries, and is against Israel. So a second superpower would therefore have been drawn in. Britain is committed to giving assistance to the United States, so she would have been drawn in, too. The other NATO countries would have had to decide what they were going to do. And China would hardly have remained on the sidelines, but would have been involved in the conflict in some way. And so, almost overnight, we would have been right there, in Zechariah 14:1–2: 'Behold, the day of the Lord cometh.... For I will gather *all nations* against Jerusalem to battle'! But it would not have been a case of 'Behold, the day of the Lord *cometh*.' It would have been the case of 'The day of the Lord *had come*'! We would have been right *there*. And the whole world would have been holding its breath! We were almost on the very brink of it happening.

But then Iran suffered a severe set-back. It was either that, or it was *God's restraining hand*—His *delaying* tactic, for a time, at any rate. Because His time was not quite yet. So it didn't happen. Not then! But that was the first time in the last few years that we have been brought to within almost a hair-breadth of seeing God gathering all nations against Jerusalem to battle.

The second time, of course, was in August 1990, when President Saddam Hussein of Iraq launched, overnight, his lightning and vicious occupation of Kuwait. Immediately he had done that, a German foreign affairs spokesman who was being interviewed on the radio on Friday evening, 10 August 1990, about the then new Middle East crisis that had been brought about by Saddam Hussein, said, 'In a very short time, it will be *the future of Israel* which will be at stake.' And that very same week the *Jerusalem Post* carried great big, black, front-page banner headlines proclaiming, 'ISRAEL—HUSSEIN'S NEXT TARGET.'

And then what happened? As the crisis increased and President Bush began to muster the coalition forces, and as the United Nations passed its resolutions pledging its support, it became more and more clear that almost every nation in the world was becoming involved in one way or another. This

immediately brought to my mind those ominous words spoken
by Almighty God in Zephaniah 3:8b:

> My *determination is* to gather the nations, that I may
> assemble the kingdoms, to pour upon them mine indig-
> nation, even all my fierce anger.

It looked as if that might be happening. The nations were
certainly all being consulted, almost without exception, and
some were being gathered and were assembling with their
armed forces in Saudi Arabia. This was a feature, which was
not present in Ayotolla Khomeinis' Gulf War. In that Gulf
War only two nations were involved—Iran and Iraq. But in
this second Gulf War, *all nations*, in one way or another, were
becoming involved. And I regarded that as most significant
from a prophetic point of view. It raised the question then in
my mind as to whether this was going to develop into the real
thing, or was it the precursor to the real thing?

Then, when the deadline for the coalition forces to launch
their 'Desert Storm' offensive drew ever nearer, and with
Saddam Hussein proudly boasting of the victory he was going
to achieve in the coming 'Mother of battles' I found myself
being repeatedly asked by anxious people everywhere, including anxious Asians and overseas people now living in this
country, 'What is it all heading up to?' In my reply at that time
I said, 'I am watching the situation very closely. It *could* lead
to Armageddon. I am not saying it *will* lead to Armageddon
but it *could* do. I am watching the situation very closely.'
When I said, 'It *could* lead to Armageddon', I meant that if
Saddam Hussein had attacked and invaded Israel it could so
easily have done. The situation was as tense as that, at one
time, and Israel itself knew it.

This, therefore, is the second time in the last few years that
we have been brought almost to the brink of seeing God
gathering all nations against Jerusalem to battle. Once again it
didn't quite happen. No doubt once again God's time was not
quite yet. But it is *going* to happen. And maybe sooner than
we think.

These two Middle East Gulf Wars which we have witnessed
in the last few years may yet prove to be the prelude, the
precursor, the run-up to the *real* thing. In any case, I don't

think we have seen the last of President Saddam Hussein. Not by a long way. And even if he were to be toppled or removed in some way, the general opinion in foreign affairs circles is that he would be replaced by someone worse, even by someone who is *far* worse in some people's opinion. For that seems to be the nature of Iraq (ancient Babylonia) at this present time. It seems to be a veritable cesspool of appalling brutality, ruthlessness and wickedness.

Everybody knows, for instance, by now, about Saddam Hussein's indescribable wickedness. Many believe he must be absolutely demonic. The question is: Is there any prophetic significance in this, and in the fact that this newly resurrected or re-emerged Babylonia seems to be the veritable seat of brutality and wickedness? I believe that there is.

With that question in mind we will turn to the Book of the Prophet Zechariah 5:5, which says:

> Then the angel that talked with me [Zechariah] went forth, and said unto me, Lift up now thine eyes, and see *what is this that goeth forth.*
>
> And I said, What is it?
>
> And he said, This is an ephah that goeth forth. He said moreover, This is their resemblance through all the earth.
>
> And, behold, there was lifted up a talent of lead: and this is a woman that sitteth in the midst of the ephah.
>
> And he said, *This is wickedness* [please notice that; he said, 'This is *wickedness*']. And he cast *it* [that is, wickedness] into the midst of the ephah; and he cast the weight of lead upon the mouth thereof.
>
> Then [said Zechariah] lifted I up mine eyes, and looked, and behold, there came out two women, and the wind was in their wings; for they had wings like the wings of a stork: and they lifted up the ephah between the earth and the heaven.
>
> Then said I unto the angel that talked with me, Whither do these bear the ephah? [Where are they taking it?, in other words].
>
> And he said unto me, To build it an house *in the land of Shinar* [note that!]: and it shall be established, and set *there* upon her own base.

My dear reader or listener! The land of Shina is *Babylon*, and Babylon is present-day Iraq. What we have here, therefore, is *wickedness* set down, right there, *in Babylon*, present-day Iraq. What we have is *wickedness* established there, and set there, upon her own base. That means Babylon is *the seat of wickedness*. It means present-day Iraq is. No wonder, therefore, that Saddam Hussein is possessed of such indescribable demonic wickedness!

It makes me ask, also, if that seat of wickedness in Babylon, spoken of in Zechariah chapter 5, is the very seat of wickedness, or *throne* of wickedness. Is it also *the seat of the Beast* mentioned in the Book of the Revelation 16:10? I merely ask the question, because the great River Euphrates is the next to be mentioned in Revelation 16:12.

At any rate, since Saddam Hussein suddenly emerged over the horizon, and began to rebuild ancient Babylon, and claimed to be a modern King Nebuchadnezzar, and the restorer of the ancient Babylonian Empire, it inevitably meant that we saw ancient Babylonia re-emerge on to the modern scene. And I believe that is not without prophetical and biblical significance, because there are prophecies in the Bible about Babylon and about the fall of Babylon which have yet to be fulfilled. So Babylon will re-emerge in some form, anyway. And we have at least begun to see it happening.

But what of the very latest developments in the Middle East as this book is being prepared for press?

I quote first from a report from the *Jerusalem Post*, dated 20th April 1991. It says:

> It is now painfully obvious that the coalition triumph in the Gulf War has been *less than complete*.

Saddam Hussein has managed to keep much of his army, perhaps its best fighting units, and a large part of his artillery, armour, helicopter gunships, air force, and missiles. So he still commands a very powerful army. His capacity to threaten his neighbours, *which include Israel*, has *not*, repeat not, been eliminated.

At home his power has been enhanced. His main domestic enemies, the Shi'ites and the Kurds, have been mercilessly decimated. The most ruthless genocidal atrocities have been committed, and the chances of their being able to raise their heads again in the foreseeable future are virtually *nil*. He has committed more brutal atrocities *since* the Desert Storm operation than he ever did before.

It becomes obvious, also, from his report to the United Nations that his chemical weapons and scud missiles have survived the war. He is giving top priority to the rebuilding of his arms factories.

The *Jerusalem Post* report says that according to the London *Observer* newspaper, Iraq has set up an operation in Jordan to illicitly buy military technology and equipment, and is smuggling spare parts and ammunition from North Korea and China which are being shipped via Singapore.

Furthermore, with the imminent withdrawal of United States troops from Iraq, Saddam Hussein's pledge to abide by United Nations Security Council resolutions which mandate the destruction of his non-conventional weapons and medium-range missiles could well prove meaningless once the only credible military threat of force is gone from circumventing inspection as cunningly as he evaded Western laws to acquire illegal arms. Also, the United States administration would like to know what happened to the enriched uranium he was known to possess. Neither did he mention anything in his report to the United Nations about his nuclear capabilities, which caused the US State Department to describe his report as 'far short of reality'! Then, with Kuwait's oil-producing capacity paralysed by him for at least a year, and with Iraq's oil wells relatively intact, it will soon be difficult to determine who really won the war! So concludes the *Jerusalem Post* report. But to continue the very latest developments in the Middle East.

Syria, too, is feverishly acquiring arms. She is a deadly enemy of Israel, and always has been. Having been granted almost all of the Lebanon, and over 2 billion dollars for joining the anti-Saddam Hussein coalition, and for pledging not to employ terrorist groups during the Gulf War, Syria has already purchased improved scud missiles from North Korea, and has completed a deal for advanced Soviet aircraft. Syria is also about to sign a strategic co-operation treaty with Iran (biblical Persia), and may already have done so by the time this goes to print. Syria does not conceal, either, her intention, when the day comes, to attack the State of Israel. And President Assad of Syria is vying for the leadership of the Fundamentalist Islam world.

In addition to what I have already quoted, *Libya's* Colonel Gaddafi is continuing to build up Libya's conventional and non-conventional arsenals and has been cunningly and subtly establishing Islamic States right across the continent of Africa.

Egypt's army has acquired a large number of F-16 aircraft *from Turkey.* They have also been given advanced Apache helicopters and sophisticated electronic equipment, whilst the American Congress has approved 1.6 billion dollars worth of F-16 aircraft to Egypt. Israel's military sources believe that such acquisitions will give Egypt parity with Israel within two years. What is the purpose of all that?, one may ask.

To Israel, Egypt's vast arms purchases are puzzling. It is true that there is a peace treaty between Egypt and Israel at the moment. But no one can rule out the possibility that *one* day, elements hostile to Israel will rise to power in Egypt. And that might agree with Bible prophecy relating to the last days.

Then there are *the Palestinian Arabs*. Saddam Hussein's survival (if, indeed, he continues to survive) could very well seduce the Palestinian Arabs into dreaming once again of Israel's destruction.

I would point out that I obtained some of this information from the *Jerusalem Post's* report, on 27th April 1991, of an interview with Israel's Foreign Minister, David Levy which took place during that week.

So that is the state of things in the Middle East today as this book is being prepared for press. To recap:

• *Iraq* is still a formidable military power and is thus a major threat to Israel. Iraq is out for Israel's eventual extermination, and the so-called liberation of the whole of Palestine.

• *Syria* also is a formidable military power and threatens to destroy Israel, especially now that she has been given almost all of the Lebanon, from which she could launch an attack against Israel. And as I go to press she is already beginning to make trouble close to the southern Lebanon Israeli border.

• *Libya*, Gaddaffi's country, is a major threat to Israel.

• *Egypt* could be a threat, and is arming alarmingly.

• *Turkey* could become a major threat to Israel, especially as she is becoming more and more fanatically Fundamentalist Islamic, and has one of the most powerful armies in the world next to the United States, although nobody seems to realise this.

Iran is now reported to be quietly building up her armies. The *Soviet Union* will unquestionably be a major threat to Israel when the time is ripe. The end-day prophecies make that plain. We need to realise, also, when considering the Soviet Union that behind Gorbachev, behind the Kremlin, behind the Politburo, lies the Soviet General Staff, the Military Generals, in other words. In fact, Mikhail Gorbachev is now surrounded by a powerful military machine led by powerful Generals. At his back is a secret army of hard-line Communist veterans and KGB men. It is these, and the Soviet General Staff, who really dictate the policy. The chief political editor of *The Daily Express*, Chris Buckland, reported from Moscow during the third week of September 1989 that the Soviet Generals are waiting in the wings to see what is going to happen with Gorbachev's *glasnost* and *perestroika* and with his reforms. And they still are!

And then what? one may ask. There could be a military take-over. Mr Tom King, Defence Minister, said on the 1 o'clock news on Wednesday October 2nd of this year 'We need to be aware that there *could* be another coup in the USSR, a Military one'. Such a take-over would be most ominous, particularly so as a new book just published in America by three policy thinkers on the staff of Harvard University, to do with strategic studies, says, 'Perestroika has thus far touched the Soviet military structure *not at all*'; and even more so when the Soviet Union has been deceiving the American administration about the destruction of armaments.

Where the Middle East is concerned, I need to stress again that the Soviet General Staff and their military have constantly held, all down the years, that Russia must become the dominant power in the Middle East. In fact, as the recent Gulf War against Saddam Hussein was developing, strong voices were being heard to say that the Soviet Union will never tolerate the United States becoming the dominant power in the Middle East. The danger then was that there might have been a confrontation. But now the United States forces have largely withdrawn.

The next move, as far as the Soviet Union and the Middle East is concerned, may well be that Russia's military will offer Iran (biblical Persia) military support and assistance when the time is ripe so that Iran can fulfil her Fundamentalist Islamic aim of taking Jerusalem, assisted by all the other Fundamentalist Islamic countries in the Middle East. Were that indeed to happen, it would bring events in the Middle East into line with the Ezekiel chapter 38 prophecy. For Persia (present-day Iran), in verse 5 of that chapter, is specifically listed as being amongst those powerful armies of the North, including those of the *far* North (Russia), which will come against the land of Israel in the latter days. It would also bring events in the Middle East well into line with Zechariah chapter 14 and indeed with Joel chapter 3. Something of that nature certainly is going to happen anyway, because that is what the Bible describes and predicts.

Once again we can see that the stage is fast being set. The various nations specifically mentioned in these end-day prophecies are taking up their positions. Ethiopia, which is also mentioned in Ezekiel chapter 38, has recently been very much in the news.

The question is, Are we about to see the last great act of human history take place before our very eyes? In other words, are we soon to witness the *real* thing, in terms of God assembling the kingdoms and gathering all nations against Jerusalem to battle to pour upon them His indignation, even all His fierce anger, as His declared determination is to do? Maybe we shall very soon see. In any event, things are very fast heading up that way.

What is the line-up as far as Israel is concerned today? The situation in Israel right now, is this:

Israel has, if you like, an *outer circle* of enemies, and an *inner circle* of enemies, which include the neighbouring Arab States. At the moment it looks as if Syria is manoeuvring her forces in the Lebanon to threaten Israel's border with Lebanon. So war with Syria could break out at any time. Iraq, being an avowedly bitter enemy of Israel, could also launch an attack against her when she has sufficiently recovered from the Gulf War. Yasser Arafat and the PLO could form a real, armed, internal enemy.

Then there is this dire threat of the Soviet Union's military making a move with *her* massive armed forces, which have in no way been diminished, but which, in fact, are fast being improved and modernised since they saw the effect which advanced, modern technology had during the recent Gulf War. The Soviet General Staff's aim in making such a move would be twofold.

1) To become the dominant and dominating power in the Middle East.
2) To seek to pacify Islamic unrest in the turbulent Islamic regions of the Soviet Union by coming against Israel, taking Jerusalem, aided by the Fundamentalist Islam countries in and around the Middle East, and then offering Jerusalem to the whole of Fundamentalist Islam as a spectacular prize.

With that in mind we need to remember that Fundamentalist Islam includes Iran (biblical Persia), Saudi Arabia, Gadaffi's Libya, all the Islamic African States that he has helped to create, and all the Islamic Arab countries who are Israel's surrounding neighbours.

We must never forget, either, that the Soviet Union could well have used President Saddam Hussein as its 'stooge', or 'puppet', to spark off the recent Gulf Crisis in the Middle East, and if so, could easily do so again. They had helped arm him to the teeth, and had a very large number of military and technical 'advisors' in Baghdad, who did not leave Iraq when the Gulf War began, when so many other countries' diplomats did.

Now that the Gulf War is over, or seems to be over, the issue of *all* issues which has been put at the top of the agenda in world affairs is Israel, and the pressurisation of Israel to commit national suicide by agreeing to have a Palestinian armed State set up within her borders, which she will never do. Whatever way the situation is viewed, therefore, the entire future of Israel is now at stake.

The nation of Israel today is very much faced with a Psalm 83 situation. Psalm 83 says:

> Keep not thou silence, O God: hold not thy peace, and be not still, O God. For, lo, *thine* enemies [notice it says *God's* enemies] make a tumult; and they that hate *thee*

have lifted up the head. They have taken crafty counsel against *thy* people, and consulted against *thy* hidden ones. They have said, Come, and let us cut them off from being a nation; that the name of Israel may be no more in remembrance.

Nothing could be more true of the situation with which Israel is being confronted today. This is the *more sure* Word of prophecy! That is *precisely* the situation today. Nothing could be more accurate!

This remarkable Psalm goes on to say:

For they have consulted together with one consent [they have reached unanimity, that means!]: they are confederate against *thee* [against Almighty *God*, that means].

Then comes *the list of the nations involved in the line-up against Israel*—the *prophesied* list. This is God's own *prestated* account of what is due to take place, His *Divinely revealed* account.

Verses 6 to 8 read:

The tabernacles of Edom, and the Ishmaelites; of Moab, and the Hagarenes [all of which are in present-day Jordan. The Ishmaelites are the Arabs—the descendants of Ishmael, the son of Abraham, whom Abraham acquired through his wife, Sarah's handmaid, Hagar, when Abraham could no longer wait for God's promise of a son by Sarah, to be fulfilled. The Hagarenes are the descendants of Hagar—also Arabs.]; Gebal, and Ammon, and Amalek [all of which are in present-day Jordan]; the Philistines [that is present-day Gaza and the Gaza Strip] with the inhabitants of Tyre [that is in the Lebanon]; Assur *also* is joined with them [that is Syria with its armies, and the region to the north *beyond* Syria to include ancient Assyria—the *nearer* armies of the North which could include present-day Iraq]: *they* have helped the children of Lot [the children of Lot are the Moabites, of course; the *mountains* of Moab are in present-day Jordan].

So that is the list of the nations involved in the line-up against Israel, as given in Psalm 83—the God-revealed list.

A *prayer* then follows from verse 9 onwards:

Do unto them *as unto the Midianites*; as to *Sisera*, as to *Jabin, at the brook Kishon*: which perished at Endor: they became as dung of the earth. Make their nobles like Oreb, and like Zeeb: yea, all their princes as Zebah, and as Zalmunna: who said, Let us take to ourselves the houses of God in possession. O my God, make them like a wheel; as the stubble before the wind. As the fire burneth a wood, and as the flame setteth the mountains on fire; so persecute them with thy tempest, and make them afraid with thy storm. Fill their faces with shame; that they may seek thy name, O Lord. Let them be confounded and troubled for ever; yea, let them be put to shame, and perish: that men may *know* that thou, whose name *alone* is *Jehovah*, art *the most high over all the earth* (vv 9–18).

The psalmist here is appealing to what God did in Israel's past history, and he is crying to God *to do it again*. What God did to the Midianites in the days of the Prophetess Deborah of Israel, and of Jabin king of Canaan, and of Sisera who was captain of the king of Canaan's armies, as recorded in the Book of Judges chapters 4 and 5, is repeatedly mentioned in different places of Scripture. It represented a mighty conflagration brought about by a direct intervention of God against the armies of the Midianites, who were captained and led by Sisera, when they amassed to attack Israel in the plain of the River Kishon at the foot of Mount Tabor, not many miles from Meggido, where the future Battle of Armageddon will take place.

God had said to Deborah in Judges 4:6–7:

Go and draw toward mount Tabor, and take with thee ten thousand men of the children of Naphtali and of the children of Zebulun. And *I will draw unto thee* to the river Kishon Sisera, the captain of Jabin's army, with his chariots and his multitude; *and I will deliver him into thine hand*.

Deborah did this, in obedience to Almighty God. Then we read in Judges 4:13:

> And Sisera gathered together all his chariots, even nine hundred chariots of iron, and all the people that were with him, from Harosheth of the Gentiles *unto the river of* Kishon.

Sisera fell into the trap, in other words! Then all heaven broke loose, at it were, for in Judges 5:20 it says:

> They fought *from heaven*; the stars in their courses fought against Sisera.

Torrents of water surged down the River Kishon and swept Sisera's mighty armies, with their chariots, all away. God must have sent a tremendous deluge down from heaven, above Mount Tabor, to cause the River Kishon to flood and burst its banks, because it says:

> The river of Kishon swept them away, that ancient river, the river Kishon (Judges 5:21).

There was such a panic caused by sheer fear among the horses, that it says:

> Then were the horsehoofs broken by the means of the pransings, the pransings of their mighty ones (Judges 5:22).

The horses hoofs were broken, no doubt, because the horses could not break free from their iron chariots when they were suddenly caught in the onrush and surge of the tide.

Habakkuk describes this as *God* coming down. He says in Habakkuk chapter 3:

> *God* came from Teman (v 3).
> Thou didst *cleave the earth* with rivers (v 9).
> The *mountains* saw thee, and they *trembled* (v 10).

It seems there was a mighty earthquake—so much so that it says:

> The curtains *of the land of Midian* did *tremble* (v 7).

It even says:

> The sun and the moon stood still in their habitation (v 11).

Habakkuk talks about burning coals raining down upon the armies, and they were smitten with pestilence:

> Before him went the *pestilence*, and *burning coals* went forth at his feet (v 5).

There must have been some mighty conflagration, because it says:

> The everlasting mountains were scattered, the perpetual hills *did bow* (v 6).

The whole earth must have been reverberating and shaking, and the rivers were boiling in furious torrents, because verse 8 says:

> Was the Lord displeased against the rivers? Was thine anger against the rivers? Was thy wrath against the sea?

So even the sea was boiling!

It says:

> Thou didst march through the land in indignation, thou didst thresh the heathen in anger. Thou wentest forth *for the salvation of thy people* (vv 12–13).

In another Scripture it says that he rained down fire and brimstone upon them from heaven, which would explain the burning coals.

All that is what is meant in Psalm 83:9 when it says, 'Do unto them as unto the Midianites; as to Sisera, as to Jabin, at the brook of Kishon: which perished at Endor: they became as dung for the earth.'

God wrought such a resounding victory on behalf of His people by a mighty, devastating, intervention that it is repeatedly referred to in their Old Testament Scriptures.

In Psalm 83:9 the Psalmist is reminding Almighty God what He did for Israel *then*, and he is crying to God to repeat it, and do it again.

And that is exactly what God *is* going to do! That is exactly what He is going to do when those armies spoken of in Ezekiel chapters 38 and 39 and in Zechariah chapter 14 come against the Land of Israel and against Jerusalem to take it. The Bible says so—this *more sure* Word of prophecy!

Let me quote some extracts from the relevant Scriptures to substantiate that.

1) Zechariah 14:3:

> Then shall the Lord go forth, and fight against those nations, *as when he fought in the day of battle*.

The day of battle is referring to this battle against the Midianites at the Brook Kishon, when Sisera and his armies with nine hundred chariots of iron and all their horses were utterly defeated at one stroke by that devastating intervention of God. That is why I have described it in such detail.

2) Ezekiel 38:18 onwards says:

> And it shall come to pass *at the same time* when Gog shall come against the land of Israel, saith the Lord God, that my fury shall come up in my face. For in my jealousy and in the fire of my wrath have I spoken, Surely *in that day* there shall be *a great shaking* in the land of Israel [that means *a mighty earthquake* and *convulsions*]; so that the fishes of the sea, and the fowls of the heaven, and the beasts of the field, and all creeping things that creep upon the earth, *and all the men that are upon the face of the earth*, shall *shake* at my presence, and the mountains shall be thrown down, and the steep places shall fall, and every wall shall fall to the ground (vv 18–20).

How devastating!

Then verse 22 says:

> And I will plead against him [Gog and all his armies]
> with *pestilence* and with blood; and I will rain upon him,
> and upon his bands [armies], and upon the many people
> that are with him, an overflowing rain, *and great hail-
> stones*, fire, and brimstone.

That is what God did with the Midianites at the Brook
Kishon when Sisera and his armies were defeated! That was
how the Lord fought *then* in the day of battle. The same
features are being mentioned: an earthquake, mighty convulsions, reverberations so that everything is shaking, pestilence
breaking out, a mighty deluge of rain, great hailstones, fire,
coals of fire, brimstone. All these features are included again.

That is how the Lord fought *then* in the day of battle, at the
Brook Kishon. That is how He is *going* to fight when He goes
forth against *these* nations. That is how He will '*persecute them
with [His] tempest, and make them afraid with [His] storm*,' to
quote Psalm 83:15. 'Let them *perish*,' prays also the Psalmist in
verse 17 of that Psalm.

Ezekiel chapter 39 tells us that they will perish to such an
extent that it will take Israel seven months to bury the enemy
dead, and seven years to burn all their devastated weapons!

3) Joel chapter 3 is about the Lord gathering *all nations* to
battle in the Valley of Jehoshaphat. It is this *same* battle, I
believe. When they are all there, Joel 3:16 says:

> The Lord also shall roar out of Zion, and utter his voice
> *from Jerusalem*; and *the heavens and the earth shall
> shake*.

This, I believe, is the same mighty shaking as that which is
mentioned in Ezekiel 38:19, when there shall be a great shaking in the land of Israel. Joel 3:16 continues by saying:

> But the Lord will be *the hope of his people*, and the
> strength of the children of Israel.

This means He is intervening on their behalf. The same

mighty shaking mentioned twice in Haggai chapter 2. Verse 6 of Haggai 2, which I have already quoted many times, says:

> For thus saith the Lord of hosts, Yet once, it is a little while, and I will *shake* the heavens, and the earth, and the sea, and the dry land; *and I will shake all nations*.

It is, therefore, a world-wide shaking. So was that which was mentioned in Ezekiel 38:19–20, because it says:

> And all the men that are upon the face of the earth, shall shake at my presence.

I believe both references are referring to the same event. They are both referring to what will happen in this great battle of the Lord against the nations that are gathered together against *God's* city, Jerusalem, in the latter days. I believe both references are referring to the same event because Haggai 2:7 goes on to say:

> And the desire of all nations shall come.

The desire of all nations is the Lord Jesus Christ.

I believe that both references are referring to the same event because, furthermore, Zechariah chapter 14 says:

> Then shall the Lord go forth, and fight against those nations, as when he fought in the day of battle. And his feet shall stand *in that day* upon the mount of Olives (vv 3–4).

The Lord Jesus is being referred to here! and it is very obvious that a mighty earthquake will *then* take place, and that there will be a great shaking in the land of Israel, because Zechariah 14:4 goes on to say:

> And the mount of Olives shall cleave in the midst thereof toward the east and toward the west, and there shall be a great valley.

Only a mighty earthquake can do that, and it certainly has not happened yet.

But there is a third reason why I believe that both of these two references are referring to the same event. The second reference, in Haggai 2:21–22, which refers to that great shaking, says:

> I will shake the heavens and the earth; and I will overthrow the throne of kingdoms, and I will destroy the strength of the kingdoms of the heathen; and I will overthrow the chariots, and those that ride in them; and the horses and their riders shall come down, *every one by the sword of his brother*.

The last words in particular should be noticed: they shall come down 'every one by the sword of his brother'. That is exactly the description given in Ezekiel 38:21 of what will happen when Gog and his armies have come against Jerusalem, and when a great shaking in the land of Israel takes place. It says, 'Every man's sword shall be against his brother.' Almost the same words are used. So I believe all these references are referring to the same event.

4) A fourth example of how God is going to do exactly what the Psalmist in Psalm 83:9 cried unto Him to do, namely, 'Do unto them as unto the Midianites, as to Sisera, as to Jabin at the brook Kishon', is found in Daniel 12:1.

You will remember from what I have already quoted that the last part of Daniel chapter 11 is about the armies of the king of the North coming against the glorious land of Israel in great fury *at the time of the end*. But then Daniel 12:1 goes on to say:

> And *at that time* shall Michael stand up, the great prince which standeth for the children of *thy* people [of Daniel's people, the children of Israel]: and there shall be a time of trouble, such as never was since there was a nation even to that same time: and *at that time* thy people [Daniel's people, Israel] shall be delivered.

They shall be delivered by a mighty and devastating intervention of Almighty God—the same almighty Divine intervention that all these other Scriptures have been talking about!

And I believe many of us who are alive today are going to see all these things taking place! And maybe before very long!

To refer back to that prayer in Psalm 83 and to that heart-rending cry to God—to do all those things to the enemies of God and of Israel, who were determined to cut Israel off from being a nation *'that the name of Israel may be no more in remembrance'*—that prayer and cry to God which the Psalmist uttered is, I say, exactly what God *is* going to do *when* all these powerful armies come against Jerusalem. And I have demonstrated that that is what He is going to do, by quoting all these Scriptures. That prayer will be answered in absolute detail, and to the letter, because it was a Divinely inspired, *prophetic* prayer. And it will be answered according to His precise timetable, in other words, at precisely His appointed time.

Chapter Nine

God's Revelation Concerning the Fast Approaching Gog and Magog War and the Coming Invasion of Israel

The question must now surely come into many peoples' minds: What is that terrible and total devastation of these powerful armies all about? It is a good and necessary question, and we need to be clear as to the answer.

In the first place, God Himself makes it clear in His Scriptures that it is about God breaking the yoke of Israel's enemies from off their necks, finally and for all time, as He has promised *on oath* to Abraham that He will do, in order that they might serve Him in holiness and righteousness before Him all the days of their life.

And *secondly*, in order that they mighty do that, it involves the *spiritual* rebirth of Israel *after* He has so delivered them.

In order to fully substantiate what I am saying, we should consider Luke's Gospel chapter 1 verse 67 and onwards, which is about what Zacharias, the father of John the Baptist, said just after John the Baptist had been born and had been named. We hear this read in our churches every year at Christmas time, so it should be very familiar to us, but I fear that we have missed noticing something which is vitally important here from a prophetic point of view. It is important, also, to notice that verse 67 says that Zacharias *'was filled with the Holy Ghost*, and prophesied'. In other words, *he spake by the Holy Ghost*. It was *the Holy Ghost* who was speaking, not Zacharias. And the Holy Ghost cannot possibly be wrong! The Holy Ghost cannot *lie*! Never!

Zacharias, speaking by the Holy Ghost, said:

Blessed be the Lord God of Israel; for he hath visited

224

and redeemed his people [that's Israel, Israel His people], and hath raised up an horn of salvation for us in the house of his servant David; as he spake by the mouth of his holy prophets, which have been since the world began (vv 67–70).

What has God spoken by the mouth of His holy prophets which have been since the world began? The next verse tells you:

That we [speaking still of God's people Israel] should be saved *from our enemies and from the hand of all that hate us* (v 71).

Notice those last twelve words. Then *verse 72* goes on to make *this* statement:

To perform the mercy promised to our fathers [fore-fathers that means] and to remember his holy covenant; *the oath* which he sware to our father Abraham (vv 72–73).

What oath? The next verse tells you:

That he would grant unto us, *that we being delivered out of the hand of our enemies might serve him without fear, in holiness and righteousness before him, all the days of our life* (v 74).

God has placed Himself *on oath* to Abraham that He will deliver His people, one day, out of the hand of their enemies, and from the hand of all that hate them, and that He will do it *for a purpose*. And that purpose is that they 'might serve him without fear, in holiness and righteousness before him, all the days of [their] life'. And He is *bound* to carry out and do what He has promised, *on oath*, to Abraham, to do. So it is *going to happen*. And I believe we will *see* it happen, maybe very soon now.

This is what the following Scriptures are all about (all of which have already been quoted or referred to): Ezekiel chapters 38 and 39; Daniel chapters 11 and 12; Joel chapter 3;

Zechariah chapter 14; and Haggai chapter 2. It is also what Isaiah 63:1–6 is all about. The passage asks certain questions, one by one:

> Who is this that cometh from Edom, with dyed garments from Bozrah? this that is glorious in his apparel, travelling in the greatness of his strength? [The answer is then given:] *I* that speak in righteousness, mighty to save.
>
> [Next question:] Wherefore art thou red in thine apparel, and thy garments like him that treadeth in the winefat? [The next answer is then given:] I have trodden the winepress alone; and of the people there was none with me: for I will tread them in mine anger, and trample them in my fury; and their blood shall be sprinkled upon my garments, and I will stain all my raiment. *For the day of vengeance* is in mine heart, and *the year of my redeemed* is come. And I looked, and there was none to help; and I wondered that there was none to uphold: therefore mine own arm brought salvation unto me; and my fury, it upheld me. And I will tread down the people in mine anger, and make them drunk in my fury, and I will bring down their strength to the earth.

To explain what the Lord is saying here, I need to point out that the 'them' that He says He will tread in His fury, and trample also in His fury, and whose blood shall be sprinkled on His garments and stain all His raiment, are the enemies of His people Israel, out of whose hand He will deliver them. Reference is also made to all who hate them. That is what is meant by 'For the day of vengeance is in mine heart' in verse 4.

Similarly, the people that He will tread down in His anger, and make drunk in His fury, and whose strength He will bring down to the earth (v 6), also refers to these enemies of His people Israel, and to all who hate them.

And when it says in verse 4, 'the year of my redeemed is come', the Lord is referring to the time being come when He will grant unto them, that they being delivered out of the hand of their enemies, and from the hand of all that hate them, will serve Him *without fear*, in holiness and righteousness before

Him all the days of their life, as He has promised *on oath* to Abraham that He *will* do.

That is also what Isaiah 66:15–16 is all about when it says:

> For, behold, the Lord will come with fire, and with his chariots like a whirlwind, to render his anger with fury, and his rebuke with flames of fire. For by fire and by his sword will the *Lord* plead with all flesh: and the slain of the Lord shall be many.

Furthermore, it is what Jeremiah 30:1–11 is all about when it says:

> The word that came to Jeremiah from the Lord, saying, Thus speaketh the Lord *God of Israel*, saying, Write thee all the words that I have spoken unto thee in a book. For, lo, the days come, saith the Lord, that I will bring again the captivity of my people Israel and Judah, saith the Lord [notice He says Israel and Judah, not just Judah! Israel and Judah refers to *all twelve tribes*, namely *the whole House of Israel*, not just the Jews.]: and I will cause them to return to the land that I gave to their fathers, *and they shall possess it* [all twelve tribes will!!]. And these are the words that the Lord spake concerning Israel and concerning Judah (vv 1–4).

There it is again: 'Concerning *Israel* and concerning *Judah*.' Nothing could be more plain. God is referring to *all twelve tribes*, namely *the whole House of Israel*, not just Judah, not just Jews. And He is most certainly not referring to the Church!

Then in verse 5 He goes on:

> For thus saith the Lord; We have heard a voice of trembling, of fear, and not of peace. Ask ye now, and see whether a man doth travail with child? wherefore do I see every man with his hands on his loins, as a woman in travail, and all faces are turned into paleness? Alas! for *that day* is great, so that none is like it: it is even *the time of Jacob's trouble*; but he shall be saved out of it. *For it shall come to pass in that day*, saith the Lord of

hosts, *that I will break his [the enemy's] yoke from off thy neck*, and will burst thy bonds, and strangers shall *no more* serve themselves of him: but they shall *serve the Lord their God*, and David their king, whom I will raise up unto them (vv 4–9).

Nothing could be more clear! This passage is all about God granting unto them, that they being delivered out of the hands of their enemies, and from the hand of all that hate them in order that they may serve *Him*, without fear (without fear of enemies or of all that hate them, that means) in holiness and righteousness before Him all the days of their life.

The reason why the Lord told Jeremiah to write all the words that He had spoken unto him *in a book* was because what the Lord was saying to him in this respect *was for a long time to come*. It would be recorded, in this book, for each and every generation to read all down the centuries until the time came for it to be fulfilled, which I might say, must be almost *now*! That is what everything that is happening in the Middle East right now is fast heading up towards!

Jeremiah 30:10 goes on to say:

Therefore fear thou not, O my servant Jacob, saith the Lord; neither be dismayed, O Israel: for, lo, I will save thee from afar, and thy seed from the land of their captivity; and Jacob shall return, and shall be in rest, and be quiet, and none shall make him afraid. For I am with thee, saith the Lord, to save thee: though I make a full end of all nations whither I have scattered thee, yet will I not make a full end of thee: *but* I will correct thee in measure, and will not leave thee altogether unpunished (vv 10–11).

To these verses I must inevitably add Jeremiah 46:28:

Fear thou not, O Jacob my servant, saith the Lord: for I am with thee; for I *will* make a full end of all the nations whither I have driven thee: but I will not make a full end of thee.

A terrible judgment of God is coming on all the nations

whither God has driven them therefore, when *that day* comes when He shall deliver them and save them from their enemies, and from the hand of all that hate them in order that they may *serve Him, without fear*, in holiness and righteousness before Him all the days of their life. And I believe that that terrible judgment of God which is coming on all those nations as He moves to deliver His people, will include, also, God taking vengeance for the terrible things that happened during the holocaust.

Yet another Scripture that is about Israel being delivered out of the hand of their enemies and from the hand of all that hate them is Daniel 12:1:

> And *at that time* shall Michael stand up, the great prince which standeth for the children of thy people [Daniel's people, the children of Israel]: and there shall be a time of trouble, such as never was since there was a nation *even to that time*: and *at that time* thy people shall be delivered, every one that shall be found written in the book.

And there are a number of other such Scriptures.

Here I need to point out that because this deliverance did not happen when the Lord Jesus came the first time—when He lived, and did what He did, amongst them—they said He could not possibly be *the Messiah*. But He was not meant to deliver them out of the hand of their enemies the first time He came, because *that time* had not yet come. It was still *future*. And it still *is*. The deliverance was not meant to happen until He came the second time, *in the latter days*. And the latter days are these days in which we are now living. So it could happen *at any time*. 'That time', to quote Daniel 12:1, could be far nearer than we think.

I need also to point out that this mighty deliverance of God's people Israel out of the hand of their enemies is the *mighty shaking* in the land of Israel described in Ezekiel 38:19—that earth-reverberating earthquake, that mighty convulsion when God will shake *all nations*, and when He totally devastates all those armies which will have invaded the land of Israel. God is going to shake the world, then. And I believe many of us will see it, and *feel* it.

So much, therefore, is it Almighty God's determined and *Divinely revealed* intention to bring about the deliverance and salvation of His people Israel from the hand of their enemies and from the hand of all that hate them, *finally and for all time*, in order that He might fulfil that *oath* that He made so long ago to Abraham, and that plan and purpose that He has for them in the future, and always has had in store for them, namely, that they should serve *Him*, without fear (of their enemies any more), in holiness and righteousness before Him all the days of their life, as the Holy Ghost, speaking through John the Baptist's father, said He would do.

In order to establish still further from the Scriptures that that is God's determined and Divinely revealed plan and purpose for His people Israel, we should look at Ezekiel 34:27b, which says:

> They [Israel] shall be safe in their land, and shall know that I am the Lord, *when* [I repeat, *when*] I have broken the bands of their yoke, and delivered them out of the hand of those that served themselves of them.

That is what God—*the God of Israel*—is saying to Israel *today*. That is what He is going to do. And it looks as if He is going to do it very soon. Where are the messengers to carry this good news to Israel right now?

Also, Isaiah 14:24–25 very emphatically says:

> The Lord of hosts hath *sworn* saying, Surely *as* I have thought, *so* shall it come to pass; and *as* I have purposed, *so* shall it stand: that I will break *the Assyrian* in *my* land, and upon *my* mountains tread him under foot: *then* shall his *yoke* depart from off them [Israel], and his burden depart from off their shoulders.

I repeat, God hath *sworn*. He hath sworn *on oath* to Abraham that He will do this. Therefore He is *bound* to do it. It is bound to happen.

The next verses of Isaiah 14 go on to say:

> This is *the purpose* that is *purposed* upon the whole earth: and this is the hand that is stretched out upon all

the nations. For the Lord of hosts hath *purposed*, and who shall disannul it? And his hand is stretched out, and who shall turn it back? (vv 26–27).

In Ezekiel 39:8b God even says in the same context, 'This is *the day whereof I have spoken*'! That means, the day of Israel's *final* and *total* deliverance from the hand of their enemies and from the hand of all that hate them.

God is working to that *great culminating point*, therefore. 'From their enemies' means, from the hand of all the nations that are *anti-Israel*. And, 'from the hand of all that hate them', means, from everyone who is anti-Semetic. So watch it Yasser Arafat! Watch it Gadaffi! Watch it, Assad of Syria!

Then when God says in Isaiah 14:26–27, 'This is the hand that is stretched out upon all the nations', it means that God's hand is stretched out upon all the nations *in judgment*—upon all the nations *except Israel*.

All these Scriptures that have been quoted are talking about, first, the day of *the God of Israel's* terrible and catastrophic judgment upon all the nations as He brings about the deliverance and salvation of His people out of the hand of their enemies. It is *the day of God's wrath and fierce anger upon all the nations*, 'the great and terrible day of the Lord', which was prophesied by the Prophet Joel (see Joel 2:31).

The second thing that all these Scriptures are talking about is what the Lord describes in Isaiah 63:4b as '*the year of my redeemed*', which, in the context of all these Scriptures, clearly means, the time when He will deliver them out of the hands of their enemies.

So Isaiah 63:4 speaks of these two things as events which will happen together: 'the day of vengeance' on the one hand, and 'the year of my redeemed' on the other. 'The day of vengeance' is the judgment of God on the nations, and 'the year of my redeemed' is God's salvation and deliverance of Israel, His people, out of the hand of their enemies.

According to all these Scriptures that I have quoted, I say again, the two will take place together. They will *coincide* with one another.

And I emphasise that I dare to believe that 'the year of my redeemed' is far nearer than we think. Indeed, throughout the period of Desert Storm, which led to the cessation of hostilities in the Gulf, there was a strong wave of feeling stirring the hearts of certain Rabbis and students in Yeshiva lecture halls in Jerusalem about the situation in the Persian Gulf having its 'linkage to Redemption', to use their phraseology. An article in the 9th March 1991 issue of the *Jerusalem Post* began by saying, 'Release and Redemption is a popular theme this year.' The article went on to say:

> To many religious Israeli Jews, a Higher Force is at work these days. True power is not in any earthly hands. Redemption belongs to God.

To the Jewish mind, 'redemption' means deliverance from the hands of their enemies. The article then went on to talk about the Divine interventions that had been experienced in Israel during the Gulf War and particularly during the scud missile attacks launched against Israel by Saddam Hussein. It said that the followers of a certain Lubavitch's Rabbi had already intimated 'the redemptive balm of the oncoming Messiah', who some were believing was due to arrive around the coming Passover period! That was the strong rumour that was going around Israel at that time! And it was creating an air of expectancy in some circles.

The article said that:

> The possibilities of Redemption and its concurrent excitement touch even the most cloistered. Rabbi Refson, head of the Neveh Yerushalayim women's yeshiva, says that 'despite the resistance (among most haredim) to explaining events in terms of a Messianic Era, one cannot deny the pre-Messianic significance of the Ingathering of the Exiles and Israel's war being fought by others.'

The article later says:

> Unquestionable signs of the Messiah at this time would validate the Zionist belief that the establishment of the State of Israel signalled the dawn of the Messianic Era.

According to the article, one afternoon during the Gulf

War, several hundred students crowded into the lecture hall of a Zionist Yeshiva in Jerusalem, and their bearded instructor began his lecture by listing parallels between the current Gulf Crisis and signs of the Messianic Age. He had come in with a pile of texts! Then, the article says:

> One of the most prominent scholars who sees the Messianic process in recent events is Rabbi Professor Leon Ashkenazi, a Jerusalem-based Sephardi scholar. He believes that 'one does not just get up and start believing in a Messianic Era just because of what happens this year.' 'I believed that process was under way a long time ago,' he says, 'because the advent of Zionism signified the Ingathering of the Exiles.'

The article then adds, 'Numerous examples and indicators of messianic movement abound.' It gives a few examples:

1) Using 1917 and the Balfour Declaration as the starting point for the Ingathering of the Exiles, the Book of Daniel predicted that 50 years after the Ingathering, Jerusalem will be reunified (1967), to be followed 25 years later by the reconstruction of the Temple [that would bring us to 1992, author].
2) The defeat by Israel of Gog, the leader of the nation of Magog, as predicted by Ezekiel, precipitates the coming of the Messiah.
3) We are living in the Jewish year 5751—the Year of Miracles. Chapter 51 of Jeremiah heralds the end of Babylon (present-day Iraq). Saddam Hussein has compared himself to the Babylonian king Nebuchadnezzar who destroyed Jerusalem and the First Temple.
4) Various prophetic descriptions of the events leading up to the Messianic Era have suggested the use of non-conventional weaponry.

The article says that Rabbi Professor Ashkenazi also notes certain other pre-messianic parallels, namely, the Gulf War occurring at the same time as the massive Soviet and Ethiopian aliya (the Ingathering of the Exiles). He refers also to

Talmudic and Kubbalistic writings which predict wars with Persia (present-day Iran) and the offspring of Ishmael (traditionally believed to be the Arabs) as preceding the Messianic Era.

'From this perspective,' says the article, 'the Arab-Jewish conflict is therefore inevitable.' Then to be as absolutely up to date as possible as this book is about to go to press, the *Jerusalem Post* in its issue of the week ending October 5th 1991 carried large black headlines over a major article on page 13 saying, 'Announcing the Days of Redemption'. Then in the first paragraph of the article it talks about the followers of the Lubaviteher Rebbe having something more important on their agenda than fear that may stalk the streets of Crown Heights, namely, The Days of Redemption, the Coming of the Messiah.

The Article then says that a giant poster or bill board was stretched out over the Ayalon highway in Tel Aviv at the Rakevet turn off, proclaiming in huge black letters in Hebrew against a yellow background, 'PREPARE FOR THE COMING OF MESSIAH.' The bill board was supposed to come down in a few days but such was the feed-back as a result of it that it was decided to keep it up longer.

So even in Jewish minds, and in the minds of some notable Jewish Rabbis and professors, 'the year of my redeemed' is far nearer than we think. All this makes me believe very strongly that many of us who are alive today will live to see 'the day of the Lord's vengeance on the nations', and 'the year of [His] redeemed' take place.

Because the return of the Lord Jesus Christ will happen at the same time—will coincide with these two momentous events—a new and glorious age would then immediately be ushered in, His Messianic Age. Hallelujah! And that could even happen before the end of this century!

Chapter Ten

Israel's Future Hope and the Glorious Culmination of This Age Seen Biblically and Prophetically

The question that now arises, however, is: What will the fulfilment of all these prophetic Scriptures to which I have been drawing your attention hold in store for Israel itself? We need to know.

The Scriptures clearly reveal that it will involve two things to begin with.

First, her *spiritual* rebirth.

Second, her *full* restoration to her land in terms not only just of the Jews but of *the whole House of Israel* which comprises of *all the twelve tribes*. A Scripture such as Ezekiel 36:24 and onwards clearly holds these two things together. It is important, too, to notice, that this is a 'Thus saith the Lord' passage:

> For [thus saith the Lord (v 22)] I will take you from among the heathen, and gather you out of all countries, and bring you into your own land.

That's the first thing that the future holds in store for Israel—their *full* return and restoration to their own land out of *all* countries, so that there are none of them left there any more. I have already pointed out that only a *partial* return has taken place so far. But a *full* and *complete* return is going to take place. And that is what is going to take place *first*.

But Ezekiel 36:25 goes on to say:

> *Then* will I sprinkle clean water upon you, and ye shall be clean: from all your filthiness, and from all your idols,

will I cleanse you. A *new heart* also will I give you, and *a new spirit* will I put within you: and I will take away the stony heart out of your flesh, and I will give you an heart of flesh. And I will put *my* Spirit within you, and cause you to walk in my statutes, and ye shall keep my judgments, and do them (vv 25–27).

That is the second thing that the future holds in store for Israel—her *spiritual* rebirth. And the Scriptures make it plain that these two things are going to take place in that order: her full restoration to her land first; and her spiritual rebirth second, after her full and complete restoration to her land has taken place.

It is quite obvious that God has not brought about Israel's *spiritual* rebirth, her *new* birth, as a nation, *yet*. For, as many people know, the majority of the Jews who are now back in their land are there in unbelief. However, God is *going* to bring about their spiritual rebirth, but not until *the whole House of Israel*, comprising all the twelve tribes, and not just the Jews, have been fully and completely returned and restored to their land, will God do that.

According to the prophetic Scriptures concerning Israel, these two things—Israel's spiritual rebirth, and her full and complete restoration to her land—will happen almost together; they will almost coincide with one another, in other words.

Furthermore, the whole of this chapter, chapter 36 of Ezekiel, is addressed to, and is referring to, *the House of Israel*. See verses 17, 21 and 22, for instance. And verse 10 makes it abundantly plain that God is addressing '*all* the house of Israel, even *all* of it' because these are the words He uses. He is not just addressing Judah and the House of Judah—the southern kingdom of Israel. So when He says in verse 28, 'And ye shall dwell in the land that I gave to your fathers; and ye shall be my people, and I will be your God', He is still addressing '*all* the house of Israel, even *all* of it', namely, the whole House of Israel, comprising all the twelve tribes. And He is most certainly *not* addressing the Church. 'The land that I gave to your fathers' wasn't a land which was given to the Church!

Israel's *spiritual* rebirth, her *new* birth, will happen, of course, in fulfilment of what is written in the Epistle to the Romans 11:26, when God has taken away the 'blindness in part that was happened to Israel' ever since the Prophet Isaiah was called to pronounce spiritual blindness upon them because of their rebellion and ungodliness, as is recorded in Isaiah 6:9–10. Here God said to Isaiah:

> Go, and tell this people, Hear ye indeed, but understand not; and see ye indeed, but perceive not. *Make* the heart of this people fat, and *make* their ears heavy, and *shut* their eyes; *lest* they see with their eyes, and hear with their ears, and understand with their heart, and convert, and be healed.

Obviously it was to be a very long-term *spiritual* blindness that was to be brought into effect, because when Isaiah cried out in amazement to God, no doubt aghast, and in great anguish, 'Lord, how long?', the Lord indicated by His reply that it would be for a very long time indeed. That spiritual blindness was still in force when the Lord Jesus was here on earth. When His disciples asked Him on one occasion why He spoke to the multitudes in Israel in parables, He replied in Matthew 13:13–15:

> Therefore speak I to them in parables: because they seeing see not; and hearing they hear not, neither do they understand. And in them is fulfilled the prophecy of Isaiah, which saith, By hearing ye shall hear, and shall not understand; and seeing, ye shall see, and shall not perceive; for *this people's* heart is waxed gross, and their ears are dull of hearing, and their eyes they have closed; *lest* at any time they should see with their eyes, and hear with their ears, and should understand with their heart, and should be converted, and I should heal them.

This spiritual blindness was still in force when the Epistles to the Corinthians were written. Speaking of the children of Israel 2 Corinthians 3:14–15 says:

> But their minds were blinded: for *until this day* remaineth the same vail *untaken away* in the reading of

the old testament; which vail is done away in Christ. But *even unto this day*, when Moses is read, *the vail is upon their heart*.

It was still in force when eventually the Apostle Paul arrived in Rome, because, after he had called the chief of the Jews in Rome together, and had persuaded them concerning Jesus, both out of the Law of Moses, and out of the prophets, from morning until evening, and after some believed and some believed not, and when they agreed not among themselves, and before they departed, Paul spake one word unto them:

> Well spake the Holy Ghost by Isaiah the prophet unto our fathers, saying, Go unto this people, and say, Hearing ye shall hear, and shall not understand; and seeing ye shall see, and not perceive: for the heart of this people is waxed gross, and their ears are dull of hearing, and their eyes have they closed; *lest* they should see with their eyes, and hear with their ears, and understand with their heart, and should be converted, and I should heal them. Be it known therefore unto you, that the salvation of God is sent unto the Gentiles, and that they will hear it (Acts 28:23–28).

In the Epistle to the Romans 11:25–26 the Apostle Paul, speaking by the Holy Ghost, made it plain *how long* this *spiritual* blindness would remain in force upon Israel. He said:

> That blindness *in part* is happened to Israel *until* the fulness of the Gentiles be come in. And so all Israel shall be saved.

In order that Israel's Divinely promised, Divinely planned, and Divinely revealed *spiritual* new birth may take place at its Divinely appointed time, Romans 11:26–27 *will* be, and *has to be*, gloriously fulfilled:

> *As it is written*, There shall come out of Sion *the* Deliverer, and shall turn away ungodliness from Jacob: *for this is my covenant* unto them, *when* I shall take away their sins.

So their *spiritual* rebirth will take place *when* The Deliverer shall come out of Zion, (which is Jerusalem), and *when* He shall turn away ungodliness from Jacob and *when* He shall take away their sins. And notice it says He has *covenanted* to do this for them (Romans 11:27). The Deliverer, of course, is the Lord Jesus Christ, when He comes again the second time. He had already ascended into heaven after His first coming, when Paul the Apostle penned this. So what Paul says here cannot possibly be referring to His first coming. It must obviously be referring to His second coming.

As to the reference to *Jacob*, I have already explained in earlier pages that Jacob is the name for unregenerate Israel. In addition, Scripture also reveals that Jacob can also mean the *whole* of Israel, that is, all twelve tribes, as it obviously does here.

Israel's *spiritual* rebirth is also what Zechariah 12:9–14 and 13:1–2 is talking about:

> And it shall come to pass *in that day*, that I will seek to destroy all the nations that come against Jerusalem. *And* I will pour upon the house of David, and upon the inhabitants of Jerusalem, *the spirit of grace and of supplications*: and they shall look upon me whom they have pierced, and they shall mourn for him, as one mourneth for his only son, and shall be in bitterness for him, as one that is in bitterness for his firstborn.
>
> *In that day* shall there be a great mourning in Jerusalem, as the mourning of Hadadrimmon in the valley of Megiddon. And the land shall mourn, every family apart; the family of the house of David apart, and their wives apart; the family of the house of Nathan apart, and their wives apart; the family of the house of Levi apart, and their wives apart; the family of Shimei apart, and their wives apart; all the families that remain, every family apart, and their wives apart.
>
> *In that day* there shall be a fountain opened to the house of David and to the inhabitants of Jerusalem *for sin and for uncleanness*. And it shall come to pass *in that day*, saith the Lord of hosts, that I will cut off the names of the idols out of the land, and they shall no more be

remembered: and also I will cause the prophets and the unclean spirit to pass out of the land.

All this refers to Israel's *spiritual* rebirth in fulfilment of Romans 11:25–27. And the repeated use of the phrase '*in that day*' in Zechariah chapters 12 and 13 tells us *when* it is going to happen. We have already seen from Ezekiel 36:24–25 that it will be *when* God has gathered *all* the house of Israel, even *all* of it, out of *all* the countries, and has brought them back into their own land. We have seen also from Romans 11:25 that it will be *when* the fulness of the Gentiles be come in. And now, in Zechariah chapters 12, 13 and 14 (which should be read as one consecutive whole), because of the repeated use of the phrase '*in that day*', we can see also that it will be *when* 'all the people of the earth be gathered together against Jerusalem' (Zechariah 12:3); *when* He has made Jerusalem a cup of trembling unto all the people round about; *when* they shall be in the siege both against Judah and against Jerusalem (Zechariah 12:2); *when* God has made Jerusalem a burdensome stone for all people, and when all that burden themselves with it shall be cut in pieces (Zechariah 12:3); *when* He seeks to destroy all the nations that come against Jerusalem (Zechariah 12:9); and *when* the Lord will, in fact, have gathered all nations against Jerusalem to battle (Zechariah 14:2).

It is *then* that the Deliverer, the Lord Himself, shall come out of Sion, devastate all those enemy nations, turn away ungodliness from Jacob, and cause Israel to be *spiritually* and gloriously reborn. It is then that these two things, the full and complete restoration and return to their land, and the *spiritual* rebirth of Israel, will have taken place.

But then there is a third thing that the future holds in store for Israel in addition to (1) their being fully returned and restored to their land; and (2) their being *spiritually* reborn, as a nation. It may surprise you to know that this third thing involves *a marvellous and actual resurrection, a literal resurrection of Israel*.

You find this referred to, for instance, in Isaiah 26:19, which is a vitally important Bible prophecy. The Prophet Isaiah says when he is speaking to, and addressing Israel:

Thy dead men shall live.

'Thy dead men' means *Israel's* dead men, in the context of what Isaiah is saying in this chapter. But Isaiah does not stop there. He goes on to say:

Together with *my* dead body shall they arise.

When Isaiah said, 'together with *my* dead body shall they arise', he was including *himself* in this statement. He is talking about his *own* resurrection. Indeed, he is *prophesying* it. So when you combine the two parts of this statement—'Thy dead men [Israel's dead men] shall live, together with *my* dead body [Isaiah's dead body]'—what do you have? You have Israel's resurrection being referred to, but not only referred to, it is being *prophesied*.

The same truth is stated again in the Book of the Prophet Hosea 13:14, where God says:

I will ransom them *from the power of the grave*; I will *redeem* them from death. O death, I will be thy plagues; O grave, I will be thy destruction.

If you study that statement in its context, you will find that 'them' unquestionably means *Israel*. 'I will ransom them [Israel] from the power of the grave; I will redeem them [Israel] from death.'

In fact, if you study this truth in the context of all those other Scriptures that I have been drawing your attention to, you will find that this is included in what '*the year of my redeemed*' will mean. It is the third thing that will be involved for Israel. Furthermore, those Scriptures make it plain that that is when this resurrection of Israel will take place.

You will no doubt recall that the *Prophet Daniel* was told that *he* would be resurrected. The Person speaking to Daniel in Daniel 12:13 said to him:

But go thou thy way *till the end be*: for thou shalt rest [that means in death], and stand in thy lot *at the end of the days*.

That he will stand in his lot after resting in death, means that God is saying He will resurrect him. In fact, God is prophesying it! And praise God, God said it would be *at the end of the days* that Daniel will be resurrected. That means, just as the new Messianic Age is about to dawn!

Furthermore, *Job* knew that he would be resurrected. Indeed, he had a very strong, firm, and unshakeable conviction about it. He said in Job 19:25–26:

> For I know that my *redeemer* liveth, and that he shall stand *at the latter day* upon the earth: and though, after my skin worms destroy this body, yet *in my flesh* shall I see God; whom I shall see *for myself*, and mine eyes shall behold, and not another.

Redemption includes being *redeemed from the power of the grave*. Job *knew* that. That is why he referred to '*my redeemer*'. Job knew that his Redeemer would do it, namely redeem him from the power of the grave; raise him from the dead, in other words. Job had a strong, firm, and unshakeable conviction that his Redeemer would do it—his Redeemer being the Lord Jesus, of course!

Redemption does not only mean being redeemed from all sin and wickedness. It means not only being redeemed from the power and stranglehold of Satan, although, of course, it does mean being redeemed from those two terrible things. But it also includes being redeemed from the power of the grave.

David, too, believed that he would be resurrected in the future. He said in Psalm 16:10–11, for instance:

> For thou wilt not leave my soul in hell; neither will thou suffer thine Holy One to see corruption. Thou wilt shew me the path of life: in *thy presence* is fulness of joy; at thy right hand there are pleasures *for evermore*.

It is true that David was prophesyng in the first place about the resurrection of God's Holy One, the Lord Jesus Christ; but he was also speaking in a secondary sense of his own resurrection. In any case, it was not likely that God would leave him there, in death, and in the grave.

But you will no doubt remember, also, Jeremiah 30:7–9,

the passage of Scripture which I quoted earlier about *the time of Jacob's trouble*. After it had said, 'But he [Jacob] shall be saved out of it', it goes on to say, 'But they shall serve the Lord their God, and David their king, *whom I will raise up unto them.*' That means, if words mean anything at all, and particularly *Divine* words, that God is going to raise up David from the dead in order that he might fulfil that particular role.

And I believe David *means* David. I believe it does in the passages of Scripture which I have quoted from the Book of the Prophet Ezekiel, where the name of David is repeatedly mentioned.

I ask: Do you not suppose that David is going to have a role to fulfil in *the regeneration*—in *the time of the restitution of all things*? I believe God has a role for David to fulfil *under* the Lord Jesus at that time—under the Lord Jesus who will be Lord of lords and King of kings, and who, *as King*, will be King over all the earth throughout His Messianic Age. We should seriously think about that, because if the twelve Apostles will have a role to fulfil throughout that time, surely David, of *all* people, will.

Furthermore, it is clear from the Scriptures and from the utterances of the Lord Jesus, that Abraham, Isaac, and Jacob are to be raised from the dead, that is, *resurrected*. The promise to Abraham was, that he should be the heir *of the world*. Romans 4:13 says:

> For the promise, that he should be *the* heir of the world, was not to Abraham, or to his seed, through the law, but *through the righteousness of faith*.

And if he is to be *the* heir of the world (which he never was when he was alive), this will involve his being resurrected.

Moreover, Jesus said to the Jewish people, scribes, and Pharisees, of His day:

> I say unto you, That many shall come from the east and west, and shall sit down *with Abraham, and Isaac, and Jacob*, in the kingdom of heaven. But the children of the kingdom shall be cast out into outer darkness (Matthew 8:11).

And in order for *that* to be fulfilled, Abraham, Isaac, and Jacob would need to be resurrected. It would involve their being raised frm the dead, in other words.

Or again, Jesus said:

> There shall be weeping and gnashing of teeth, when ye shall see *Abraham*, and *Isaac*, and *Jacob*, and *all the prophets* in the kingdom of God, and you yourselves thrust out (Luke 13:28).

So not only will Abraham and Isaac and Jacob be resurrected, that is, raised from the dead, but the Lord Jesus' statement here involves *all the prophets*—the *Old Testament* prophets, all of whom I have listed on a previous page—being raised from the dead, that is, resurrected, as well. Jesus said so, in Luke 13:28!

But did you know, also, that this resurrection is *the hope of Israel*? Paul the Apostle knew! Read the accounts in the Acts of the Apostles of his trials before Annanias the High Priest in Jerusalem, and before Felix and before King Agrippa in Acts chapters 23 to 26, and what do you find there?

In Acts 23:6, for instance, he said in his defence:

> Men and brethren, I am a Pharisee, the son of a Pharisee: *of the hope and resurrection of the dead* I am called in question.

It was a *hope*. To him it was a *glorious* hope—a hope to look forward to. He was sure of it. Unquestionably sure.

When he was brought before Felix in Acts 24:14–15, again in his defence, he said:

> So worship I the God of my fathers, believing all things which are written in the law and in the prophets: and have *hope* toward God which they [the Jews] also allow, *that there shall be a resurrection of the dead*, both of the just and of the unjust.

Then in verse 21 of that same chapter, he says:

> *Touching the resurrection of the dead* I am called in question by you this day.

Yet again in his defence before King Agrippa, in Acts 26:6–8, he says:

> And now I stand and am judged for *the hope of the promise made of God unto our fathers*: unto which promise *our twelve tribes*, instantly serving God day and night, *hope to come*.

So he is talking about the *hope* of the resurrection, the *promise* of the resurrection, and the resurrection to which *all the twelve tribes of Israel* hope to come. To him it was not just a hope, a *personal* hope, a *glorious* hope, and a *hope to look forward to*, but it was, indeed, *the hope of Israel*. And he *knew* it!

And when he said, 'unto which promise *our twelve tribes* . . . hope to come', he was not just talking about the Jews, about Judah! He was talking about *all* the House of Israel, even all of it, the *whole* House of Israel, even all twelve tribes!

Who can say that God has no further plan for Israel?! Paul the Apostle most certainly did not say that!

He also said to King Agrippa in Acts 26:8:

> Why should it be thought a thing incredible with you, *that God should raise the dead*?

The issue of all issues, therefore, in these trials of Paul the Apostle, and in his defence in each one of them, was the question of this resurrection—the hope of Israel.

Continuing his defence before Agrippa, Paul went on to say to him in Acts 26:22–23:

> Having obtained help of God, I continue unto this day, witnessing both to small and great, saying none other things than those which the prophets and Moses did say should come: that Christ should suffer, and that he should be the *first* that shall *rise from the dead*, and should shew light unto *the people* [meaning the people of Israel], *and* to the Gentiles [that is everybody else].

Then he said to Agrippa in verse 27:

> King Agrippa, believest thou *the prophets*? I know that thou believest.

And that almost resulted in King Agrippa becoming a Christian!

But then in Acts 28:20, which is the account of what happened when the Apostle Paul eventually arrived at Rome, and to which I have already referred, he said to all the chief of the Jews whom he had gathered together for a whole day's conference:

> [I have] called for you, to see you, and to speak with you: because that *for the hope of Israel* I am bound with this chain.

In view of all these Scriptures, there is no question but that, concerning Israel's future resurrection, Paul the Apostle most certainly had a strong and unshakeable conviction that this is indeed *the hope of Israel*. That is why he stood so firmly in defence of it, at all three of his trials.

And this resurrection is exactly what Ezekiel chapter 37 is all about. This chapter is an account of the vision of dry bones which the Prophet Ezekiel was given. The Lord set him down in the midst of the valley which was full of bones. There were very many of them in the open valley, and they were very dry. Now dry bones are the bones of *dead* people! And this valley was *full* of them! God said to Ezekiel, 'Son of man, can these bones live?' And Ezekiel answered and said, 'O Lord God, thou knowest' (Ezekiel 37:1–3). That is the background.

In verse 11 and onwards God provides His own interpretation of the vision. And as I proceed to quote it, I need to lay down this principle: we must *never* spiritualise what God never intended to be spiritualised. Never!

> Then He said unto me, Son of man, these bones *are the whole house of Israel* (v 11).

God is telling Ezekiel exactly what these very many bones are! They are the whole House of Israel. And when God said they were the whole House of Israel He *meant* they were the whole House of Israel. That is the first point.

Then God says in verse 12:

> Therefore prophesy and say unto them, Thus saith the Lord God: Behold, O my people, I will *open your graves*, and cause you to come up *out of your graves*, and bring you into the land of Israel.

When God says '*graves*', He *means* graves! We must never spiritualise what God never intended to be spiritualised. *Never!* When God says, 'I will *open* your graves,' He means 'I will open your graves', open them *literally*. Furthermore, when God says, 'I will *cause you to come up out of your graves*', He means 'I will cause you to come up out of your graves', after He has opened them, that is!

This vision is all about *the resurrection—Israel's* resurrection! The resurrection to which all Israel's twelve tribes hope to come, as God has promised they will come. This is what the Apostle Paul was talking about—*the hope of Israel*!

The God of Israel goes on, in verses 13 and 14, to say:

> And ye shall *know that I am the Lord, when* I have *opened* your graves, O my people, and brought you up *out of your graves* [my people is the people of Israel]. And shall *put my spirit* in you, and ye shall *live*, and I shall place you in your own land: then shall ye know that I the Lord *have spoken it*, and *performed it*.

In Ezekiel's vision—a vision given to him by God about what God was going to do for Israel in the future—these very many bones *lived*, and stood upon their feet, '*an exceeding great army*' (Ezekiel 37:10).

Yes, indeed, they *would* be an exceeding great army if they comprised *the whole House of Israel*, which God Himself said they did, in verse 11; and especially as the hope of Israel is this resurrection to which their twelve tribes are hoping to come!

And if somebody has a problem as to where all this exceeding great army of people is to be put, when God has, indeed, opened their graves and has brought them up out of their graves, and has then brought them into the land of Israel, God even seems to have taken care of that in advance. Speaking to Zion (which is Jerusalem) in Isaiah He says:

> Lift up thine eyes round about, and behold: all these gather themselves together, and *come to thee*. As I live, saith the Lord, thou shalt surely *clothe thee with them all*, as with an ornament, and bind them on thee, as a bride doeth. For thy waste and thy desolate places, and the land of thy destruction, *shall even now be too narrow by reason of the inhabitants*, and they that swallowed thee up shall be far away. The children which thou shalt have, after thou hast lost the other, shall say again in thine ears, The place is too strait [narrow] for me: give place to me that I may dwell.
>
> Then shalt thou say in thine heart, Who hath begotten me these, seeing I have lost my children, and am desolate, a captive, and removing to and fro? and who hath brought up these? Behold, I was left alone; these, where had they been? (Isaiah 49:18–21).

So the problem of space will arise! But God has already provided the answer by saying to Abraham, originally in Genesis 15:18, *by covenant*:

> Unto thy seed [descendants] have I given this land, *from the river of Egypt unto the great river, the river Euphrates*.

And God has continually repeated that, in several other Scriptures. For instance, in Deuteronomy 1:6–7, God said to Moses and to the children of Israel:

> Take your journey, and go to...the land of the Canaanites, and unto Lebanon, *unto the great river, the river Euphrates*.

God repeated this when He said in Deuteronomy 11:24:

> Every place whereon the soles of your feet shall tread shall be yours: from the wilderness and Lebanon, *from*

the river, the river Euphrates, even unto the uttermost sea shall your coast be.

So that should be space enough!

Only very recently it was said in a Middle East news report that Israel could soon, very easily, see her borders literally becoming from the river of Egypt to the Euphrates. She would do nothing to precipitate that happening. But God has His *own* way of seeing that His Word is fulfilled when *His* time is ready.

In any case, however, all of God's promises to Abraham, to Isaac, and to Israel herself, all down the years and centuries, *demanded* their resurrection. And here, in all these Scriptures, God is saying, 'I have *spoken* it. It is going to be *performed*. I myself am going to *raise them up*!'

That is why the promise of God to Daniel, in Daniel 12:1, to the effect that '*at that time*' Daniel's people (Israel) would be delivered, is followed so closely by a statement about *the resurrection*. The righteous ones among them will be resurrected and raised from the dead in order that they may enter into their newly liberated and cleansed land as the Lord ushers in His Kingdom in His Messianic Age; and the others among them will be resurrected to shame and everlasting contempt.

And so, I repeat, Ezekiel 37:10 says of those very many dead bones which God said were *the whole House of Israel*:

The breath came into them, and they *lived*, and stood upon their feet, *an exceeding great army*.

That means there was a *massive* army of them. And it was all brought about by a mighty work of the Holy Spirit of God. And when God specifically told Ezekiel, 'These bones are the whole House of Israel', I *believe God*! And so did Ezekiel!

What the prophetic Scriptures hold in store for Israel in the future, therefore, includes at least these three things:

1) Her being delivered from the hand of her enemies and from the hand of all that hate her, finally and for all time, in order that she may serve Him *without fear* in holiness and righteousness before Him all the days of her life.
2) Her spiritual rebirth.
3) Her dead men, living, ie, their resurrection.

All this must surely coincide with Our Lord Jesus Christ, the Son of Man, ushering in His Kingdom in direct fulfilment of what was long ago prophesied in the vision of that great image which King Nebuchadnezzar of ancient Babylon had, as is recorded in Daniel 2:34–35, and verses 44 and 45. The stone 'cut out without hands' (which refers to the Lord Jesus) smites that great image upon his feet, and then, through *Him*—the Lord Jesus—the God of heaven sets up a kingdom which shall never be destroyed to replace the thrones and governments of this earth.

And it will also be in direct fulfilment of the prophecy in Daniel chapter 7, when, after the thrones of this world were cast down, the Ancient of Days—God Almighty—gave to His Son dominion, and glory, and a kingdom, that all people and nations and languages, should serve Him. That dominion is to be an everlasting dominion, which shall not pass away, and His kingdom that which shall never be destroyed.

Also, it should be noted, that at the end of Daniel chapter 7 it says:

> And the kingdom and dominion, and the greatness of the kingdom *under the whole heaven* [so it is a kingdom *on earth*, if it is under the whole heaven], shall be given to the people of the saints of the most High, whose kingdom is an everlasting kingdom, and all dominions shall serve and obey him (Daniel 7:27).

Haggai 2:21–27 supports what I am saying. In that passage God says:

> I will shake the heavens and the earth: and *I will over-throw the throne of kingdoms*, and *I will destroy the strength of the kingdoms of the heathen*; and I will over-throw the chariots, and those that ride in them; and the horses and their riders shall come down, every one by the sword of his brother.

That means the *armies* of these kingdoms shall be thrown down *as well as the throne of kingdoms*. So Haggai 2:21–22 is fulfilled at this point, and falls into place.

This also is where Revelation 11:15 falls into place and is fulfilled, when it says:

> The kingdoms of this world are become the kingdoms of our Lord, and of his Christ; and he shall reign for ever and ever.

It is the time when the Beast, the Anti-Christ, the world power of Daniel chapter 7 and of Revelation chapter 13 will be slain, and his body be destroyed, and given to the burning flame. This will also be in fulfilment of Daniel 7:11, and Revelation 19:19–20.

It is the time when the prophecy of Revelation 11:17–18 will take place, when the Lord God Almighty has taken to Himself His great power and is reigning; the time when, according to that prophecy, His *wrath* is come (that wrath which John the Baptist said people should flee from).

It is the time when the hour of His judgment has come (see Revelation 14:7). And:

> The time of the dead, that they should be judged, and that Thou [O Lord God Almighty], shouldest give reward unto thy servants the prophets, and to the saints, and them that fear thy name, small and great; and shouldest destroy *them which destroy the earth* (Revelation 11:18).

It is the time when all true believers, Old Testament ones and New Testament ones alike—right up to this present time—as *heirs of God* and *joint heirs* with Christ, will enter into the glory of their inheritance in that kingdom, when Abraham, Isaac, Jacob, Moses, Joshua, Samuel, Job, Isaiah, Daniel, David, and *all the prophets*, and many, many others, will *all* have a part in that kingdom, and will all be resurrected and raised from the dead in order that, indeed, they *may* do so. And in addition, all the saved people of God, including ourselves, if we are saved, will have our part in it also, as *heirs of God*, and *joint-heirs with Christ* of His Kingdom!

And all this will usher in:

- The time of the restoration or restitution of all things.
- The time when the creature itself also shall be delivered

from the bondage of corruption into the glorious liberty of the children of God.

• The time when the wolf shall lie down with the lamb and the lion shall eat straw like the ox.

• The time when the Lord will rebuke strong nations from afar off, and men shall beat their swords into ploughshares, their spears into pruning hooks. Nation shall not lift up sword against nation, neither shall they learn war any more.

• The time when all nations shall go up to Jerusalem to worship, because the *Lord* is there!

• The time when the Lord Jesus shall be King over all the earth.

• The time when the earth will be filled with the glory of God as the waters cover the sea.

All this, is *the great culminating point* towards which God is working!

How absolutely *wonderful*! How fantastically *marvellous* all this will be!

All of this constitutes *the* Gospel, even *all* of it! It *all* constitutes *the* Good News, even *all* of it. Yet the half of it is never preached!

Why do we *limit* it? *Why? Why? Why?* Especially when that great and marvellous culminating point may be reached very, *very* soon? And, by the way, who said you can preach it all in twenty minutes?!

The question is: How near are we?

I believe we are far, far, nearer than we think. Maybe within less than a hair's breadth of the very heavens suddenly being rent assunder, and the Lord Jesus appearing in all His Glory, coming in the clouds, surrounded by multitudes and multitudes of angels, and accompanied by all His redeemed people who are already in heaven, with the Lord Jesus Himself giving a shout. With the voice of the archangel, and with the trumpet of God sounding to raise the dead which are in Christ first, and then to catch up we which believe in Him and are still alive, together with them, into the clouds, to meet Him in the air.

How wonderful that will be! for all those who are saved!

But how near are we?

Dr Martyn Lloyd Jones said, you will remember, when he was interviewed shortly before he went to be with the Lord, 'I don't think we have twenty years to go.' He went to be with the Lord in 1981. That is now over ten years ago. So if he was right, we have less than ten years left. I repeat, if he was right!

The question is: Are we ready? *How* ready?

If Jesus were suddenly to appear, would we be so ready that we would be prepared to leave everything behind? And everybody?

To put it this way: a Captain of a P&O liner, who was an outstanding Christian, was on the bridge as the liner was cruising off the coast of South Africa. Suddenly he saw a huge whirlwind developing inshore. As it spun round and round in a huge spiral, it was taking up with it everything which was not firmly anchored to the ground. Turning to his First Mate, he pointed inshore to the whirlwind, and said, 'First Mate, that is exactly what it will be like when the Lord Jesus Christ returns. Everything that is lightly attached to the earth will be taken up, and everything which is firmly anchored to the earth will be left behind.' Then he said, 'How do *you* stand, First Mate?' That is a question which each and every one of us should be asking ourselves. 'How do *we* stand?

When Dr Martyn Lloyd Jones was being interviewed, after he had said, 'I don't think we have twenty years to go', his interviewer asked him, 'What then do you consider should be the message for the rising generation?' He said, 'There is only *one* message. Flee from the wrath to come. And put your trust in the Lord Jesus Christ for your eternal salvation.'

Have *you* done that, you who are reading this and are still unsaved, and who still have not been born again of the Holy Spirit of God.

Have *you* done that?

Have you fled from the wrath to come? Have you fled to *Jesus*?

Have you put your trust in the Lord Jesus Christ for your personal, and eternal salvation?

If not, you need to do so. And you need to do so *now*.

God says, '*Now* is the accepted time. Behold *now* is the day of salvation.' Don't put it off until tomorrow. Satan is a past master at getting people to put it off. There might never be a tomorrow. Tomorrow may be too late. Trust in the Lord Jesus Christ to save you *now*, and when you do, He will save you for all eternity.